Edmund Spenser

Edmund Spenser

Essays on Culture and Allegory

Edited by
Jennifer Klein Morrison and Matthew Greenfield

Ashgate

Aldershot • Burlington USA • Singapore • Sydney

Published by

Ashgate Publishing Ltd
Gower House, Croft Road,
Aldershot, Hampshire GU11 3HR
England

Ashgate Publishing Company
131 Main Street
Burlington, Vermont 05401
USA

Ashgate website: http://www.ashgate.com

ISBN 0 7546 0227 3

British Library Cataloguing-in-Publication Data
Edmund Spenser: essays on culture and allegory
   1. Spenser, Edmund, 1552?–1599 — Criticism and interpretation
   I.   Morrison, Jennifer Klein II. Greenfield, Matthew
   821.3

US Library of Congress Cataloging-in-Publication Data
Library of Congress control number: 00-103146

This volume is printed on acid-free paper.

Printed and bound in Great Britain by MPG Books Ltd, Bodmin, Cornwall

Contents

Afterword

List of Illustrations

Notes on the Editors and Contributors

Paul Alpers is the Class of 1942 Professor of English at the University of California, Berkeley. His most recent book, *What is Pastoral?* (1996), received the Christian Gauss Award. He is also the author of *The Poetry of* The Faerie Queene (1967) and *The Singer of Eclogues: A Study in Virgilian Pastoral* (1979), and of numerous articles in various journals including *Critical Inquiry, English Literary History* and *Representations*. He has edited two collections, *Elizabethan Poetry: Modern Essays in Criticism* (1967) and the Penguin Critical Anthology *Edmund Spenser*. He is a fellow of the American Academy of Arts and Sciences.

Leonard Barkan is Samuel Rudin University Professor of the Humanities and Professor of English and Fine Arts at New York University. He is the author of *Transuming Passion: Ganymede and the Erotics of Humanism* (1991), *The Gods Made Flesh: Metamorphosis and the Pursuit of Paganism* (1986), which won the Christian Gauss Award, and of the forthcoming *Unearthing the Past: Archaeology and Aesthetics in the Making of Renaissance Culture*. He is a fellow of the American Academy of Arts and Sciences.

Nicholas Canny is Professor of History at National University of Ireland, Galway. He is the author of *Kingdom and Colony: Ireland in the Atlantic World, 1560-1800* (1987), *From Reformation to Restoration: Ireland 1534-1660* (1987), *The Upstart Earl: A Study of the Social and Mental World of Richard Boyle, First Earl of Cork, 1566-1643* (1982), and *The Elizabethan Conquest of Ireland: A Pattern Established* (1976); his largest volume to date, *Making Ireland British, 1580s-1650s*, will be published by Oxford University Press in 2000. He has also edited or co-edited four important anthologies including *The Origins of Empire* (1998) which is the first volume of the *Oxford History of the British Empire*. He has published over thirty articles in various American and British journals and collections. He is a Vice-President of the Royal Irish Academy, and a Member of Academia Europaea, and he has held fellowships at the Institute for Advanced Study and the National Humanities Center.

Donald Cheney is Professor of English at the University of Massachusetts, Amherst. He is the author of *Spenser's Image of Nature: Wild Man and Shepherd in* The Faerie Queene (1966) as well as articles in *Spenser Studies* and *Spenser's Life and the Subject of Biography* (1996), which he also co-edited. He is a member of the editorial board of *English Literary Renaissance* and a senior co-editor of the monumental *Spenser Encyclopedia* (1990). He is currently co-editing a forthcoming edition and translation of the work of Elizabeth Jane Weston with Brenda Hosington.

Matthew Greenfield is Assistant Professor of English at Bowdoin College. His publications include articles in *English Literary Renaissance, Shakespeare Quarterly* and *Raritan*. He has held fellowships from the Whiting and Mellon Foundations. He is currently working on a book called *Satire and Social Memory in Early Modern England*.

Linda Gregerson is Associate Professor of English at the University of Michigan, where she directs the Master of Fine Arts Program in Creative Writing. She is the author of *The Reformation of the Subject: Spenser, Milton and the English Protestant Epic* (1995) and of articles in *English Literary History, Milton Studies, Criticism, Prose Studies*, and numerous other journals. She has also published two books of poetry, *The Woman Who Died in Her Sleep* (1996) and *Fire in the Conservatory* (1982). She is currently at work on two critical projects, *Nationalism and Subjectivity in Early Modern England* and *Among the Wordstruck: Essays on Contemporary American Poetry*.

Kenneth Gross is Professor of English at the University of Rochester. He is the author of *The Dream of the Moving Statue* (1992) and *Spenserian Poetics: Idolatry, Iconoclasm and Magic* (1985) and has written on Dante, Milton, Shakespeare, Marvell, American poetry and puppet theater in journals including *English Literary History, Publications of the Modern Language Association of America, Modern Language Notes, The Yale Review* and *Raritan*. His next project, *Shakespeare's Noise*, is forthcoming.

Andrew Hadfield is Lecturer in Medieval and Renaissance Studies in the Department of English at the University of Wales, Aberstwyth. He is the author of *Literature, Politics and National Identity: Reformation to Renaissance* (1994) and *Edmund Spenser's Irish Experience: Wild Fruit and Savage Soyl* (1997), and co-editor of *A View of the Present State of Ireland: From the First Edition* (1997), *'Strangers to that Land': British Perceptions of Ireland from the Reformation to the Famine* (1994) and *Representing Ireland: Literature and the Origins of Conflict, 1534-1660* (1993).

Willy Maley is Professor of Renaissance Studies in the Department of English Literature at the University of Glasgow. He is author of *A Spenser Chronology* (1994), and *Salvaging Spenser: Colonialism, Culture and Identity* (1997), and co-editor of *Representing Ireland: Literature and the Origins of Conflict, 1534-1660* (1993), *Postcolonial Criticism* (1997), and *A View of the Present State of Ireland: From the First Published Edition* (1997).

Richard McCabe teaches English Literature at Merton College, Oxford. He is the author of *Joseph Hall: A Study in Satire and Meditation* (1982), *The Pillars of Eternity: Time and Providence in* The Faerie Queene (1989) and *Incest, Drama and Nature's Law, 1550-1700* (1993), and co-editor of *Presenting Poetry: Composition, Publication, Reception: Essays in Honour of Ian Jack* (1995).

Jennifer Klein Morrison is Assistant Professor of English at Regis College and Lecturer at Harvard University's Extension School. She served as guest-curator for the exhibit, *Spenseriana: From Illustrated to Spurious Spenser* (1996), at the Beinecke Rare Book and Manuscript Library; she is Assistant Editor of *The Proceedings in the Opening Session of the Long Parliament* (Boydell and Brewer, forthcoming, Yale Center for Parliamentary History), and she has published in the *Yale University Art Gallery Bulletin.*

Maureen Quilligan is Judith and Howard Steinberg Professor of English at the University of Pennsylvania. She is the author of *The Allegory of Female Authority: Christine de Pizan's* Cité des Dames (1991), *Milton's Spenser: The Politics of Reading* (1983) and *The Language of Allegory: Defining the Genre* (1979), as well as numerous articles. She was co-editor of two influential anthologies, *Rewriting the Renaissance: Discourses of Sexual Difference in Early Modern Europe* (1986) and *Subject and Object in Renaissance Culture* (1996).

Susanne L. Wofford is Professor of English at the University of Wisconsin, Madison. She is the author of *The Choice of Achilles: The Ideology of Figure in the Epic* (1992), in addition to various articles on *The Faerie Queene*, Spenser, and Shakespeare. She edited *Hamlet: Case Studies in Contemporary Criticism* (1994) and *Shakespeare: The Late Tragedies* (1996), and is currently at work on two projects: *The Apparent Corpse: Fantasies of Substitution on the Renaissance English Stage* and *Fictions of Disfigurement in the Renaissance: Boccaccio to Cervantes.*

Acknowledgments

The essays in this volume were first written for the Yale University conference *The Faerie Queene* in the World, in memory of A. Bartlett Giamatti (1996). We wish to thank Elizabeth Fowler, who conceived of the conference, presided over its organization and encouraged the production of this volume, and Patrick Cheney, who served as a co-organizer. Without grants from the James M. and Marie-Louise Osborn Collection, curated by Stephen Parks at the Beinecke Rare Books and Manuscript Library at Yale University, the Yale Center for British Art, the Pennsylvania State University, Major League Baseball, Inc. and the Spenser Society of America, neither the conference nor this book would have been possible.

Introduction:
Spenser and the Theory of Culture

Matthew Greenfield

In 1980 Stephen Greenblatt called for the development of a new "cultural poetics."[1] In responding to this call, literary critics have frequently emphasized the "cultural" and neglected the question of "poetics." The project of this volume involves a return to a recognition of the mutual dependence of the two terms: each of the essays in the volume travels through poetics to the theory of culture. The volume's contributors share a conviction that the close reading of Spenser can play a crucial role in developing a richer tool-kit for cultural analysis. To explain the roots of this conviction will require a few words about the history of Spenser criticism and its influence on anthropological thought.

One commentator has suggested that the 1980s saw the beginning of a "movement to include theoretical and interdisciplinary approaches" in Spenser studies.[2] In fact, though, Spenserian criticism has had a markedly theoretical character at least since the 1950s. Spenser studies has always been the site of some of the most advanced literary theory, a high-technology laboratory for the development of new thinking about allegory and related topics including representation, narrative, genre, and agency. In addition to a number of splendid books focused on *The Faerie Queene*, the important contributions to this tradition include Northrop Frye's *Anatomy of Criticism: Four Essays*, Angus Fletcher's *Allegory: The Theory of a Symbolic Mode*, Maureen Quilligan's *The Language of Allegory: Defining the Genre*, Patricia Parker's *Inescapable Romance: Studies in the Poetics of a Mode*, and Alastair Fowler's *Kinds of Literature: An Introduction to the Theory of Genres and Modes*.[3] None of these works focuses exclusively on Spenser, but each developed out of an engagement with Spenser studies and a close reading of Spenser's poetry. Frye, for example, explains that the *Anatomy of Criticism* began as "a study of Spenser's *Faerie Queene*," but "became an introduction to the theory of allegory, and that theory obstinately adhered to a much larger theoretical

---

[1] *Renaissance Self-Fashioning: From More to Shakespeare* (Chicago, 1980).

[2] Mihoko Suzuki, "Introduction," *Critical Essays on Edmund Spenser* (New York, 1996), p. 5.

[3] Northrop Frye, *Anatomy of Criticism: Four Essays* (Princeton, 1957); Angus Fletcher, *Allegory: The Theory of a Symbolic Mode* (Ithaca, 1964); Maureen Quilligan, *The Language of Allegory: Defining the Genre* (Ithaca, 1979); Patricia Parker, *Inescapable Romance: Studies in the Poetics of a Mode* (Princeton, 1979); and Alastair Fowler, *Kinds of Literature: An Introduction to the Theory of Genres and Modes* (Cambridge, Mass., 1982).

structure" (p. vii). Similarly, Fletcher and Fowler each wrote books on Spenser before or after producing their *summae,* and Quilligan and Parker both made significant professional and intellectual investments in Spenser studies at the beginning of their careers. In his contribution to this volume, Leonard Barkan tells a story similar to Frye's: setting out to write a dissertation on *The Faerie Queene,* he became fixated on a single episode in which Spenser presented an allegory of the functioning of the human body. In the end, his dissertation became a book called *Nature's Work of Art: The Human Body as Image of the World,* which treated a broad range of authors.[4] Like Frye, Barkan found his thinking about Spenser unfolding into a treatment of a more general question of literary theory. This experience clearly has something to do with the intensely theoretical qualities of Spenser's poetry, the way it continuously reflects on its own operations as well as on the structure of the world around it. Barkan found in *The Faerie Queene* not only a fascinating allegorical representation of the body but the kernel of a theory of the representation of the body. Spenser's writing has an uncanny power to turn practical critics into theorists, close readers into the developers of large ideas.

Spenserians have been among literary criticism's leading exporters of intellectual energy. Collectively, their works have had an enormous influence on not only literary criticism but also other disciplines. Anthropology provides a particularly striking example. When Clifford Geertz graduated from Antioch College in 1950 with a degree in philosophy and English literature, he carried some ideas from literary criticism into the social sciences and developed the new methodology now known as interpretive anthropology.[5] "Doing ethnography," Geertz suggested, "is like trying to read (in the sense of 'construct a reading of') a manuscript—foreign, faded, full of ellipses, incoherencies, suspicious emendations, and tendentious commentaries, but written not in conventionalized graphs of sound but in transient examples of shaped behavior."[6] This revolt against positivism has had enormous repercussions for many disciplines, and it paved the way for literary critics to begin borrowing ideas back from anthropology several decades later. In making anthropology into an interpretive discipline, Geertz drew especially heavily on the thought of two literary critics. Northrop Frye was one of them.[7] Although phrases like "symbolic system" and "deep structure" have complex ancestries, it is difficult to avoid hearing in Geertz's use of them the influence

---

[4] *Nature's Work of Art: The Human Body as Image of the World* (New Haven, 1975).

[5] See Geertz, *After the Fact: Two Countries, Four Decades, One Anthropologist* (Cambridge, Mass., 1995), esp. p. 98.

[6] *The Interpretation of Cultures* (New York, 1973), p. 10.

[7] The other crucial critic was Kenneth Burke. A partial sample of Geertz's references to Frye would include *The Interpretation of Cultures,* pp. 446, 450; *Local Knowledge: Further Essays in Interpretive Anthropology* (New York, 1983), pp. 4, 29; Richard Schweder and Robert A. LeVine, eds., *Culture Theory: Essays on Mind, Self, and Emotion,* (Cambridge, 1984), p. 10; and *After the Fact: Two Countries, Four Decades, One Anthropologist,* p. 3.

of Frye's *Anatomy of Criticism*. And Geertz's student James Boon used the discussion of romance in *The Anatomy of Criticism* as the theoretical foundation for his own first book, *The Anthropological Romance of Bali, 1597-1972: Dynamic Perspectives in Marriage and Caste, Politics and Religion*.[8]

The body of literary theory developed in the laboratory of Spenser studies played an even more prominent role in the next significant development in anthropological theory, the self-reflexive turn of the 1980s. In 1986 the publication of *Writing Culture: The Poetics and Politics of Ethnography* helped crystallize the notion that anthropologists needed to become more conscious of the literary, formal, and generic features of their work.[9] This anthology has exerted an enormous pressure on the shape of the discipline. Even anthropologists who reject the volume's conclusions have been forced to become more self-conscious about the forms in which they write, the stories they tell, and, most destabilizing of all, the allegorical dimension of even the writing of social scientists.[10] One of the crucial contributions of *Writing Culture* was to introduce anthropologists to the concept of allegory. In "On Ethnographic Allegory," James Clifford argued that "Once the ethnographic process is accorded its full complexity of historicized dialogic relations, what formerly seemed to be empirical [and] interpretive accounts of generalized cultural facts (statements and attributions concerning 'the !Kung', 'the Samoans', etc.) now appear as just one level of allegory."[11] Clifford describes several of the allegories that frequently inform anthropological writing. The most ubiquitous of these is what Clifford calls "salvage, or redemption, ethnography," which imagines the ethnographic writer as preserving the memory of disappearing cultures: "Every description or interpretation that conceives of itself as 'bringing a culture into writing', moving from oral-discursive experience (the 'native's', the fieldworker's) to a written version of that experience (the ethnographic text) is enacting the structure of 'salvage'. To the extent that the ethnographic process is seen as inscription (rather than, for example, as transcription, or dialogue) the representation will continue to enact a potent, and questionable, allegorical structure" (p. 113). As with Geertz, the work of Spenserians played a crucial role in the formulation of a new direction for the theory of culture. Although Clifford also cites Paul de Man, his primary influences seem to be Northrop Frye and Angus Fletcher. And among the five people Clifford thanks at the end of his essay is the Spenserian Harry Berger, Jr., who was at the time also on the faculty of the University of California at Santa Cruz. Clifford, who co-edited the volume, seems to have helped introduce other cultural theorists to literary

---

[8] *The Anthropological Romance of Bali, 1597-1972: Dynamic Perspectives in Marriage and Caste, Politics and Religion* (Cambridge and New York, 1977).

[9] James Clifford and George E. Marcus, eds., *Writing Culture: The Poetics and Politics of Ethnography* (Berkeley, 1986).

[10] For criticism of the agenda of *Writing Culture*, see the essays collected in Richard G. Fox, ed., *Recapturing Anthropology: Working in the Present* (Santa Fe, 1991).

[11] "On Ethnographic Allegory," in *Writing Culture*, p. 109.

criticism. Several of the other contributors to the volume make use of Clifford's idea of "ethnographic allegory." Stephen Tyler discusses the now largely discredited but still influential "evolutionary allegory" that undergirds comparisons of "primitive" and "modern cultures."[12] Similarly, Vincent Crapanzano discusses the allegorical frames of three ethnographic texts, and Michael Fischer argues that "the conventions of realism, especially as practiced in traditional ethnography, themselves contain and are made coherent through allegorical metaphors."[13] However crude some of these uses of literary theory may be, clearly the concept of allegory has had a powerful and enabling effect within anthropology.

Like Clifford, Crapanzano, Fischer, and Tyler, the contributors to this volume understand cultural description as a form of allegory. This belief makes the reading of Spenser a peculiarly fruitful enterprise. Spenser is not only a powerful theorist of allegory and poetics more generally, he is also a profound and subtle ethnographer of both England and Ireland. These two species of theory, the poetic and the cultural, have more than a casual relationship in Spenser's work: each depends on the other. This explains how the essays in this volume can each begin with close reading and end by challenging the ethnographic allegories that shape our own knowledge of early modern Britain.

The first section of the book, "Allegories of Cultural Development," questions the narrative that tells of the emergence of "the modern." The volume begins with Leonard Barkan's essay "Ruins and Visions: Spenser, Pictures, Rome," which centers on Spenser's translations of Du Bellay's *Songe ou Vision* and *Antiquitez de Rome*. Barkan describes these works as the terminal point for a series of translations of cultures across boundaries— transfers of energy from ancient Rome to France to early modern England, from poetry to visual culture and back, and from Catholic to Protestant aesthetics. By the end of Barkan's essay, the binary division between medieval and early modern has come to seem inadequate as a description of the transmission and development of culture. In "Spenser's Currencies," Donald Cheney, writing on *The Shepheardes Calender*, focuses on the idea of literary works as commodities circulated within a market-place. Cheney reveals that this concept of the function of literature and the career of the poet, which is so frequently described as developing in the early modern period, in fact develops in ancient Rome: "Horace addresses his book, his *liber*, as if it were a favorite slave, also a *liber*, who is eager to expose himself to a broader public . . . the well-known dealers there, the Sosii brothers, are seen as pimps offering for sale a *liber* which has been polished with pumice, a substance used to prettify both books and boys. Both offer themselves for sale (*prostare*), and both, the poet

---

[12] "Post-Modern Ethnography: From Document of the Occult to Occult Document," in *Writing Culture*, p. 127.

[13] Crapanzano, "Hermes' Dilemma: The Masking of Subversion in Ethnographic Description," in *Writing Culture*, pp. 51-76; Fischer, "Ethnicity and the Arts of Memory," in *Writing Culture*, p. 198.

warns, are subject to the fluctuations of market demand." Maureen Quilligan's essay, "On the Renaissance Epic: Spenser and Slavery," also locates the uncanny persistence of Roman thought in a set of ideas that are often characterized as emerging in the early modern period: in her discussion of *The Faerie Queene*, she shows how Spenser's representation of a developing mercantile, wage-based economy depends on classical epic's attempt to mediate the social contradictions engendered by slavery. As in the essays of Barkan and Cheney, social formations generally considered distinctively "modern" are revealed as exhumations or simulacra of the classical past.

The second section of the book, "Allegories of Cultural Exchange," focuses on Spenser's complex narratives about the relations between England and Ireland. Together, the essays in this section call into question the idea of a distinctively "English" early modern culture. Richard McCabe's essay is called "Translated States: Spenser and Linguistic Colonialism." Discussing Renaissance theories of cultural and linguistic change, McCabe describes Spenser's anxiety about "an alarming tendency for the marginal to displace the central and for the central to decline into 'barbarity.'" McCabe traces an ambiguous, threatening infiltration of Irish words and Irish culture into Spenser's writing and English literature more generally. "Colonials Write the Nation: Spenser, Milton, and England on the Margins," Linda Gregerson's essay, centers on tensions and contradictions within the idea of a Protestant nation: the nation depends on the drawing of boundaries, while the religion makes universalist claims. English nationalism thus stands "outside the normative domestications of cultural and material practice"—it has only provisional, tentative connections to the English state and its territory. Nicholas Canny's essay, "The Social and Political Thought of Spenser in his Maturity," focuses on Spenser's theories about how English culture might be transported to Ireland and imposed on the Irish. Canny situates Spenser's thought within a series of ongoing debates within Renaissance pedagogy and political philosophy. Like McCabe and Gregerson, Canny suggests that cultural energy flows across political boundaries in ways that render problematic the idea of a unified national culture.

The third section of the book, "The Functions of Allegory," raises questions about the nature of the cultural work performed by literature. Kenneth Gross's essay, "The Postures of Allegory," suggests that allegory has a powerful defamiliarizing effect: reading a poem like *The Faerie Queene* disorients one, making one's social world and even one's own body seem foreign and strange. Allegory blurs, corrodes, and transmutes the symbolic systems out of which cultures are composed: the allegorist creates new cultural possibilities, new "postures." Susanne Wofford also complicates historicist understandings of Spenser's epic in an essay called "The Enfolding Dragon: Arthur and the Moral Economy of *The Faerie Queene*." Wofford suggests that the description of the dragon on Arthur's helmet is the site of one of a number of deep fissures within the poem. Ultimately, Wofford argues, the allegorical systems of theology and chivalric romance cannot be merged into a common project. Historicist readings of *The Faerie Queene*, which often rely on an insufficiently cautious understanding of allegory, have failed to adequately account for the doubleness of the poem's politics. In "'Work fit for an Herauld': Spenser in the '90s," Paul Alpers offers a related discussion of the complexity of the cultural work performed by Spenser's poetry. Building on the historicizing Spenser criticism of the 1990s, Alpers argues that attention to Spenser's social and material position can deepen our understanding of the formal and aesthetic properties of his late poetry. Alpers analyzes the complex fragmentation and proliferation of authorial personae in the political allegory of the fifth book of *The Faerie Queene* and in the public poetry of the "Epithalamion" and the "Prothalamion."

The volume concludes with Andrew Hadfield and Willy Maley's "A View of the Present State of Spenser Studies: Dialogue-Wise." In a pastoral debate that mimics the form of Spenser's own *View of the Present State of Ireland*, Hadfield and Maley situate Spenser within his overlapping cultures— Irish, English, Scottish, and New World—and then go on to debate the relation of his writing to these contexts. "What is the nature of fairyland in the poem?" Hadfield asks of *The Faerie Queene*. "It might be best to suggest that it represents a series of alternative Englands and Britains, past, present, future (as has long been recognized), plus a series of displaced and possible nations which overlap, conflict, and mingle." The contributors to this volume have developed new instruments for navigation within this complex space. It is our hope that these instruments will prove useful to other readers of literature and other theorists of culture.

Part I

Allegories of Cultural Development

1

Ruins and Visions:
Spenser, Pictures, Rome

Leonard Barkan

Anniversaries, even when they belong to poems rather than to persons, inspire historical reflection. In this case, the history is my own. The last time I attempted a project that was wholly dedicated to *The Faerie Queene* was in 1967, when I wrote the prospectus for my dissertation. I failed. And I have failed again this time. Not that I wish to suggest there is a jinx operating here; it's just that Spenser seems to enact a peculiar sort of self-effacement within my scholarly imagination. Thirty years ago I planned a critical/interpretive thesis on *The Faerie Queene* that was going to observe Spenser's habit of breaking down entities into their minute constituent parts. I talked a lot about prisms, and I took my title from the proem to Book III, where the poet invites Queen Elizabeth to observe herself figured in "mirrours more then one"—that is, Gloriana as queen, Belphoebe as chaste maid. My plan was to devote the first third of the first chapter to what I considered the most basic act of Spenserian prismatism, the allegorical breakdown of the human body in the Castle of Alma episode in Book II. After a year or so of research into the background for this third of a chapter, I started to feel that maybe I should write my whole dissertation about the human body, fitting in *The Faerie Queene* as best I might. I suppose I broke Spenser down into his constituent parts and threw most of them away. When I next essayed a large-scale project, this time about metamorphosis, I cannot say that *The Faerie Queene* played quite such a formative role. Yet as I was sending the manuscript off to the publisher and composing the foreword, I looked back a dozen or so years to the inception of the work and declared that my personal rediscovery of Ovid had inspired me because I found in the *Metamorphoses* the place of origin for everything I liked best about the Renaissance.[1] What I might just as well have said is, everything I liked best about Spenser.

There is no need to go on with this autobiography of an apostate but always secretly faithful Spenserian, a sort of *Faerie Queene* Marrano. My real point is to observe a particular way that this poem functions, at least upon me.

---

[1] These books are *Nature's Work of Art: The Human Body as Image of the World* (New Haven, 1975) and *The Gods Made Flesh: Metamorphosis and the Pursuit of Paganism* (New Haven, 1986).

Perhaps because *The Faerie Queene* is unfinished, perhaps because it is so hybrid, perhaps because of its belatedness in a whole series of contradictory traditions ranging from medieval allegory to humanistic classicism to Renaissance *realpolitik*, it never seems to stand still for me as an object in itself. While for others Spenser's poem may (justly) represent a tracing sheet for ideologies, in me it produces a kind of passion for etiologies—that is, a longing to go back to origins, to consider not just its sources in the narrow sense but the whole fabric of literary and esthetic culture that made it possible. When I was relatively new to the profession I remember being ridiculed by a couple of senior colleagues because I chanced to say I wanted to "account for" *The Faerie Queene*. In a sense they were right: it is at once a trivializing and a presumptuous activity. You account for a leak in the ceiling, and then you fix it and get rid of it. I do not mean to be getting rid of Spenser, or attempting to explain him away. But I do find that he offers the most fascinating of studies in the processes, the ratios, the directionality of cultural transmission.

Two related passages in *The Faerie Queene* reveal the poet himself imagining just this sort of movement. In the Book of Chastity, at the beginning of what will be the story of Amoret and Belphoebe, Venus is described as having lost her "little sonne, the winged god of loue." To find him,

> she left her heauenly hous,
> The house of goodly formes and faire aspects,
> Whence all the world deriues the glorious
> Features of beautie …

> First she him sought in Court, where most he vsed
> Whylome to haunt, but there she found him not …

> She then the Citties sought from gate to gate,
> And euery one did aske, did he him see;
> And euery one her answerd, that too late
> He had him seene, and felt the crueltie
> Of his sharpe darts and whot artillerie …

> Then in the countrey she abroad him sought,
> And in the rurall cottages inquired,
> Where also many plaints to her were brought …
> And eke the gentle shepheard swaynes, which sat
> Keeping their fleecie flockes, as they were hyred,
> She sweetly heard complaine …

> But when in none of all these she him got,
> She gan auize, where else he mote him hyde:
> At last she her bethought, that she had not
> Yet sought the saluage woods and forrests wyde,

In which full many louely Nymphes abyde,
Mongst whom might be, that he did closely lye.[2] (3.6.11-16)

More briefly, in the Book of Courtesy it is not Venus seeking Cupid but
Calidore seeking the Blatant Beast:

Him first from court he to the citties coursed,
And from the citties to the townes him prest,
And from the townes into the countrie forsed,
And from the country back to priuate farmes he scorsed.

From thence into the open fields he fled ...
Him thether eke for all his fearefull threat
He followed fast, and chaced him so nie,
That to the folds, where sheepe at night doe seat,
And to the litle cots, where shepherds lie
In winters wrathfull time, he forced him to flie. (6.9.3-4)

These narrative quests, which are also developmental histories of poetic
materials, have the same structure. The object of pursuit moves from its
essential place of origin through an ever wider geography of concentric
circles—court, city, country, deep country, and so on—until it ends up in what
Spenser is defining as his own poetic milieu, which, in the case of Book III, is
"the saluage woods and forrests wyde" and, in the case of Book VI, is the
sheepcote. What I find noteworthy about these versions of the literary or
aesthetic *translatio studi* is not so much that they culminate in Spenser's own
universe (that is hardly surprising) but that he generously allows all the
preceding literary milieux their own privileges. In other words, the narrative of
Spenserian etiologies is one in which the sources are not dissolved once the
poetic destination has been attained.

Rather, it is one in which the journey matters as much as the arrival. As
Spenser stages these episodes, literary influence itself becomes a quest, and
one in which the endpoint is not the rejection of earlier stages but their
fulfillment and integration. My own experience of stopping short of *The Faerie
Queene*, or of losing myself in its origins, is, after all, one of the inevitable
shapes of the quest (a particularly Spenserian shape, to be sure). I place
Spenser's poem inside a stretch of cultural geography, and I find myself
providing a sort of meta-literary map, not of Faeryland but to it. Nor is the map
entirely meta-literary or metaphorical. At the midpoint of both Venus's and
Calidore's searches, you may recall, was the city. It is not a milieu with which
we always associate Spenser, even though he was by birth as much a Londoner
as Ben Jonson was. But I take permission from these topographical narratives

[2] Citations to Spenser, with the exception of his translations from the *Theatre for
Worldlings*, are taken from the *Poetical Works*, ed. J.C. Smith and E. De Selincourt (London,
1969).

to design a map of my own with two focal points: Rome, and the poet who brought Rome to Spenser, Joachim du Bellay.[3]

Spenser encountered du Bellay at a quite astonishingly young age. In 1568 the Calvinist Dutch *émigré* Jan van der Noot published a patchwork of prose and verse under the title *A Theatre for Worldlings*.[4] In the English version of this collection, published in 1569, Spenser, still a schoolboy, provided blank-verse translations of eleven sonnets from those that make up du Bellay's *Songe ou Vision*, itself first published only eleven years earlier. At some later moment—but still early in his career, according to most scholarly opinion—he fashioned a new and this time complete translation of the *Songe*, now in sonnet form like the original; in addition, he produced a translation of du Bellay's *Antiquitez de Rome*, which had been closely joined to the *Songe* in the original 1558 French publication. Beyond the question of these particular translations, the pervasiveness of du Bellay's influence on Spenser is signaled by the 1591 volume in which "The Ruins of Rome by Bellay" and "Bellays Visions" appear. The book itself is called *Complaints*, while du Bellay's Rome lyrics had been published along with a sonnet cycle entitled *Les Regrets*; and other works in the Spenser volume, especially the *Tears of the Muses* and *The*

---

[3] I have benefited from a considerable body of valuable scholarship on the du Bellay sequences, from which I would especially single out Daniel Russell, "Du Bellay's Emblematic Vision of Rome," *Yale French Studies* 47 (1972), 98-109; Wayne Rebhorn, "Du Bellay's Imperial Mistress: *Les Antiquitez de Rome* as Petrarchist Sonnet Sequence," *Renaissance Quarterly* 33 (1980), 609-22; Sharlene M. Poliner, "Du Bellay's *Songe*: Strategies of Deceit, Poetics of Vision," *Bibliothèque d'humanisme et Renaissance* 43 (1981), 509-25; Thomas M. Greene, *The Light in Troy: Imitation and Discovery in Renaissance Poetry* (New Haven, 1982), pp. 220-41; G.W. Pigman III, "Du Bellay's Ambivalence toward Rome in the *Antiquitez*," in *Rome in the Renaissance: The City and the Myth*, ed. P.A. Ramsey (Binghamton, 1982), pp. 321-32; P.M. Martin, "Les Rome de Joachim du Bellay, à travers les 'Antiquitez de Rome' et les 'Regrets,'" *Etudes classiques* 51 (1983), 133-50; Margaret Ferguson, "'The Afflatus of Ruin': Meditations on Rome by Du Bellay, Spenser, and Stevens," in *Roman Images: Selected Papers from the English Institute*, ed. A. Patterson (Baltimore, 1984), pp. 23-50; E. MacPhail, "The Roman Tomb or the Image of the Tomb in du Bellay's *Antiquitez*," *Bibliothèque d'humanisme et Renaissance* 48 (1986), 359-72.

[4] Within a year, the original Dutch version and translations into French and English all appeared in London. All included poetic materials from Petrarch (as rendered by Marot in the French) and du Bellay. Quite apart from signaling Spenser's première as a poet a full decade before the appearance of *The Shepheardes Calender*, the *Theatre for Worldlings* has considerable importance as a work of Protestant polemics that is none the less sensitive to recent developments in Continental poetics. The illustrations that are paired with the poetry, of which more below, have also led some scholars to refer to this volume as the first English emblem book. Spenser's authorship of the translations, which has occasionally been doubted on account of his youth and the fact that he is nowhere mentioned in the book, can be treated as reasonably certain given the similarities to his versions of these poems in the *Complaints* of 1591, whose title page refers to the Petrarch materials as "formerly translated." See J.A. van Dorsten, *The Radical Arts: First Decade of an Elizabethan Renaissance* (Leiden, 1970); C.J. Rasmussen, "'Quietnesse of Minde': *A Theatre for Worldlings* as a Protestant Poetics," *Spenser Studies* 1 (1980), 3-27. On the place of the *Complaints* volume in Spenser's career and chronology, see H. Stein, *Studies in Spenser's* Complaints (New York, 1934).

Ruins of Time, imitate the visionary, the satirical, and the topographical aspects of the French poet's art.[5]

That du Bellay should be the starting point for a map like mine is not coincidental. He is, after all, the great sixteenth-century theorist of literary influence, who pushed into yet more paradoxical territory all of Petrarch's notions of attaining an individual personal voice by following in the footsteps of classical models. Territory occupied by du Bellay—and Spenser can be assumed to know this realm of theory quite well, since it was being adapted into English terms by Richard Mulcaster, the same teacher at the Merchant Taylors' school who may have obtained the van der Noot opportunity for the young poet—is saturated, one might almost say overdetermined, by challenging injunctions concerning what it means to imitate predecessors.[6] More than that, the issues as du Bellay presents them in the *Deffence et illustration de la langue françoyse* are set in the context of translation, which becomes at once the necessary and the impossible step in a transmission of cultures.[7]

What happens when you translate someone who has famously theorized the problematics of translation? Du Bellay's strictures were, of course, focused on the move from classical to modern tongues. But his arguments, which postulate an essential core to each language—the *naïf*, which is cognate to "native"—cast a complicating shadow on all transcultural linguistic moves. Not that his own practice always conforms to his theories or to any sort of rigorous self-consciousness. Du Bellay's stay in Rome during the 1550s, the same period that witnesses the composition of the *Antiquitez* and the *Songe*, becomes the occasion for a considerable production of Latin verse, which even his contemporaries recognized as some sort of contradiction to the manifesto of the *Deffence*. In response, he wrote (among other things) an introductory verse *Ad lectorem* in which he compares the writing of verse in French to legitimate marriage and the writing of verse in Latin to a delicious episode of adultery: "Illa [the one over there—that is, the French girl, since he is writing this from Italy] quidem bella est, sed magis ista placet."[8] But what kind of adultery—or other sexual unorthodoxy—is involved in writing of the ruins of Rome, in French, and in the poetic mode famous for its examination of extramarital

---

[5] On the relations between du Bellay and Spenser, in addition to Ferguson as cited above in n. 3 and below in n. 6, see Anne Lake Prescott, *French Poets and the English Renaissance: Studies in Fame and Transformation* (New Haven, 1978), pp. 46-52, and Lawrence Manley, "Spenser and the City: The Minor Poems," *Modern Language Quarterly* 43 (1982), 203-27.

[6] Concerning Mulcaster's work on native, foreign, and classical linguistic traditions along with their relations to both du Bellay and Spenser, see M.W. Ferguson's superb entry under "du Bellay" in *The Spenser Encyclopedia*, ed. A.C. Hamilton, et al. (Toronto, 1990), pp. 83-5. For Mulcaster's most important work, first published in 1582, see *Mulcaster's Elementarie*, ed. E.T. Campagnac (Oxford, 1925).

[7] The discussion of translation is to be found especially in book 1, chs. 5 and 6. See the subtle analysis of this work in Margaret Ferguson, *Trials of Desire: Renaissance Defenses of Poetry* (New Haven, 1983), pp. 18-53.

[8] See du Bellay, *Poésies latines et françaises*, ed. E. Courbet (Paris, 1918), p. 453.

desire, during the same period when, as he says, he is more turned on by his Latin mistress? The matter is further entangled by the fact that in the *Deffence* du Bellay frequently characterizes failed translation, or other sorts of inferior modern production, as a plundering or profanation of classical relics.[9] Which almost makes the *Antiquitez*, with its enumerations of decayed and destroyed antique remains, into an allegory of bad literary imitation.[10]

But let us move off the starting point and on to the quest. Our first, and most minute, map of directionalities consists simply in the transit from du Bellay to Spenser in the *Theatre for Worldlings* and then to Spenser in the *Complaints*. My interest is not so much in verbal relations between French and English or between the two English versions. Rather, I wish to trace some throughlines among these three points. Petrarch, for instance: the first set of poems that Spenser produced for the van der Noot volume, there entitled *Epigrams*, is in truth a translation of *Rime* 323 ("Standomi un giorno"), itself by way of Clément Marot's version, which had been rendered into Dutch for the original edition of van der Noot's book. In the English volume, *Rime* 323 is devolved from *canzone* form into six separate sonnet-like lyrics plus an envoy, in effect deconstructing Petrarch's alternative poetic forms. Perhaps more interesting is the fact that "Standomi un giorno" is clearly the source for the whole visionary mode of du Bellay's *Songe*, the translation of which follows it almost without break in van der Noot's publication. The relations turn again in the *Complaints* volume, where the original authors are credited explicitly in the titles, where the whole descent from Petrarch to du Bellay to Spenser himself is represented—again literary influence as integration rather than rejection—and where "Standomi un giorno" is itself reintegrated into the status of a single poem in multiple stanzas, though with an original Spenserian ending.

Alternatively, we may consider the spin on these lines of progression offered by the presence of van der Noot himself. The *Theatre for Worldlings* is a 200-page sermon attached to a handful of brief lyrics; it is also a zealously Protestant project constructed on the basis of Catholic poetry, much of which glorifies Rome. Granted that the opposition is not quite so stark as this suggests: Du Bellay is himself quite capable of moral outrage at the behavior of the Roman clergy. And van der Noot alters the material by omitting some of

---

[9] "O Apollon! O Muses! prophaner ainsi les sacrées reliques de l'Antiquité" (Joachim du Bellay, *La deffense et illustration de la langue françoise*, ed. H. Chamard [Geneva, 1969], pp. 96-7).

[10] It is, of course, at the same time a work of good imitation—that is, deeply in touch with its own classical intertextuality. A study like the present one that focuses on relations between du Bellay and Spenser can hardly fail to mention the originary work's own origins. The *Antiquitez*, more than the *Songe* (not surprisingly), is a tissue of intertextualities going back to Ovid, Lucan, and Horace but equally dependent on du Bellay's neo-Latin contemporaries including George Buchanan and Janus Vitalis. In fact, *Antiquitez* 3, of which much is made below, is virtually a translation from the *Elogia* of Vitalis. On all these relations, see R. Schwaderer, *Das Verhältnis des Lyrikers Joachim du Bellay zu seinen Vorbildern* (Würzburg, 1968), K. Lloyd-Jones, "Du Bellay's Journey from *Roma Vetus* to *La Rome Neufve*," in *Rome in the Renaissance*, pp. 301-19, and, especially, George H. Tucker, *The Poet's Odyssey: Joachim du Bellay and the* Antiquitez de Rome (Oxford, 1990).

the seemingly more Catholic sonnets in the *Songe*, replacing them with more acceptable visionary materials based on the Book of Revelations.[11] In fact, the sermon works hard to tease out all possible negative readings of Rome, including some quite original ones, for example, that Romulus and Remus "sucked all manner of crueltie and beastlynesse" out of the she-wolf's teats.[12] Still, why go to the trouble of further disseminating relatively new Catholic verse only to have to wrench it into new meanings? I cannot answer the question for van der Noot. But what is important for our purposes is that Spenser will receive du Bellay through the necessary refraction of a hermeneutic tradition that is determined to turn Catholic materials into Protestant ones and to exploit the glory of Rome *in malo*. But as with the reappearance of Petrarch, we must recall that Spenser's second version of the *Songe*, this time with the *Antiquitez*, will not shy away from all the dangerously Catholic elements in the original and will, of course, omit the Protestantizing sermon; in short, it will once again reintegrate itself with its origins.

Then there is the matter of verse forms, which also undergo a sequence of mutations from the French original onwards. Du Bellay's great innovation, in both the *Songe* and the *Antiquitez*, was to take the sonnet (and more particularly the sonnet sequence), which Petrarch had perfected as the supreme expression of erotic subjectivity, and use it as the medium for theological, visionary, and historical expression. In truth, the erotic is by no means abandoned in the *Antiquitez*—a fact that complicates the terms in which both Rome and the lamenting poet–speaker are presented. In the England of 1569, with Petrarchan sonnets on erotic themes as familiar a medium as they are in du Bellay's France, the young Spenser renounces the opportunity to repeat du Bellay's innovation and experiments instead with a different new form, which we might call the blank verse sonnet. To the extent that this is a departure from the source, it is a swerve-as-*hommage*, since Spenser is translating what was original in du Bellay into his own imitative form of originality, the curious hybrid of blank-verse and sonnet bearing precisely the same mix of erotic and elegiac possibilities. The wheel turns again in 1591 when Spenser returns all these lyrics to the sonnet form, by which time that

---

[11] It is not so much that the omitted poems are theologically objectionable to Protestants as the fact that they make more direct reference—and not always approvingly—to the Catholic church. Sonnet 6 begins with a conceit on the she-wolf who suckled Romulus and Remus, an episode that van der Noot allegorized as the Roman church *in malo*. Sonnet 8 weaves together the seven hills of Rome and the seven-headed beast of Revelations. Sonnets 13 and 14 recount a mythologized history of the Catholic church, including the sufferings it has sustained from corrupt clerics on the one hand and the Protestant Reformation on the other. In effect, van der Noot is removing some of the Book of Revelations subtext from du Bellay and replacing it with his own explicit version in the four poems that he appends seamlessly to the eleven sonnets from the *Songe*. This completes the orthodox Augustinian picture of history, according to which the rise and fall of Rome are stages on the way to the final Apocalypse.

[12] Jan van der Noot, *Theatre for Worldlings*, facsimile edition, ed. W.A. Jackson and L.S. Friedland (New York, 1939), 15[v].

verse form is the reigning medium for erotic expression in Spenser's national language.

We may follow this trajectory one more time in regard to the form in which the poems are presented in publication. Du Bellay's own volume prints his poems one after the other, merely broken into two sequences, as he expresses it on the title page:

> LES ANTIQUITEZ DE ROME
> CONTENANT UNE
> GENERALE DESCRIPTION DE SA GRANDEUR
> ET COMME
> UNE DEPLORATION DE SA RUINE:
> PLUS
> UN SONGE OU VISION
> SUR LE MESME SUBJECT[13]

Van der Noot, on the other hand, not only divides up Petrarch into separate poems but also publishes each of the resulting "Epigrams" and "Sonets" with an illustration on the facing page. These images—for instance, the mannerist river god that illustrates *Songe* 7 (fig. 1.1)—have been variously attributed to Marcus Gheeraerts the Elder and Lucas de Heere; they had begun as etchings for the pre-English versions of the *Theatre for Worldlings* and were recreated as woodcuts for the volume in which Spenser's translations appeared.[14] In either form, they are of remarkably high quality, both in conception and realization—compared, say, to the *Shepheardes Calender* woodcuts of a few years later (fig. 1.2). Owing both to their excellence and their prominence in the book's design, they form a significant partnership to the verses. It is not surprising that van der Noot would have added such images as part of his revision of the alien Catholic materials: the resulting book pages come to embody an evangelical habit of combining a set of verbal truths that appeal to the sophisticated literate Christian and visual representations that appeal to the common person.

In this process, what was Petrarch or du Bellay becomes a particularly attractive form of emblem book; indeed, an emblem book in which the visual element is exceptionally well integrated. After all, in the van der Noot version

---

[13] Citations to the *Antiquitez* and the *Songe* are taken from *Les Regrets et autres oeuvres poëtiques*, ed. J. Jolliffe and M.A. Screech (Geneva, 1974). English versions given here are Spenser's, in the *Complaints* version, except when the material was not included there; in that case the translation is by the present author.

[14] Both these artists can be connected to the milieu of the *Theatre for Worldlings*. Gheeraerts was, like van der Noot, an exile in London, while de Heere had written a poem that appears within the prefatory material to the Dutch edition. See Louis S. Friedland, "The Illustrations in *The Theatre for Worldlings*," *Huntington Library Quarterly* 19 (1956), 107-20, and M. Bath, "Verse Form and Pictorial Space in Van der Noot's *Theatre for Worldlings*," in K. J. Höltgen, et al., eds., *Word and Visual Image: Studies in the Interaction of English Literature and the Visual Arts* (Erlangen, 1988), pp. 73-105.

Figure 1.1
Songe 7, Jan van der Noot, *Theatre for Worldlings* (London, 1569)

Figure 1.2
"Januarye" woodcut from Edmund Spenser's *Shepheardes Calender* (London, 1591)

each of these twenty-one poems is a separate vision. And each of the woodcuts
is the vision. We do not see the dreamer (as one did frequently in this genre);
in fact, the one poem out of the twenty-two that has no accompanying image is
the first of the *Songe*, where the situation of the dreamer is established. Rather,
each picture leaps directly to the visionary conclusion.

Figure 1.3
"At my right hande, a Hinde appearde to me" [15]
Jan van der Noot, *Theatre for Worldlings* (London, 1569)

---

[15] Spenser's translations from the 1569 *Theatre for Worldlings* are cited from Joachim du Bellay, *Antiquitez de Rome translated by Edmund Spenser as Ruines of Rome*, ed. M.C. Smith (Binghamton, 1994).

Figure 1.4
"Then heauenly branches did I see arise"
Jan van der Noot, *Theatre for Worldlings* (London, 1569)

Figure 1.5
"I saw a Phoenix in the wood alone"
Jan van der Noot, *Theatre for Worldlings* (London, 1569)

Figure 1.6
"A frame an hundred cubites hie
I sawe, an hundred pillers eke about"
Jan van der Noot, *Theatre for Worldlings* (London, 1569)

Figure 1.7
"I saw raisde vp on pillers of Iuorie …
The double front of a triumphall arke"
Jan van der Noot, *Theatre for Worldlings* (London, 1569)

Figure 1.8
"Then I behelde the faire Dodonian tree"
Jan van der Noot, *Theatre for Worldlings* (London, 1569)

Figure 1.9
"Vpon a hill I saw a kindled flame"
Jan van der Noot, *Theatre for Worldlings* (London, 1569)

Figure 1.10
"I saw the great Typhaeus sister come"
Jan van der Noot, *Theatre for Worldlings* (London, 1569)

The image, which is located on the right-hand page, realizes, in every sense of the term, the visionary language of the poem that is facing it on the left. It also contrasts with the text, supplants it, short-circuits it, supplements it—in short, all those effects that images have upon words. But following our theme of directionality, perhaps the most telling matter, then, is the absence of these images in the 1591 volume. As in other respects, Spenser's more mature version reverts to du Bellay. Whether, following our pattern of the cumulative quest, the visual force of the image can be said to have integrated itself into the totality of the poems' effect: that is, in a sense, the lurking question in regard to everything I am discussing here—not only for the *Complaints* but also for *The Faerie Queene.*

I offer a possibly circuitous step toward this matter by touching upon one more piece of directionality, this time within the work of du Bellay, between the *Antiquitez* and the *Songe*. I say "between," but it is important to remember that we can establish no definitive chronological priority between the two cycles.[16] Both groups of poems were written during du Bellay's stay in Rome in the mid-1550s. They were published together in a single volume when he had returned to France. The *Antiquitez* are presented as the primary work, but the title page, as we have seen, includes the *Songe* in a featured role, declaring it to be "sur le mesme subject." That statement is true in regard to the title page's own account of the *Antiquitez* as "une generale description de sa grandeur et comme une deploration de sa ruine"; but in other ways the two works seem to emerge from quite different traditions, roughly comparable to elegy and dream vision. Perhaps a better way to distinguish them, albeit retrospectively, is to note that Spenser first translated the *Songe* and then the *Antiquitez*—though in keeping with my notions of the cumulative literary quest, it is more accurate to say he first translated the *Songe* and then the *Antiquitez* and the *Songe* together. The *Songe*, in short, conforms to earlier, medievalizing poetic modes that are perfectly in keeping both with the young English poet's predecessors and with the religious purposes of the volume in which his translations appeared; hence the ease with which theologically questionable sonnets could be replaced with visions in the style of the Book of Revelations. The *Antiquitez* conform rather to newly developing humanist modes of poetic expression; and though they, too, contain theological traps, it would have been more difficult to find ready-made substitutions.

But my interest is in one particular matter as it refracts between the two works. We have already observed—with pictures—how each sonnet in the *Songe* consists of a different dream vision; and we noted that the woodcuts in the van der Noot volume omitted the dreamer, focusing only on the dream.

---

[16] The work of V.-L. Saulnier, "Commentaires sur les *Antiquitez de Rome*," *Bibliothèque d'humanisme et Renaissance* 12 (1950), 114-43, has been significant in demonstrating that du Bellay's varying responses to Rome represented alternative points of view rather than a sequence of changing opinions. This is all the more likely considering that he spent only four years in Rome.

There is another omission from these images: in every case, the glorious object of the vision is destroyed in the last lines of the sonnet, and that is never visible in the images. The hundred-column Doric temple (see figure 1.6) is destroyed by "un soudain tremblement [qui] / Renversa ce beau lieu depuis le fondement" ("an earthquake ... overthrew this frame with ruine great"). A diamond obelisk 10 feet square topped with a golden vase containing the emperor's ashes (fig. 1.11) meets its end when the dreamer sees "du ciel la tempeste descendre, / Et foudroyer ce brave monument" ("a tempest from the heaven descend, / Which this brave monument with flash did rend").

Figure 1.11
"A sodaine tempest from the heauen, I saw,
With flushe stroke downe this noble monument"
Jan van der Noot, *Theatre for Worldlings* (London, 1569)

The memorial arch with alabaster capitals and crystal frieze (see figure 1.7) with Victories and triumphal chariots for emperors is "d'une soudaine cheute ... reduict en poudre" ("with sodain fall to dust consumed quight"). And finally a whole city "quasi semblable à celle / Que vid le messager de la bonne nouvelle" is undone when "du costé de Nort vint le cruel orage" which overturns "les foibles fondemens de la grande Cité" ("a citie like unto that same / Which saw the messenger of tidings glad"; undone "when from the northern coast a storm arose," which overturns "the weake foundations of this Citie faire.")

This sonnet, the last vision before the dreamer wakes up, Spenser did not translate in the *Theatre for Worldlings* version (and it was therefore not illustrated). That should not surprise us, since du Bellay seems here to be weaving the Rome of the earlier visions together with the heavenly Jerusalem of the Apocalypse; furthermore, the agent of destruction, the cruel storm from the North, might seem uncomfortably close to a representation of the Protestant Reformation. Whatever the revisionary purposes may have been in 1569, this sonnet points precisely toward the differences between du Bellay's two sequences, even as it starts to erase them. The almost mechanically repeated act of destruction in the *Songe* is firmly in the mode of the magical and visionary. If we are to understand "le mesme subject" here as a description of the grandeur of Rome and a "deploration de sa ruine," then Rome is in this case the stuff of transhistorical Christian vision and the ruin is a magic act that follows only the logic of prophetic dreams.

The accounts of the fall of Rome in the *Antiquitez* are quite different. There is a fairly steady progression. In the early sonnets, the causes tend to be the general and inexorable flow of time: "Ce qui est ferme, est par le temps destruit" (3: "That which is firm doth flit and fall away"); "Toute chose au dessous de la Lune / Est corrompable et sugette à mourir" (9: "All things which beneath the Moone have being / Are temporall, and subject to decay"). Later there are much more particularized accounts:

> Ces grands monceaux pierreux, ces vieux murs que tu vois,
> Furent premierement le cloz d'un lieu champestre,
> Et ces braves palais, dont le temps s'est fait maistre,
> Cassines de pasteurs ont esté quelquefois. (18)

> These heaps of stones, these old wals which ye see,
> Were first enclosures but of salvage soyle,
> And these brave Pallaces which maystered bee
> Of time, were shepheards cottages somewhile.

The shepherds, according to this sonnet, became kings, the kings became emperors; but heaven opposed this aggrandizement, and "Mist ce pouvoir es mains du successeur de Pierre" ("Her power to *Peters* successor betooke"), such that they are, in effect, shepherds once more. From that somewhat mythic account, du Bellay moves toward explanations that are more firmly grounded.

In another version of the city with pastoral origins, he declares of Rome that "Son pouvoir dissipé s'écarta par le monde" (20: "Her power disperst, through all the world did vade"), which is an extremely sophisticated explanation of the weakening of empire. Later he invokes the politics of destroying or not destroying Carthage—a city that was ruined by quite different circumstances and whose destruction rendered Romans "un peuple ocieux" in whom "void-on ... / L'ambition facilement s'engendre" (23: "a people given all to ease, / [in whom] Ambition is engendred easily"). Finally, he sums up the phenomenon in a past-and-present account that could have found itself in the most up-to-date humanist version of Rome's story:

> Ainsi de peu à peu creut l'empire Romain,
> Tant qu'il fut despouillé par la Barbare main,
> Qui ne laissa de luy que ces marques antiques,
> Que chacun va pillant. (30)

> So grew the Romane Empire by degree,
> Till that Barbarian hands it quite did spill,
> And left of it but these olde markes to see,
> Of which all passers by doo somewhat pill.

A quite sophisticated account proceeding through the rise of Rome, the barbarian invasions, the remaining emblems of former greatness, and the modern dangers of their further decay.

In short, one of these sonnet cycles is visionary; the other is historical. In one of them, a city allusively but not always directly associated with Rome—the title *Songe ou Vision* avoids saying what the subject of the vision is precisely—consists of magical structures built out of gold and crystal and allegorical representations; and it comes tumbling down through thunderclaps of visionary inevitability. In the other sonnet cycle, a Rome that is explicitly named contains, just to pick one list, "Ces vieux palais, ces monts audacieux, / Ces murs, ces arcz, ces thermes et ces temples, / ... / Ces vieux fragmens [qui] encor servent d'exemples" (27: "These haughtie heapes, these palaces of olde, / These wals, these arcks, these baths, these temples hie, / ... / these old fragments [that] are for paternes borne"). When this city enters a state of ruin, it is through a sequence of civil and foreign wars, of political realities, of weakening authority, and of a continuing power vacuum.

But the most important thing about establishing these distinctions is to observe the reconcilability of the alternatives. The combination of the two sequences in du Bellay's original and the reintegration of them in Spenser's *Complaints* volume signify that all those visionary episodes of rise and fall, generally owing their origins to the Book of Revelations, can be grafted on to the narrative of history. In that narrative, the city of Rome—with or without the pros and cons of its place in theology—forms the crowning example for a modern practice of reading the past both as different from the present and as contributing through a logical series of steps to the making of that present. The origins of this combination go back to Dante's *De Monarchia* (a term cited in the *Antiquitez*) and, especially—once again—to Petrarch, who was, not coincidentally, the author both of visionary lyrics whose object could be transferred from Laura to Rome and of theories of the past that could frame Rome in its proper historicity.[17] Du Bellay, to be sure, is the carrier of this genetic material; through him Spenser will inherit—and realize in the grand imaginative fictions of *The Faerie Queene*—the possibility of integrating the visionary with the historical. But like the quests of Venus and Calidore, this line must travel through the city.

All roads, they say, lead to Rome; none of them, as it turns out, is a one-way street. If Rome plants itself squarely at the point of opposition and reconciliation between the visionary and the historical, that is because it lies at the heart of all the problematics of cultural inheritance for which I am attempting to provide a pathway.[18] Du Bellay is Spenser's Man in Rome, and the matter of Rome is transmitted decisively through the lyric and the visionary qualities of the *Antiquitez*. Consider some of the most famous lines in du Bellay's sequence, which present themselves as (dare I say?) always already proverbial:

> Nouveau venu, qui cherches Rome en Rome
> Et rien de Rome en Rome n'apperçois:
> Ces vieux palais, ces vieux arcz que tu vois,
> Et ces vieux murs, c'est ce que Rome on nomme …
> Rome de Rome est le seul monument,
> Et Rome Rome a vaincu seulement. (3)

> Thou stranger, which for *Rome* in *Rome* thou seekest,
> And nought of *Rome* in *Rome* perceiv'st at all,
> These same olde walls, olde arches, which thou seest
> Olde Palaces, is that which *Rome* men call …
> *Rome* now of *Rome* is th'onely funerall,
> And onely *Rome* of *Rome* hath victorie.

> Rome seule pouvoit à Rome ressembler,
> Rome seule pouvoit Rome faire trembler. (6)

---

[17] On the specific case of *monarchy* as an abstract term for universal power centered on Rome, see *Antiquitez* 16: "Et comme on void la flamme ondoyant en cent lieux / Se rassemblant en un, s'aguiser vers les cieux, / Puis tumber languissante: ainsi parmy le monde / Erra la monarchie." As for the possible homology between Petrarch the love poet and Petrarch the reviver of Rome, the subject is a very large one. My own sense of it is based partly on Thomas Greene's notion of "subreading," used to characterize the poet's relation to Roman antiquities and then applied to the sort of lyric poetry that he is writing (*Light in Troy*, pp. 88-103), and partly on the ideas of Nancy Vickers concerning a fundamentally fragmentary vision of the beloved, which I would associate as well with the fragmentary state of antiquity ("Diana Described: Scattered Woman and Scattered Rhyme," *Critical Inquiry* 8 [1981], 265-79).

[18] These arguments concerning the status of ancient Rome as history, myth, and repository of classical relics are taken from my *Unearthing the Past: Archaeology and Aesthetics in the Making of Renaissance Culture* (New Haven, 1999); see that work for a fuller account of these matters.

Rome onely might to *Rome* compared bee,
And onely *Rome* could make great *Rome* to tremble.

Rome fut tout le monde, et tout le monde est Rome.
Et si par mesmes noms mesmes choses on nomme,
Comme du nom de Rome on se pourroit passer
La nommant par le nom de la terre et de l'onde,
Ainsi le monde on peult sur Rome compasser,
Puisque le plan de Rome est la carte du monde. (26)

Rome was th' whole world, and al the world was *Rome*,
And if things nam'd their names doo equalize,
When land and sea ye name, then name ye *Rome*,
And naming *Rome* ye land and sea comprize:
For th'auncient Plot of *Rome* displayed plaine,
The map of all the wide world doth containe.

It is a sort of mini-poetics of the impossible, translating all of the darkest implications of the *Deffence* and attaching them to the name of Rome. It all goes back to what I take to be a rather innocent turn of phrase in a widely influential Petrarch letter—"For who today are more ignorant about Roman affairs than the Roman citizens. Sadly do I say that nowhere is Rome less known than in Rome"—which perhaps du Bellay read as personal permission for a foreigner to know more or care more about Rome than the Romans do.[19] At all events, with three or four decades of deconstruction behind us, it is almost too easy to read these lines. Rome is the unfindable, the nonpareil. It is the map of the world, but it cannot be mapped and therefore renders the world unmappable. It is the only possible vanquisher of itself, but it is also the tomb of itself: the living Rome was entombed in or under the seven hills; what survives of Rome is literally tombs, while to render Rome in poetry may be to extract it from the tomb or simply to provide another kind of tomb. Rome is the very definition of name—that is, of language—a claim which is abetted by all the kinds of rhyme available among "Rome," *nomme*, and *nom*, but if it is the quintessential name, it can only be the name of itself, and therefore it defines but also defies signification. In its very repetition the word becomes part mantra, part nonsense.

But there is something very real behind these incantatory turns of phrase, which du Bellay may have been the first to have the historical distance to perceive. From the twelfth century onwards a set of often-repeated tag lines, based on an elegy by Hildebert of Lavardin, declared that nothing could equal Rome, even though she was in total ruin: "Roma quanta fuit ipsa ruina docet."[20] What is distinctive in this very persistent mentality is not the flat

---

[19] *Familiares*, 6.2, cited from Francesco Petrarca, *Letters on Familiar Matters*, trans. A.S. Bernardo (Baltimore, 1985), 1: 293.

[20] For Hildebert's poem, which does not actually contain the quoted line, see *Oxford Book of Medieval Latin Verse*, ed. F.J.E. Raby (Oxford, 1959), p. 220. On the phrase itself, see Salvatore Settis, "Continuità, distanza, conoscenza: tre usi dell'antico," in *Memoria dell'antico*

comparison but the ratio, or what we might term exponential thinking: however ruined Rome is now, by that much more do we need to multiply the once living city in our imaginations. The ruins of Rome thus contribute to a living text of epic similes whereby that which is seen becomes aggrandized through a ratio of comparisons to that which cannot be seen. And what cannot be seen decisively shifts from the realm of the visual artist to that of the poet.

In the same famous letter that spawned the repeated chanting of "Rome," Petrarch uses the desolation of the city (which he somewhat exaggerates) as a *tabula rasa* on which to impose his own living history in words, recreating the ruined urban landscape. With two more centuries of antiquarianism, humanism, and the aesthetic exploitation of the example of antiquity, du Bellay is able to understand the subject of Rome as the paradigm of imagination, that is, of seeing what is not there and supplanting the absent images with present language.

> Peusse-je aumoins d'un pinceau plus agile
> Sur le patron de quelque grand Virgile
> De ces palais les protraits façonner:
> J'entreprendrois, veu l'ardeur qui m'allume,
> De rebastir au compas de la plume
> Ce que les mains ne peuvent maçonner. (25)

> Or that at least I could with pencill fine
> Fashion the pourtraicts of these Palacis
> By paterne of great *Virgils* spirit divine:
> I would assay with that which in me is,
> To builde with levell of my loftie style,
> That which no hands can evermore compyle.

That Virgil is the paradigm of portraiture—not just Virgil, as Spenser has it, but "quelque grand Virgile"—and that du Bellay's "pattern" is also a patron (again, not available to his translator) suggests not only the familiar business of the poet who invents in words a new and more lasting visual experience; it also signifies the ongoing, or transitive possibilities of this kind of poetic creation. And here we arrive at the nub of the matter—the sign of directional alternatives that are also subject to summation. At least within what I am calling the Matter of Rome, what produces the energy to carry on the Great Tradition is not merely the prestige of the past nor the attractions associated with theories of imitation; it is what we might call the energy gap—the sparking distance—that exists between material visuality and verbal re-imagination. The poet contemplating Rome can "encompass" (du Bellay's word, Englished) the visual experience of antiquity and then leap beyond it.

---

nell'arte italiana (Turin, 1986), 3: 375-8 and Nicole Dacos, *Roma quanta fuit: tre pittori fiamminghi nella Domus Aurea* (Rome, 1995), esp. pp. 5-13.

That, as it happens, is the claim in the very opening lines of the *Antiquitez*, and it is the last of the directionalities that I shall attempt to map here. It should be noted that this is the one poem out of all forty-eight that Spenser never translated—being the dedication to the French King Henri II— but that hardly suggests he never read it.

> Ne vous pouvant donner ces ouvrages antiques
> Pour vostre Sainct-Germain ou pour Fontainebleau,
> Je les vous donne (Sire) en ce petit tableau
> Peint, le mieux que j'ay peu, de couleurs poëtiques,
> Qui, mis sous vostre nom devant les yeux publiques,
> Si vous le daignez voir en son jour le plus beau,
> Se pourra bien vanter d'avoir hors du tumbeau
> Tiré des vieux Romains les poudreuses reliques.

[Not being able to give you those antique works for your palace of Saint Germain or for Fontainebleau, I give you them, Sire, in this little tablet, painted, as best I can, in poetical colors. The which, if you deign to see it in its sharpest light, may well boast of having extracted from the tomb the crumbling relics of the ancient Romans.]

The entire poetic production—both *Antiquitez* and *Songe*—is presented here as an alternative to something that the poet cannot provide, namely the *ouvrages antiques* that might fill up and decorate the royal abodes. I recognize the formulaic aspects of this move, and I do not imagine that du Bellay had spent four years cruising the Esquiline wishing he had a shovel instead of a pen. But it would be unwise to allow our latter-day historical sophistication to move us past this opening too rapidly.

In this segment of the transmission of cultures, the material remains of ancient Rome are the thing itself. Nowhere else in Europe are those remains at once so desired and so unobtainable as they are in France. Du Bellay's reference to Fontainebleau, which was the seat not of Henri II but of Francis I, should recollect to us the persistent efforts of the earlier king to acquire ancient sculpture for his palace. Vasari tells a delicious anecdote about the efforts of François's emissaries to obtain the *Laocoön* as a gift from Pope Clement VII.[21] The wily Medicean pontiff arranges to have Baccio Bandinelli—here playing the role of papal plagiarist-in-chief—produce a perfect replica of the famous statue. But Clement likes the work so much that he ships it to a more conveniently located city that also wishes to possess the ancient *Ding an sich*, namely Florence. The French king is left to send Cellini and Primaticcio (Italians, no less) to make castings of the major sculptural antiquities. And these plaster replicas will bear witness for centuries to the grandeur and inaccessibility of the masterpieces that live on the other side of the Alps. In my

---

[21] See Giorgio Vasari, *Le vite de' più eccellenti pittori scultori ed architetti*, ed. G. Milanesi (Florence, 1906), 6: 145, translated by Gaston duC. deVere as *Lives of the Painters, Sculptors and Architects* (New York, 1996), 2: 272-3.

view, these replicas will help determine the famously academic course of French art for a long time. Nor is it a coincidence that the only French head of state in the future who really can dictate to all of Europe, Napoleon, will stipulate the transport of 100 major works of art, mostly antiquities, from Italy to the Louvre, where they will remain until the Congress of Vienna ships most of them home again.[22] But, to return to the sixteenth century, Francis I succeeds up to a point, with replicas and Italianate painting *all'antica*; Henri, with more aggressively imperial ambitions, is less able to achieve this particular sign of success.

Du Bellay installs himself in this space, defining his poetic project and placing it in relation to the monarch. In explicit terms, the *Antiquitez* begins with an admission of failure and an act of substitution. The "tableau / peint" and the "couleurs poëtiques" signal limits but they also stand as the perpetual sign that the poet might have some real material thing to give to his monarch. The poem is an alternative to a world of material objects; it is also defined as some sort of replication of them. These material objects, as it happens, are in ruins, even if one could lay one's hands on them. The poem is not in ruins and indeed, as du Bellay will suggest in later sonnets, appears in a medium intrinsically less likely to be ruined. But the poem sets itself the task of compensation. It engages in a vast cultural act of *energeia* that will make absent things present and will overcome its own belatedness in relation to the unobtainable material remains of antiquity because it can present these things both as ruined and as (to use the Renaissance term) repristinated—that is, like new.

Not that the project is easy—and it gets harder for Spenser. The fantasies of reinventing Rome are created by a descendancy of displaced persons: Dante and Petrarch who were not Romans and who were banished even from their own city; then du Bellay, who felt exiled and dispossessed in Rome. Drift, in other words, occurs not merely between the points on this line but within each one. And du Bellay will respond to its challenge in the very last lines of the *Antiquitez* by juxtaposing the mutability of marble and porphyry with a decisive act of self-assertion:

> Vanter te peuls, quelque bas que tu sois,
> D'avoir chanté le premier des François,
> L'antique honneur du peuple à longue robbe. (32)

> Well maist thou boast, how ever base thou bee,
> That thou art first, which of thy Nation song
> Th'olde honour of the people gowned long.

---

[22] See Francis Haskell and Nicholas Penny, *Taste and the Antique* (New Haven and London, 1981), pp. 108-16.

But England is beyond the circle even of mutability and displacement, beyond the transit from the greatness of Rome to the ruins to the transportable ruins to the compensation for untransportable ruins into a realm where the whole project is further attentuated by theological problematics.

Yet the more radical the drift—that is, the longer the literary quest-line—the more potent the energies of compensation—that is, the possibility of a summing-up, of an "all of the above." The modality of compensation defines both the relations between ancient and modern and the relations between verbal and visual art. It is also an exponential trope in just the way of "Roma quanta fuit ipsa ruina docet": that is, it builds its own presence on a multiplication of absence. Reviving antiquity on the one hand and, on the other, composing verse that is filled with ecphrasis, with prosopopoeia, with the invention of grand visual shows that arise out of nothing and return to nothing: these are not by mere happenstance the great poetic subject that Spenser inherits. What happens to it in his hands, what he can present in compensation to his monarch, is the grafting of visuality onto visionariness, the simultaneity of an antiquity materially renewed and a mutability permanently re-enacted. That is as far as du Bellay and his Elizabethan translator can take us toward the major poem; like so many of Spenser's other heroes, I stop short of the goal, which is to say, *The Faerie Queene* itself.

2

Spenser's Currencies

Donald Cheney

It may seem unnecessary today to affirm the value of Spenser's poetry, at a time when so many exchanges of information, evaluation, and appreciation are taking place in what seems, by and large, a strong and even inflationary market; but it may be useful to consider the degree to which Spenser's original decision to go public, to go into print with his enterprise, was taken with full awareness of both its risks and its necessity. *The Shepheardes Calender* concludes with a riddling motto: *Merce non mercede*. Whether this is to be rendered as the Yale editors have suggested, "Judge by the goods, not the price," or perhaps taken as contrasting the market value of a book with its patronage value as a privately circulated manuscript in the old way, the "grace and favour" of a courtly dedication, the words seem to locate the volume explicitly as merchandise, and as constituting a risky venture, at that.[1] I would suggest that the *Calender*'s strategies of presentation, as domestic almanac and as an eclogue book with full apparatus in imitation of the classics, place it within an Augustan tradition whereby poetic survival is couched in economic terms (as currency), in calendrical terms (as recurrency), and in terms, too, of the characteristically Spenserian signature of a poetry attuned to the natural currents of river or waterfall. At the same time, I shall propose more sketchily that when the 1579 prospectus of the *Calender* is recalled explicitly in *The Faerie Queene*, Spenser can expect the reader to recognize simultaneously the monumental achievement of his project and its commitment to the workings of mutability.

E.K.'s final notes on the *Calender* address Colin's tantalizingly absent emblem or motto to "December," which may well have been (as Hughes first suggested in 1715)[2] a line attributed to Vergil: *Vivitur ingenio, caetera mortis erunt*, "One lives on in one's genius, all else will be mortal." Whether or not the Renaissance Vergil is in fact being invoked here, as witnessing that poet, poem, and patron will survive when all else must yield to death, E.K. clearly

---

[1] W.A. Oram, et al., eds., *The Yale Edition of the Shorter Poems of Edmund Spenser* (New Haven and London, 1989), p. 213. Cooper's *Thesaurus* of 1584 lists as meanings for *merx, mercis*: "Any kind of marchandise; chaffer; ware that is bought and solde." For *merces, mercedis*: "Wages; the reward of service; rent; reuenewes; domage or hurt that foloweth of a thing." Cicero is cited: "*Fidem cognoscere hominum magna mercede*. With great losse and domage to know how truly men are." The emphasis on risk here recalls Ariosto's comparably riddling epigram to the *Orlando furioso, pro bono malum*.

[2] *Shorter Poems*, p. 209.

intends to identify the new poet as emulating and indeed fulfilling an Augustan program:

> The meaning whereof is that all thinges perish and come to theyr last end, but workes of learned wits and monuments of Poetry abide for ever. And therefore Horace of his Odes a work though ful indede of great wit and learning, yet of no so great weight and importaunce boldly sayth.
>
> Exegi monimentum ære perennius,
> Quod nec imber nec aquilo vorax etc.
>
> Therefore let not be envied, that this Poete in his Epilogue sayth he hath made a Calendar, that shall endure as long as time etc. folowing the ensample of Horace and Ovid in the like.
>
> Grande opus exegi quod nec Iovis ira nec ignis,
> Nec ferrum poterit nec edax abolere vetustas etc. (p. 212)

The reference to Ovid's claim at the end of the *Metamorphoses*, "Iamque opus exegi" (slightly garbled by E.K.), reminds the reader that Spenser has just completed a calendrical work like Ovid's incomplete *Fasti*, which was apparently abandoned by the Roman poet after six books at the end of June. And anyone with a view of the full shape of Spenser's later career will surely observe that where the new poet has thereby (rather incidentally, to be sure, by comparison to the more salient aspect of his project, the imitation of Vergilian pastoral) completed or restored an antique ruin, the mature Spenser will begin his 1596 installment with a completion of a Chaucerian fragment, the Squire's Tale, but break off his own vast metamorphic project, his own *carmen perpetuum*, after six books. The daisy-chain of completions and incompletions continues in him, and through him.

What is more, the second half of Spenser's twelve-line epilogue to the *Calender*, beginning "Goe lyttle Calender, thou hast a free passeporte," echoes the envoi, "Goe little booke," placed at the opening of the volume. The most immediate and obvious source of this envoi is Chaucer's conclusion to *Troilus and Criseyde*, itself an imitation of Boccaccio. Like Chaucer, Spenser humbly proposes to follow his predecessors by a lowly gait, "farre off"; in Spenser's case it is his English Tityrus, Chaucer himself, whose footing he follows here—as he will also do in Book IV of *The Faerie Queene*. Meanwhile, Chaucer had used the same formula to define his own relationship to antique models:

> But litel book, no makyng thow n'envie,
> But subgit be to alle poesye;
> And kis the steppes where as thow seest pace
> Virgile, Ovide, Omer, Lucan, and Stace. (5.1789-92)

Mention here of *Stace*, Statius, reminds us that the ending of the *Thebaid* similarly proposes to follow worshipfully in the steps of Vergil. So, by a commodious *vicus* of recirculated texts, we find that Spenser's Romish

Tityrus, Vergil, the principal member of his Augustan triad of authorities, also lies buried in this tribute.

It is the third member of the triad, however, to whom I now turn, for a consideration of a Horatian matrix to Spenser's poetics.[3] E.K. has cited Horace's conclusion to the third book of his *Odes*, *Exegi monumentum*, as a source of the *Calender*'s epilogue; and I want to look more closely at it, along with Horace's comparable envoi to the first book of his *Epistles*, which Ellen Oliensis has recently discussed insightfully.[4]

In *Epistles* 1.20, Horace addresses his book, his *liber*, as if it were a favorite slave (also a *liber*) who is eager to expose himself to a broader public. Statues of Vertumnus and Janus mark the booksellers' neighborhood in Rome, and the well-known dealers there, the Sosii brothers, are seen as pimps offering for sale a *liber* which has been polished with pumice, a substance commonly used to prettify both books and boys. Both offer themselves for sale (*prostare*), and both, the poet warns, are subject to the fluctuations of time and market demand:

> My liber, you seem to be gazing on Vertumnus and Janus; obviously you want to go on sale there, polished by the pumice of the Sosii. You resent the lock and seal that a modest *liber* would accept gracefully, you moan at being seen by so few people and you praise being in the public eye, though you were not brought up that way. Go ahead, where you want to go; but once you are let out there will be no returning. You will say, 'Alas, what have I done? What did I want?' when you get hurt and you find yourself put on the shelf when some admirer tires of you.[5]

The poet goes on to prophesy that the *liber* will be treasured in Rome until its youth is past, but that once it has become shopworn by much handling it will either be abandoned and consumed by lice (like pumice, something that attaches itself equally to books and boys) or shipped off to the provinces; then the protector it had scorned earlier will have the last laugh. In old age, it will even find itself used as a text for schoolboys.

Finally, in the third part of this envoi, the poet envisions a more mellow time that will find the *liber* surrounded by an audience that wants to hear about

---

[3] Angus Fletcher's term, "matrix," seems apt here: Spenser is like an earlier Stephen Daedalus in seeing matrix love as at once objective and subjective genitive, sources that embrace his text as much as they are embraced by it. *The Prophetic Moment: An Essay on Spenser* (Chicago and London, 1971).

[4] "Life after Publication: Horace, *Epistles* 1.20," *Arethusa* 28 (1995), 209-24.

[5] Vertumnum Ianumque, liber, spectare videris,
scilicet ut prostes Sosiorum pumice mundus.
odisti clavis et grata sigilla pudico;
paucis ostendi gemis et communia laudas,
non ita nutritus. fuge quo descendere gestis.
non erit emisso reditus tibi. 'quid miser egi?
quid volui?' dices, ubi quid te laeserit, et scis
in breve te cogi cum plenus languet amator.

the identity of the poet. Horace asks to be described as himself a freedman's son, *libertino nato patre*, who was able to escape the straitened circumstances of his birth and achieve fame and respect. "If someone asks you when I lived," he concludes, "tell him I completed my forty-fourth December when Lepidus was chosen as Consul alongside Lollius."[6]

This poem deserves a fuller treatment than it can receive here, where its role as a Spenserian source must seem dangerously close to what the poet feared in prophesying that it might become a schoolboy text. Horace has begun by suggesting that his book, cherished and shaped by its maker, has now grown impatient and demands publication, a manumission that its loving owner or parent, (counsellor, *monitor*, in the Latin), knows to be ill-advised, even fatal, though he is powerless to deny it autonomy. The speaker looks forward, with parental superiority, to the satisfaction of being proven right when the prodigal comes to grief. Yet he goes on to imagine a time when the book regains its audience and indeed achieves a oneness with its author, so that it can speak of the poet in terms very like those the poet has used of it: Horace was himself a freedman's son who further liberated himself by virtue of his talents. Poet and poem are both expressions of a parent's desire, and both must exercise their own desire to escape it. In short, what I am calling the "matrix" of Horatian allusion here is an awareness of how a poem must escape its origins and thereby affirm and be atoned with them.

His pun on *liber* has enabled Horace to develop a family romance of authorship and publication that Spenser partly translates in his envoi and then more broadly incorporates into the *Calender* itself. The new poet's little book is addressed at the outset as a "child whose parent is unkent," and who needs to flee Envy's bark and find succour and tutelage under Sidney's wing. Like Horace, however, Spenser looks forward to a happier time when it will be past jeopardy and when favorable reviews will make possible an expanded dialogue between poet and book, and further publications: "Come tell me, what was sayd of mee: / And I will send more after thee."

Both E.K. in his commentary, and Hobbinol in the pastoral fiction, take on some of the role of parent, lover, and *monitor* assumed by the speaker in Horace's envoi; there are elements of both comedy and pathos in the efforts by these loving and particular friends to contain and comprehend the prodigious ephebe that is both the new poet and the new poetry. Meanwhile, Colin shares with Horace's *liber* the condition of willful exile from paradise ("June," 9-16). And like Adam, both exiles have fled, or been liberated, manumitted, into a world of time. Roman booksellers are fittingly situated near the statues both of Janus (god of beginnings and associated with Genius, itself a figure of generation, from *gignere*) and Vertumnus, the god of the changing year and its products, and of exchange or trade: the seasons of the year are comparable to

---

[6] forte meum si quis te percontabitur aevum,
me quater undenos sciat implevisse Decembris
collegam Lepidum quo duxit Lollius anno.

the public's changing tastes. Horace's poem, like the *Calender*, moves from Janus in the first line to mention of the poet's own forty-four Decembers in the last, and it shares some of the same ironies as to the way poets and poems can be identified with the months.

Though the English language does not allow Spenser to develop Horace's pun on *liber*, I think that the complex of ideas that Horace generates flows into his poetry in numerous ways. The nourishing possessiveness of the pederastic tutor or *monitor* appears in the fictional figure of Hobbinol, as well as in the conveniently available fact of Gabriel Harvey's eagerness to publicize his friendships and hand out advice. Though the desire to move out of the nest is seen in Colin's love for Rosalind rather than in the *liber*'s desire for street-corner hustling, it is no less fraught with perils, and it will take a knight of courtesy to protect against Envy, both in the envoi to the *Calender* and in Book VI of *The Faerie Queene*, where Calidore not only confronts the Blatant Beast but also provides first aid, largely conversational, to several of its victims.

An important aspect of the Horatian matrix to Spenser's poetry, as I see it, is the slipperiness of allusion in both poets, who hint or seem to hint at unsoundable depths of meaning beneath the tranquil and highly-polished surface of their lyrics. It is hard to see just how Horace moves from the master–slave relationship in the first two sections of his poem, to the oblique autobiography of its conclusion, with its appearance of a colophon putting a date and an end to the book; but it feels right and strangely true to life, as do the teasing references to an unspecified poetic identity in the *Calender*, or the returns of Colin Clout in 1595 and 1596.[7] In all these cases, the parent–child or master–slave drama is resolved by a reminder of its inherent circularity, its containment within a romance cycle of mutual changes.

A key to Spenser's view of a world, or an art, that is eternal in mutability can be found in these figures of cyclical change and return or recurrency that I have been attributing to the Horatian matrix. In *Epistles* 1.20, the *liber* survives through a winter of neglect and looks forward to a later, more mellow time of recollection and (as it were) republication with commentary, now as a "classic." When Spenser claims in his epilogue to have made a calendar for every year, "That steele in strength, and time in durance shall outweare," he is echoing (as E.K. observes) another, more famous poem by Horace, the conclusion to the third book of the *Odes*, which claims to have completed a monument more lasting than bronze, *Exegi monumentum aere perennius*.

Of course, it is clear enough that a perpetual calendar like Spenser's embodies the changing seasons; being eternal in mutability is its subject as well as its attribute; Horace, by contrast, seems to be talking about simple durability, a monument that is unchangeable. Yet there may be another way of reading this famous claim. Bronze, or the other alloys included in the Latin *aes*, was not only (perhaps, not even primarily) the stuff of monuments. *Aes*

---

[7] *Colin Clouts Come Home Againe, Faerie Queene* 6.10.

was also the material of money, and a word for it.[8] Similarly, *perenne* contains the word for the year, *annus*, and so, at least by implication, it may be rendered as "enduring the changing seasons," just as Spenser's calendar does. I would suggest that Horace's line may be understood as claiming to have created a work "more current than currency," in the sense that it is perennially refreshed, made newly current for each new generation of readers. In fact, the poem does go on to speak of the poetic monument's surviving the endless chain of years and the flight (or flow) of time. Finally, the poet claims of himself, "I shall not wholly die ... ever shall I grow, fresh [or restored, *recens*] from my fame in later times."[9] At the very least, it seems that Spenser is echoing Horace more closely and subtly than might be at first apparent.

In an earlier essay,[10] I suggested a context that might make sense of two famous cruces in the *Calender*'s "November" eclogue: the lament for a Dido who has perished by water ("drent") rather than fire ("brent") and the location of a November sun in Pisces ("Fishes haske"). Near the midpoint of his six-book *Fasti*, Ovid treats the Ides of March, a date that might be of obvious pertinence to a *Calender* that was appearing in the midst of a lively debate over reforming the Julian calendar by submitting to a more recent Roman tyrant, Pope Gregory. Ovid refers only glancingly to the event that we, and Spenser, would associate with the Ides of March; instead, he identifies the date with Dido's sister Anna, who fled from Carthage to Rome and then escaped Lavinia's jealous wrath by transforming herself into the Roman river goddess Anna Perenna, a figure of the changing, perennial year (*amnis perenne*). A recognition of this Ovidian source for a piece of the Dido romance that lives on in Aeneas's Rome, both as a figure of the hero's earlier Carthaginian adventure (a survival of the *veteris vestigia flammae* that he has carried with him from Troy) and as a condition of Rome's fertility, would be a further instance of a familiar Spenserian theme. From his first public beginnings in 1579, Spenser has identified the wellspring of his poetry with the springtime of his impulse as poet of love, and typically, insistently, has tuned his verses "unto the Waters fall" ("Aprill," 36). In doing so, he expresses his anxiety at the workings of mutability, and a joyous readiness to go with its flow. We shall not soon be done with negotiating the currents, or currencies, that underlie the polished but densely intertextual surface of his verse.

---

[8] Renaissance dictionaries typically devote much space, in their entries under *aes*, to *aes alienum*, no doubt reflecting an increased consciousness of questions of debt and credit in a burgeoning money economy.

[9] non omnis moriar ... usque ego postera crescam laude recens.

[10] "The Circular Argument of *The Shepheardes Calender*," in G.M. Logan and G. Teskey, eds., *Unfolded Tales: Studies in Renaissance Romance* (Ithaca and London, 1989), pp. 137-61.

3

On the Renaissance Epic:
Spenser and Slavery

Maureen Quilligan

It is not often remembered, but the Renaissance was a time for the renascence of slavery in the economics of many Western European powers (if not actually in Northern Europe itself). Not often thought of as sharing with antiquity this particular aspect of economic organization, the Renaissance is more usually regarded as a time of the birth of the free and autonomous individual. Yet, if we push some of Fredric Jameson's arguments about genre to their logical conclusions, we might better understand how the Renaissance was rightly named for a rebirth of some classical forms and that, indeed, the resurgence of the genre of the epic in the Renaissance speaks to the resurgence of slavery, by which European powers were building their new Atlantic empires. Given Jameson's understanding of genre, we may be enabled to see how, in two strangely parallel scenes, *The Faerie Queene* may be aiming to do the work which epic poems usually do, to wit, mediating the contradictions (that is, the internally irrational elements) of a slave economy, particularly as slavery was just becoming an element in the overseas economy of Renaissance England's growing imperial interests. By inspecting these two episodes, Guyon's confrontation of Mammon in Book II (the Book of Temperance) and Britomart's slaying of the Amazon Queen Radigund in Book V (the Book of Justice), I hope to show how a properly theorized notion of genre can force us to adopt far more culturally embedded and site-specific reading practices. While I can only begin to articulate the range of problems raised by such a global suggestion—about an entire genre in a quickly-changing historical period—it will be useful to begin by asking how we must read the text to find the relationship of this particular late sixteenth-century English epic, by a would-be courtier to Queen Elizabeth I, to the activity of pan-Atlantic slavery during the Renaissance. Interestingly, the two episodes in which Spenser seems most specifically to meditate on the problem of slave and wage labor are cruces in the only books of his epic to focus on any of the twelve classical Aristotelian virtues, that is, the books of Temperance and Justice (unlike, for example, Holiness, or Chastity which Aristotle does not, of course, mention). In such a way the epic appears to insist that in these episodes it deals most specifically with issues which have resonance back to Greek times.

In *The Political Unconscious*, Fredric Jameson observes that "genre is essentially a socio-symbolic message"; in other words, "form is immanently and intrinsically an ideology in its own right." When a form is "reappropriated and refashioned in quite different social and cultural contexts," Jameson explains, "this message persists."[1] In other words, the real contradictions of the first historical moment for which the genre was designed to provide an imaginary solution may continue to supply a shape for ensuing potentialities of the form. Thus, in Jameson's example, the point of origin for romance as a genre was that moment when maurauding bands of soldiers finally joined forces and formed themselves into a cohesive class, the feudal nobility: romance is thereby the genre which insists that the alien enemy is not "other," but the same as oneself.[2] Romance thus takes the older contrast between good and evil in the *chanson de geste* and shows how two enemies can recognize each other as being part of the same group. The typical plot of romance provides this solution when an unknown hostile knight, often in disguise, is bested in a contest and asks for mercy by telling his name, "at which point," Jameson argues, the knight is "reinserted into the unity of the social class" and "he becomes one more knight among others and loses all his sinister unfamiliarity."[3] From this formal viewpoint epic might be seen as the diametrical opposite of romance: epic is that genre which, in making the "same" into an "other," allows one group to fight, conquer, and subject an enemy. It is the genre of nation-building when the construction has imperial purposes. Relying somewhat more remotely on Jameson than I do here, David Quint makes a parallel argument when he argues that the instituting moment for epic is Virgil's transformation of a "recent history of civil strife into a war of foreign conquest" in the *Aeneid*, that is, the turning of the same into an other.[4] It was Christopher Kendrick who first applied Jameson's thesis specifically to epic; he made a more narrowly Marxist claim that epic as a genre was designed to speak to the contradictions experienced by Greek and Roman societies which relied on the imperial conquest and subsequent enslavement of subject peoples.[5] Epic, in other words, is the genre of the slave mode of production. In the context of *Paradise Lost*, Kendrick argues that the "peculiar attachment of fate to military action may ... be linked to slavery ... for the classical mode of production ... required a perpetual replenishment of its basic labor force, chiefly manifested ... as the need for foreign conquest" (p. 108). Intent on tracing the amalgam of genres in Milton's poem, Kendrick

---

[1] Fredric Jameson, *The Political Unconscious: Narrative as a Socially Symbolic Act* (Ithaca, 1981), p. 141.

[2] Jameson, p. 118.

[3] Jameson, pp. 118-19.

[4] *Epic and Empire: Politics and Generic Form from Virgil to Milton* (Princeton, 1993), p. 123. Quint does not derive this insight from Jameson, however, instead insisting that the "equation of power and the very possibility of narrative" is the "defining feature of the genre" of epic; he locates two different forms of the genre in the "winners' epic" and the "losers' epic."

[5] Christopher Kendrick, *Milton: A Study in Ideology and Form* (New York, 1986).

never questioned whether the issue of actual slavery may have been important to Milton's contemporaries. Neither Jameson nor Kendrick (nor indeed Marx himself) take up the question of how gender plays into these issues, or what, indeed, specifically happens when the male knight in a romance turns out to be a woman, as so often happens to the paradigmatic romance scene when it is reorganized for use in the Renaissance epic. My main point here is that the complicated work done by the figure of the woman warrior in *The Faerie Queene* bears most forcefully on this epic's mediation of the contradictions of New World slavery at the moment when England first embarked on its overseas empire.

It is comparatively easy to argue—as I have in a recent essay—that *Paradise Lost* as an epic rehearses some of the potentialities sedimented in the form and thereby is able to deal with the problems attendant upon the slave trade as well as actual slavery. It is in part possible to make such an argument historically and directly if only because, in buying Barbados from the Dutch, Cromwell's government had added to England's possessions an actual slave colony. Milton's complex meditations on freedom and on labor in that epic may thus be quite interestingly contextualized by the problem of labor in the New World and also by the expanding Atlantic slave trade which aimed to solve that problem, itself an economic activity which England was to monopolize for a century and half subsequent to the publication of Milton's poem.[6]

It is relatively more difficult to make the case for the importance of slavery to Spenser's epic, not merely because England's participation in the slave trade had only just begun in the 1590s. Much of the very best work being done on Spenser now is focused on his particular imperialist context, Ireland, and the transatlantic trade in human labor is not so important as it in fact later became, when groups of rebellious Irish were sold into slavery in the West Indies as they were during the seventeenth century.[7] So too, Spenser's epic

---

[6] "Freedom, Service and the Trade in Slaves: The Problem of Labor in *Paradise Lost*," in *Subject and Object in Renaissance Culture*, ed. Margreta de Grazia, Maureen Quilligan, and Peter Stallybrass (Cambridge, 1996), pp. 213-34. J. Martin Evans, *Milton's Imperial Epic: Paradise Lost and the Discourse of Colonialism* (Ithaca, 1996), pp. 77-82, takes up the question of indentured servitude, but does not broach the issue of slavery, although he provides a much needed argument about the embeddedness of Milton's epic in New World discourses.

[7] Recent particular attention to *The View of the Present State of Ireland* has tended to de-emphasize Ireland as being but one piece in England's Atlantic enterprise. See Andrew Hadfield, *Edmund Spenser's Irish Experience* (Oxford, 1997) and Willy Maley, *Salvaging Spenser: Colonialism, Culture and Identity* (London, 1997). In a number of studies, Nicholas Canny has argued that the two must be seen as part of a single enterprise: "almost every promoter of English settlement in Ireland ... compared their work to that of those contemporaries who were attempting to settle among the North American Indians," *Kingdom and Colony: Ireland and the Atlantic World 1560-1800* (Baltimore, 1988), p. 2; K.R. Andrews, N.P. Canny, and P.E.H. Hair, eds., *The Westward Enterprise: English Activities in Ireland, the Atlantic, and America 1480-1650* (Liverpool, 1978). Early New Historicist studies of Spenser stressed the New World context; see especially Stephen Greenblatt, *Renaissance Self-Fashioning: From More to Shakespeare* (Chicago, 1980), pp. 179-85.

does not, in fact, take the form of the single-heroed classical epic where there is one enemy to conquer and subjugate, but rather inhabits that hybrid space between epic and romance, a generic blend which may speak to the problematically feudal arrangements being tried out in various New World venues and ventures, themselves a rehearsal in a different key of the same evolving set of economic changes which Richard Halpern has followed Marx in terming "primitive accumulation." Most important for my purposes here is Halpern's emphasis on the "freeing" of labor, or the slow and certain creation of a class of workers who, in being (violently) denied their former access to the means of production, ended with only their labor to sell in the metropolitan center.[8] I think the Mammon episode tells us that this change in labor practices needs to be contextualized by New World labor experiences.

Guyon's argument with Mammon before his descent into the cave is an interesting meditation on the predicament of a pedestrian, that is, a non-chivalric venturer in these new, non-feudal, economic conditions. I do not mean to turn their conversation into an economic allegory—but I do think the discussion interesting if only because Milton chooses to stage a strangely similar kind of chat about the different economics of labor between Adam and Eve just before she goes off to face her temptation by the Devil, famously alone (Milton's mistake in remembering Guyon's lack of company in Spenser's episode may not be so much a precursor to his staging of a temptation between Satan and Abdiel as Harold Bloom has argued, but a proleptic enactment more specifically, of that between Satan and an Eve who already thinks of her work as wage-labor).[9]

Guyon meets Mammon sunning his gold, a huge heap of metal in various forms, stamped, unstamped, coins, ingots, and mere raw lumps. I stress the physical state of the metal because Spenser does and it may, indeed, have been the sheer physical increase in the amount of gold circulating in Europe to which this moment in part refers. Guyon is not, in fact, interested in what the metal means—its value—but rather in where it comes from, especially given its bulk:

> What secret place (quoth he) can safely hold
> So huge a masse, and hide from heauens eye?
> Or where hast thou thy wonne, that so much gold
> Thou canst preserue from wrong and robbery?
> Come thou (quoth he) and see. (2.7.20)

Intrigued by the place, Guyon goes—just as Eve follows Satan to see the tree. The issue of place is an important one in Book II. Mammon's cave is clearly a classical-cum-Dantesque infernal region; but as Spenser begins Book II with coy questions about place, it may be useful to think of the proem in the context

---

[8] Richard Halpern, *The Poetics of Primitive Accumulation: English Renaissance Culture and the Genealogy of Capital* (Ithaca, 1991).

[9] Harold Bloom, *A Map of Misreading* (Oxford, 1975), pp. 127ff.

of Guyon's question about the location of all this gold. Spenser explains that Faeryland is also a previously unknown place, but insists that just because no one knows it, that doesn't necessarily mean it does not exist as, for example, no one knew of the New World until quite recently:

> Many great Regions are discouered,
> Which to late age were neuer mentioned.
> Who euer heard of th'Indian *Peru*?
> Or who in venturous vessell measured
> The *Amazons* huge riuer now found trew?
> Or fruitfullest *Virginia* who did euer vew? (2. proem 2)

"Peru" gives a nice rhyme with "trew"and "vew," but one may wonder why it should make the list of newly discovered places, particularly because the two other *loci* are so allegorically resonant, the Amazon river carrying the entire gendered script of Artegall's imperialist conquest of Radigund's kingdom in Book V and the other complimenting Spenser's Irish neighbor, Walter Ralegh, who had named English North America "Virginia" for Elizabeth, a proper set of places to be mentioned at the outset of Guyon's imperialist voyage to suppress a threatening feminized space.[10]

It was one of the paradoxes of the Spanish conquest of the New World that the closer the aboriginal civilization to that of the conquistadors, the easier was the conquest. Thus, two of the first regions to fall were the Aztec empire of central Mexico and the Inca empire of Peru. It was, of course, primarily about the Caribbean islands and Mexico that Bartolomé de las Casas wrote when he lamented the destruction of the Indies, later arguing in front of Charles V against Bishop Sepulveda that the Indians were human, and had rights not to be enslaved, victims first of illegal war and then worked to death in the mines and cities of the New World.[11] The argument was famous and would have been known in England at the time and later through an English translation of las Casas, which appeared in 1581 as *The Spanish Colonie*.[12]

Peru had become newly important in the mid-sixteenth century because of a sudden, drastic economic change when huge silver mines were discovered in the Andes; while 100 per cent of metallic exports from New Spain were gold until 1530, they became 85 per cent silver from 1530–60. Perhaps more importantly, Peru was the site of the only large mercury deposit, which had become fundamental to a new and more economical process of smelting silver,

---

[10] See Louis Montrose, "The Work of Gender in the Discourse of Discovery," in *New World Encounters* (Berkeley, 1993), pp. 177-217.

[11] Bartolomé de Las Casas, *In Defense of the Indians* (DeKalb, Ill., 1992) p. xxi. Las Casas had dedicated his compendium of the arguments to Philip II (son of Charles V) just before Philip would have traveled to England to become the consort of Mary Tudor in 1552.

[12] James Aleggrodo, the translator, explains that he undertook the task "to serve as a President and warning to the xii Provinces of the lowe Countries," *The Spanish Colonie* (London, 1583), A2v.

smelting silver, suited to an environment short on wood.[13] Augustine Zarate's
The Discoverie and Conquest of the Provinces of Peru had also been translated
and printed in London in 1581, the last chapter of which describes the rich
mines at Potossi: "The vains of these Mines is of sutche qualitie, that the Owre
wil not melt with ye winde of Bellowes, as in other Mines are accustomed: but
their meltyng is in certain litle Furnaaces, called Guayras, wherein they vse to
melt with coles and sheepes dung with the only force of the ayre, with out any
other instrument" (Aa.ii-v). Figure 3.1, a plate depicting Peruvian goldsmithing
from Theodor De Bry's *America*, printed in 1596, while it is not a graphic
vision which would have been current among readers of the first installment of
The Faerie Queene, does represent a very contemporary view of what the
reader of the 1581 imprint might have imagined the activity to look like.[14]

Spenser is not so much concerned with metallurgy, but his vision of the
demonic labor which is the "source" of the gold Mammon shows Guyon is a
scene of frenzied activity:

> One with great bellowes gathered filling aire,
> And with forst wind the fewell did inflame;
> Another did the dying bronds repaire
> With yron toungs, and sprinckled oft the same
> With liquid waues, fiers *Vulcans* rage to tame,
> Who maistring them, renewd his former heat;
> Some scumd the drosse, that from the metall came;
> Sopme stird the molten owre with ladles great;
> And euery one did swincke, and euery one did sweat.
>
> But when as earthly wight they present saw,
> Glistring in armes and battailous aray,
> From their whot worke they did themselues withdraw
> To wonder at the sight: for till that day,
> They neuer creature saw, that came that way.
> Their staring eyes sparckling with feruent fire,
> And vgly shapes did nigh the man dismay,
> That were it not for shame, he would retire,
> Till that him thus bespake their soueraigne Lord and sire. (2.7.36-7)

Mammon tells him this is what he had wanted to see:

> Behold, thou Faeries sonne, with mortall eye,
> That liuing eye before did neuer see:
> The thing, that thou didst craue so earnestly,
> To weet, whence all the wealth late shewd by mee,

---

[13] *A History of New Spain.*

[14] Theodor de Bry, *America* (Frankfurt, 1596), G4. Parts 1-3 of de Bry's volumes
were published in 1590, the year of the publication of the first installment of *The Faerie
Queene*; the remaining three parts were published variously, but all was complete with part VI
printed in 1596, the year of the six-book version of Spenser's epic.

Figure 3.1
Peruvian goldsmithing
Theodor de Bry, *America* VI (Frankfurt, 1596)

Proceeded, lo now is reueald to thee.
Here is the fountaine of the worldes good. (2.7.38)

What Guyon sees is not merely the gold itself but the labor—done by demonic slaves, hardly human, who both repel and frighten Guyon. What Guyon had wanted to know was whether the gold was obtained by good or evil means; the text makes no comment beyond Guyon's refusal and request to be able to follow his "emprise." In looking so like the picture of New World conquest—naked workers surveyed by armed knights—this vision presents New World wealth as it really was, without the erasure of its base in forced labor. In the images which circulated with the New World texts in Theodor de Bry's vast compilation (published simultaneously with the publication of *The Faerie Queene*), we see what that labor, as it was described in verbal pictures, would have looked like to Spenser's contemporaries. (Figures 3.2 and 3.3 show gold mining and sugar refining in the Spanish "islands" from part V of *America* [1595], A2; A3.) Part V is De Bry's printing of a translation of Girolamo Benzoni's *La Historia del Mondo Nuovo* first printed in Venice in 1565, and thus the verbal descriptions of the enslaved labor of African slaves could well have been current among Spenser's first readers. Benzoni's descriptions of the laboring Africans include a full discussion of the specific practices of cruelty with which the Spanish—necessarily, as Benzoni notes—treated their slaves; his verbal details suggest the particulars of de Bry's pictures; in other instances de Bry's engraver simply follows the outlines of the woodcuts in the Italian volume.

In Mammon's cave, Guyon confronts the source, as it were, not merely of the gold metal which had doubled in actual mass throughout Europe at this time, fueling a grueling inflation which had eaten away at aristocratic fortunes based in land; he also confronts the way this metal changed working conditions. A knight who prefers to spend his days in "der-doing arms" (2.7.10) ought not to have to care that a feudal gift economy of service has been transformed into a wage economy. But Mammon makes him care, dismissing his classical arguments against avarice and forcing him to confront the moment:

> ... leaue the rudenesse of that antique age
> To them, that liu'd therein in state forlorne;
> Thou that doest liue in later times, must wage
> Thy workes for wealth, and life for gold engage. (2.7.18)

It is this argument which makes Guyon take notice. In figure 3.4—the fascinating frontispiece to part V of *America*—one can see how the "work" of the slave-driving Europeans becomes almost indistinguishable from that of the burdened slaves. They are both doing the work of empire.

Slaves are not always others in *The Faerie Queene* as are the demons in Book II; in Book V Artegall himself is turned into a wage slave by the Amazon Radigund, dressed in women's clothes and forced to sew to earn his meals. The

Figure 3.2
Negroes gold mining in the Spanish "Islands"
Theodor de Bry, *America* V (Frankfurt, 1595)

Figure 3.3
Sugar plantation labor
Theodor de Bry, *America* V (Frankfurt, 1595)

Figure 3.4
Frontispiece
Theodor de Bry, *America* V (Frankfurt, 1595)

contrast between knightly freedom and the ignoble slavery of the thrall could hardly be made greater and repeats with a fascinating variation the confrontation between the deformed shapes of the demons and Guyon's glistering armor. The contrast is not between their "ugly shapes" but between proper male and female attire. He sees many brave knights

> Spinning and carding all in comely rew,
> That his bigge hart loth'd so vncomely vew.
> But they were forst through penurie and pyne,
> To doe those workes, to them appointed dew:
> For nought was giuen them to sup or dyne,
> But what their hands could earne by twisting linnen
> twyne. (5.5.22)

The narrator comments on the proper "comliness" of the orderly row in which the knights sit, spinning and carding. What is "uncomely" about the operation is that such comeliness and order is inappropriate to knights; in itself it is not unattractive but in fact good, because it is rationally organized labor. The row is "comely," but perhaps even more so when the rows are made up of women workers, for whom labor in the production of textiles is appropriate. In part, then, what Britomart assists Artegall in achieving when she frees him from this slavery ("so hard it is to be a woman's slave") is not merely the reorganization of the *polis*, which repeals from women their unlawful sovereignty, but, I think we are allowed to imagine, a regendering of this labor force. It is right for the women to be enslaved in rational, comely rows.

It is important to notice the similarity between an armed Guyon looking on the naked demon slaves in Mammon's cave and an armed Artegall regarding the cross-dressed sewing knights: the parallel creates a self-commenting moment whereby the poem asks us to analyze the similarities between the two scenes. Both Guyon and Artegall watch a labor they themselves morally should never perform; to work this way, either to succumb to the avaricious desire for the wealth so produced in Guyon's case or to become entrapped by the sexual interaction which initially tricks Artegall by its mimicry of his desire for Britomart—to do either sort of labor is to become enslaved. Both challenges in each hero's life have to do with earning one's way in a world which is supposed to be feudal—where, like Don Quixote, the knight does not have to pay his way. Guyon's and Artegall's epic quests are defined in quite specific detail in contrast to this sort of activity: the refusal defines them specifically, that is, as distinct from the species of creature which perform the labor, in Guyon's case demons, and in Artegall's case, women.

The biggest difference from the slavery fundamental to classical epic is that Renaissance slavery is only mercantile, the originary violence—heretofore the stuff of heroism and therefore the proper subject of epic—lost in the internal bartering within the continent of Africa. Unlike Roman troops in Gaul, English armies did not fight in Africa, enslaving the conquered enemies;

having heard that "Negroes were very good marchandise in Hispaniola," John Hawkins managed "partly by the sword, and partly by other meanes" to get "into his possession ... 300 Negroes ... besides other marchandises" and then to set sail, in 1562, to the West Indies. He not only made good bargains throughout the islands, he explains, he was able to fill up his ships again with ginger, sugar, pearles, hides, "and like commodities" so that he ended by returning to England "with prosperous success and much gaine to himself, and the aforesaid adventurers."[15]

The fundamental difference between the slavery of classical conquest and the racially-based slavery of the mercantilistic transatlantic trade, which occasions a loss of heroism—can be traced in *The Faerie Queene* most immediately, I think, in the function of what I am going to christen with Jameson's term the "ideologeme" of the woman warrior. As David Quint quite brilliantly points out, it is the figure of the woman, specifically Cleopatra in Virgil's epic, who turns what was actually a civil war among equal triumvirs into an epic war against others, thereby making an epic where the winners tell the story out of romance.[16] Like Cleopatra in this, the proper woman warriors, Penthesilea and Camilla, fight on the losing side, Camilla warring specifically to stop any intermarriage from taking place between Aeneas and Lavinia. It is different in Ariostan Renaissance epic where it is the women warriors who are the winners; they fight on the right, triumphant side, our side—Bradamante, Marfisa, Britomart. This change in the side on which the woman warrior fights is one of the greatest differences between classical and Renaissance epics. A brief glance at figure 3.5 reveals Theodor de Bry's engraving of John White's image of a Pictish woman warrior which he included in his series of watercolors depicting the Lost Colony at Roanoke. When De Bry published his first volume of America, it was of the English colonial enterprize—in chronological fact, one of the last enterprizes—illustrated with engravings of White's watercolors, done for Walter Ralegh's Lost Colony at Roanoke and which, therefore, Spenser may well have seen. One sees the idea of the New World in De Bry's two frontispieces for the whole project of *America*, part I (figures 3.4 and 3.6): importantly, White's woman warrior is part of this set of images (De Bry even imports an image of another woman warrior by a French artist).

Denise Albanese has recently made a very interesting argument about the inclusion of pictures of a male Pict in White's series. Her main point is that to draw an analogy, as White does, between the antique English native and the contemporary American native is to "propose a Foucaultian conjunction of power and knowledge: this early modern modeling of history is not the pliant and playful 'rehearsal' of culture for which the Renaissance has been a recent

---

[15] Richard Hakluyt, *The Principall Navigations, Voyages and Discoveries of the English Nation* (London, 1589), p. 522.

[16] See above, n. 4.

Figure 3.5
Pictish woman warrior
Theodor de Bry, *America* I (Frankfurt, 1590)

Figure 3.6
Frontispiece
Theodor de Bry, *America* I (Frankfurt, 1590)

referent, but the making of one culture through the expenditure of another."[17]
Albanese's argument rests on some very pointed reasoning:

> Although the Pict is brought in as a proximate avatar for the
> precursors of the English Race, his temporal distance from any site
> of contemporary reading seems as significant as the common ground
> upon which he is purported to stand. The opposite is true for the
> Algonkian: while he shares the temporal frame of those who might
> gaze upon his reproduced image, he is distanced as much the by
> status of primitivism attributed to his culture as by geography. Seen
> from the vantage of the seventeenth century, the English 'then'—
> when savage Picts were the prime inhabitants of Britain—becomes
> the (north) American 'now.' (p. 28)

Albanese does not take into account the problematic accompaniment of the
image of the Pict by pictures of women warriors, and her point that De Bry's
version of the drawings by White "provide no depiction that commemorates
European interactions with the inhabitants they observe" so that the portrayals
tend therefore to make the difference between English and American one of
"time as well as space," is true only with reference to the first part of *America*
(p. 28). In subsequent volumes, as we have seen, there are many interactions
between Americans and Europeans portrayed. Because the pictures of female
antique warriors outnumber the images of male, one is pressed to consider that
the Picts appear in the series in order to provide a rationale for showing women
warriors.

Two questions need to be asked: 1) why does the representation of
native Americans need to be accompanied by pictures of women warriors? and
2) why does the woman warrior become one of us rather than (like Cleopatra,
like Penthesilea, Camilla) an other? De Bry's *America* images a subtle but
crucial difference between the use of this figure in classical and in Renaissance
epics, and it may well have something to do with the historical difference in
the slave mode of production between the classical period and the
Renaissance—that is, with the greater reliance of Renaissance slavery on
unheroic barter and trade and its far greater element of racism.[18] It is of course
true that there was no slavery in North America at the time White drew his
pictures; but as the rest of the volumes show, the project was already very
much one of European dealings with two subjected races, the native American
and the imported African. If Jameson's understanding of genre is accurate and
it is responsive to changes in historical circumstance, we may find that an
analysis of the different functions from one period to another of the

---

[17] Denise Albanese, "Humanism, Colonialism, and the Gendered Body in Early
Modern Culture," in *Feminist Readings of Early Modern Culture*, ed. Valerie Traub, M.
Lindsay Kaplan, and Dympna Callaghan (Cambridge, 1996), pp. 16-43.

[18] In assuming the greater racism in the Atlantic slave trade than in classical slavery, I
am relying on work by, among others, Robin Blackburn, *The Making of New World Slavery
1492-1800* (London, 1997).

ideologeme of the woman warrior can tell us something about crucial differences between those periods. The women warriors may also help us to understand something about the contrasts between English and Romance language-speaking attitudes towards racial differences. David Quint's fascinating argument about Tasso's Clorinda, a Renaissance epic woman warrior who fights (more classically) on the losing side, is a very suggestive case in point. As a woman warrior whom Spenser seems specifically to be remembering in the episode of Artegall's enslavement when he gives Radigund's enamored maid the name "Clarinda," Tasso's Clorinda is an interesting transition point in the evolution of the ideologeme. Because she seems to stand behind the signal moment of the Radigund episode in Book V, it is necessary to spend some time troubling over her remarkable hybrid nature.

Born of black Christian Ethiopian parents, white Clorinda is raised a Muslim, and is only baptized into the Christian faith into which she was born moments before she dies. She is therefore a very complicated amalgam of racial and ideological differences, racial differences here becoming an apt means for visualizing ideological differences. David Quint has interestingly argued that the hero's baptism of his beloved after he tragically slays her, thinking her a man, gestures at the Roman Catholic Church's problems with the heretical Ethiopian Church's emphasis on multiple baptisms (pp. 237-47). The hero baptizes her with water carried in a helmet, a helmet being that which kept her identity from him. In this gesture of a knight's baptizing his Ethiopian beloved, Quint points to Tasso's discomfort with the Counter-Reformation Church's need to make heretical Christians into enemies, that is to "other" those who are, in some fundamental way, the same. While Quint is correct to point out the function of the woman warrior as epic ideologeme to "other" the enemy—and the complications of this process for the Counter-Reformation are surely caught up in Clorinda's complicated genealogy—an even more fundamental generic function for that figure is to articulate what finally is always and everywhere basic to gender difference, that is, the division of labor.

Spenser's Amazon episode is quite different from Tasso's because first of all it is bound up with Elizabeth I and Spenser's concern to contain her gynecocracy.[19] This is what is local to Britomart and Radigund's story, specifically tied to Spenser's British, as opposed to Tasso's Mediterranean, context. But the moment when Britomart slays Radigund is also part and parcel of the fundamentally generic use of the woman warrior as epic ideologeme. The differences between Tasso and Spenser's use of the item of the helmet—that which makes the female other look momentarily like the same, that is, a male knight—can help to make the issue clear. Britomart kills Radigund by

---

[19] Susanne Woods, "Spenser and the Problem of Woman's Rule," *Huntington Library Quarterly* 48 (1985), 141-58; Mary Villeponteaux, "'Not as women wonted be': Spenser's Amazon Queen," in *Dissing Elizabeth: Negative Representations of Gloriana,* ed. Julia M. Walker (Durham, N.C., 1998), pp. 209-25.

attacking her when she is down, not allowing her to regain consciousness and to begin fighting again.

> She her so rudely on her helmet smit,
> That it empierced to the very braine,
> And her proud person low prostrated on the plaine.
>
> Where being layd, the wrothful Britonesse
> Stayd not, till she came to her selfe againe,
> But in reuenge both of her loues distresse,
> And her late vile reproch, though vaunted vaine,
> And also of her wound, which sore did paine,
> She with one stroke both head and helmet cleft.
> Which dreadfull sight, when all her warlike traine
> There present saw, each one of sence bereft,
> Fled fast into the towne, and her sole victor left. (5.7.33-4)

Unlike Tasso's hero, Britomart has no desire to intermarry with the enemy. If the other is an Ethiopian Christian, the problem of ideological difference is not insuperable. But if one needs a subject population to act as a workforce, to make the newly conquered territory profitable, then it is important for one to feel that the population is not one with whom one would ever want to intermarry. Spenser's sophistication about how one might go about creating native populations into racial others—and how dangerous intermarriage is to the colonial enterprize—is on view in the *View of the Present State of Ireland*.[20]

However awful the British colonization of Ireland was and is, it was not, of course, a simple case of slavery. What is specific to slavery, according to Orlando Patterson's suggestive analysis, is what he calls "social death," the "natal alienation" of the slave where the slave has no legitimate kin relations whatsoever, no socially signifying associations with ancestors, and therefore no relations to pass on to children.[21] Amazons are, of course, already skewed in their kinship systems, but they may, like Penthesilea's loyalty to the losing Trojan side, demonstrate the violence necessary before the Trojan women can be led off into slavery. When the woman warrior is on our side, not othered as an enemy but the same, and when, as with Britomart, she slays another woman, we have a far more distinct racial bar constructed; there is no intermarriage possible here—not merely because, as with Penthesilea, the Myrmidons slay her before they can take her home to be the wife they wish their own wives resembled—but because there can, finally, be no dynastically significant physical congress between them.[22] They may never intermarry and create a

---

[20] Hadfield, *Spenser's Irish Experience*, pp. 108-112.

[21] Orlando Patterson, *Slavery and Social Death: A Comparative Study* (Cambridge, Mass., 1982).

[22] Quintus Smyrnaeus, *The Fall of Troy*, trans. Arthur S. Way (London, 1913), 1: 669-74: "The warriors gazed, and in their hearts they prayed / That fair and sweet like her their wives might seem, / Laid on the bed of love, when home they won."

new race of Romans out of Trojan and Rutulian blood; instead, one group enslaves the other as a group racially distinct from itself. Spenser's emphasis is on the crucial moment of the cleaving of head and helmet, that is, the moment which repeats Artegall's realization that Britomart herself is a woman when he falls in love with her in Book IV, itself a rehearsal of another moment involving helmets—when Tasso's hero recognizes his beloved Clorinda. Artegall goes through the same process again when he fights with Radigund, shearing off her helmet, revealing her beauty, and succumbing to it. Britomart does not make that mistake.

What does Britomart actually do with the helmet and the head? She cleaves them both. Does this mean she decapitates the head, removing it from the body, or does it mean she splits the helmeted head in two? In a book which specifies that Munera's hands and feet are nailed up for all to view, and Pollente's head is placed punningly on a pole, the exact dismemberment enacted may be important. The emphasis on the head, of course, doubtless recalls all the parliamentary wrangling about whether or not Elizabeth I could call herself "Head" of the Church, her solution being enshrined in the witty "etc." standing at the head of Spenser's poem in its dedication to her. The problem of a female head of state provides part of the violence behind Britomart's blow.

Yet what is more generically fundamental to this moment is what the head accomplishes. The Medusa-like image may be either a Perseus-like decapitated head, or it may be a head split open; it hardly matters which because either way the image reveals a castration: either Medusa or the doubled cleft mark of the female genitals. Elizabeth once lamented that she was passed over for rule in favor of her younger brother because she was "cloven." Whatever the actual physical appearance of Radigund's head, its function is to terrify the Amazon mob. Talus pursues this fleeing army and begins a piteous slaughter that leaves such heaps of carcasses Britomart takes pity on them and makes him stop. After freeing the captive cross-dressed knights, Britomart restores the women who have not been slaughtered to "men's subjection." The response of all—Amazon nation and freed men—is to adore Britomart as a goddess. Restored to a natural subjection, the Amazon nation is, according to the narrator, made finally just. To call this "slavery" does not somehow sound right, because the only work we see anyone doing, carding and sewing, is, after all, women's "natural" work. It is only slavery when feudal knights do it. The Amazons, I would like to suggest, stand in for colonized laborers who all work like women—women, Indians, or Africans.

The result of the death of the woman warrior is thus quite different from the moment in Tasso's epic. There, love can cross any barrier: the hero and his slain beloved are both Christians (however much one may be heretical) even though they began as racial others and even though she dies. Unlike the dead Muslim Clorinda in Tasso's epic, the spared Amazonian nation of Spenser's are easily subjected—they do not fight once their leader is conquered. In a sense one does not even have to mount a just war against them in order rightfully to subject and enslave them, their subjection being natural because they are women. Britomart kills no one else in the epic. I used to think she killed a version of herself, that is, the woman who would take advantage of the self-enthralling courtly knight, thus fitting her for a wifehood that is far more powerful in early modern Protestantism than it was in the medieval Catholic preference for virginity, and therefore more needful of internalized policing. But when Britomart kills off Radigund the poem also puts women into two groups, Britomart's divinely obedient woman and women who are othered into a most violently imposed political subjection. By such gendered means a racial difference between the two groups becomes constructed.

Let us consider for a moment how Jameson's point about the romance ideologeme of the enemy knight's forced self-naming, helmet off and identity finally known, whereby the enemy-other is now recognized as the same and therefore not evil, is changed when the warrior is a woman. The revelation of her identity, that she is in fact a woman, is always something of a shock. Although she may be "one of us," the woman warrior can never be purely the same as the warrior knight. The generic result of romance, then, that is, turning the enemy other into another member of the same feudal class, is complicated when the chivalric challenger is shown to be a woman. The fundamental otherness carried by the ideologeme of the woman warrior is, I suggest, profoundly deepened, as Spenser achieves it, when the fight is between two women. The Myrmidons can admire the dead Penthesilea and imagine her a wife; Aeneas can intermarry with the people for whom Camilla fights; Tancredi can fall in love with Clorinda and baptize her. In contrast a woman-to-woman combat insists upon the lack of any possible dynastically significant intermarriage. Ariosto's acute use of this function of the figure in another Italian epic, *Orlando Furioso*, is comically presented in the woman knight Marfisa's experiences in Alessandretta. Marfisa can successfully fight off the numbered knights in combat, but she is unable to fulfill the second part of the challenge, that is, to sleep with the requisite number of women. To imagine fighting with warriors from a realm of women as Greek mythology does, is to imagine foreign others whom one can conquer and with whom one can intermarry as Theseus famously does. To imagine a realm of women with whom one's own women fight is to establish a group of racial others whose difference is policed by gender. To add to this combat the surrounding context of men enslaved into doing a forced labor which is ordinarily done by women, as Spenser does, is to come very close to articulating the fundamental historical reason for creating this racial otherness, that is, a cultural need to create a group of lesser beings for whom such labor is their natural calling. Gender is the greatest divider of labors. As I have suggested, the remarkable and heretofore unnoticed parallel between the two scenes of Book II and Book V, and the prominent concern with "wages" in both, indicates that they are doing the same generic work.

The persistent racism of the English-speaking world is not only practiced most immediately through gender politics, it is here constructed through them. That this is broadly true may be indicated by the briefest mention of the most explicitly New World text closely contemporaneous with Spenser, Shakespeare's *The Tempest*. A racial difference means there can be no appropriate intercourse between Miranda and Caliban. Ferdinand is a love-slave; Caliban is a slave-slave, indeed an African (his mother is from Algiers).[23] While they both do the same kind of work, Ferdinand as "patient logman" distinguishes himself specifically by the legitimacy of his union with Miranda. Caliban's worst and most damning act before attempting to overthrow Prospero is his attempted rape of Miranda. Here he demonstrates the rightness of his punishment in enslavement.

That the successful discourse of racism is best erected, as Spenser does it, by differentiating between different "races" of women may be demonstrated by a final very quick glance at one of the most interesting contemporary readers of Spenser, Mary Wroth.

In her long prose romance, *The Countess of Mountgomerie's Urania* (1621), Wroth revises a number of Spenser's densest allegorical moments when she has the enchantment in the Castle of Love include Urania's maid's vision of her lover in the arms of a black woman: "Urania's maide beheld as she beleev'd Allimarlus in the second Tower, kissing and embracing a Black-moore; which so farre inraged her, being passionately in love with him, as she must goe to revenge her self of that injurie."[24] Kim Hall has interestingly argued that in this moment we see Wroth's paradigmatic enunciation of a cultural concern about the exoticism of all epic adventure into new worlds, a concern that the adventurer will "go native." As Hall notes, "the introduction of racial otherness serves to distinguish" groups of women.[25] Wroth here seems self-consciously to articulate through this fantasm how women are culturally made to assume the burden of policing racial difference through their own sexual jealousy. As a woman, Wroth reads the racial script that is being constructed in texts such as Spenser's and makes it explicit in her own. (In a fascinating sonnet on sunburn, Wroth meditates on the relations of the Indian's red skin color to gendered subjection.)

I do not mean to suggest here that epic is reduceable to this one function; surely the complications of each individual text and the compli-cations of their explicit and inexplicit recall of each other makes for a far more

---

[23] Stephen Greenblatt, *Learning to Curse: Essays in Early Modern Culture* (New York, 1990), pp. 24-5, discusses the colonialist issue in terms of the mutual unintelligibility of languages. For a discussion of the relations between Miranda, Caliban, and Prospero in terms of Gayle Rubin's understanding of the traffic in women, see Jyotsna G. Singh, "Caliban versus Miranda: Race and Gender Conflicts in Postcolonial Rewritings of *The Tempest*," in *Feminist Readings of Early Modern Culture*, pp. 191-209.

[24] *The First Part of the Countess of Montgomery's Urania*, ed. Josephine A. Roberts (Binghamton, 1995), p. 40.

[25] Kim F. Hall, *Things of Darkness: Economies of Race and Gender in Early Modern England* (Ithaca, 1995), p. 189.

various set of relations than one having to do with a single set of economic conditions. But genre is a powerful cultural tool and when genres have such interesting histories, appearing, disappearing, and then reappearing over such long stretches of human time, it is interesting to ask why they do and what they are doing, culturally, when they do. Our English-speaking Western Hemisphere racism is such a powerful and long-lived construct that it stands to reason that our most powerful cultural tools were used in its construction. And we have little hope of finally undoing it without understanding how, and with what tools, it was made.

Part II

Allegories of Cultural Exchange

4

Translated States:
Spenser and Linguistic Colonialism

Richard A. McCabe

Commenting in *A View of the Present State of Ireland* upon what he regards as the "degeneracy" of the Old English families that have adopted the Gaelic language, Spenser observes that "wordes are the Image of the minde So as they procedinge from the minde the minde must be nedes affected with the wordes So that the speache beinge Irishe the harte muste nedes be Irishe for out of the abundance of the harte the tongue speakethe" (p. 119).[1] Similarly, Fynes Moryson regarded the adoption of the Gaelic language as a "tuchstone" of "inward affection" demonstrating an unwillingness on the part of the "English Irish" to "apply themselves any way to the English, or not to followe the Irish in all thinges."[2] These remarks activate habits of linguistic discrimination stretching back to the ancient Greeks for whom "barbarism" was primarily a semantic concept: originally "barbarians" were those who could not speak Greek but made incomprehensible "babbling" noises (like *bar bar*).[3] By extension, "barbarians" were those who did not share in what were held to be the superior cultural attainments of the Greek-speaking world. Latin speakers were initially regarded as "barbarians" but, after the conquest of Greece and the consequent Hellenizing of Roman civilization, the Romans redefined the notion of barbarity in such a way as to exclude themselves but to embrace all those living beyond the boundaries—and against the perceived values—of the Graeco-Roman world. The category of the "barbaric" was therefore fluid and changeable, constructed and deconstructed as the need arose, and entirely dependent upon cultural, and to a large extent linguistic, perspectives. As St. Paul observed, "if I know not the meaning of the voice, I shall be unto him that speaketh a barbarian, and he that speaketh shall be a barbarian unto me" (1 Corinthians 14.11).

---

[1] All quotations of *A View* are from *The Works of Edmund Spenser*, ed. Edwin Greenlaw, et al., Variorum Edition (Baltimore, 1932-58), *The Prose Works* 9 (1949). All quotations of the poetry are from the same edition.

[2] *Shakespeare's Europe: Unpublished Chapters of Fynes Moryson's Itinerary*, ed. Charles Hughes (London, 1903), p. 214. Hereafter Moryson.

[3] Eric Cheyfitz, *The Poetics of Imperialism: Translation and Colonization from* The Tempest *to* Tarzan (Oxford, 1991), pp. 89-90.

Adopting an attitude very similar to that of the ancient Greeks and Romans, Richard Stanyhurst observed that

> the inhabitants of the English pale have beene in old time so much addicted to their civilitie, and so farre sequestered from barbarous sauagenesse, as their onelie mother toong was English. And trulie, so long as these impaled dwellers did sunder themselves as well in land as in language from the Irish: rudenesse was daie by daie in the countrie supplanted, civilitie ingraffed ... and in fine the coine of a yoong England was like to shoot in Ireland.[4]

Owing to their incorporation into Holinshed's *Chronicles*, Stanyhurst's views were generally regarded as authoritative, and the association between geographical segregation, linguistic difference and cultural inferiority was commonly taken for granted—hence the passage into common parlance of the term "beyond the pale."[5] Yet, as both Stanyhurst and Spenser recognized, the boundaries of the original Pale were so fluid and shifting as to render entirely relative all notions of "beyond" and "within." Spenser notes that areas once considered central now constituted "the moste outboundes and abandoned places in the Englishe pale, And inded [are] not Counted of the Englishe pale at all" (p. 61). His terminology serves to remind us that the sense of a boundary, and particularly an unstable boundary, implies not merely a spatial division but also a point of contact, an area of ambiguity which is neither beyond, nor within, but between. In cultural terms it suggests all that is hybrid and ambivalent, a sense of otherness all the more disturbing for being uncannily familiar. The arguments adduced in Holinshed ignore the fact that the early Norman settlers had leveled the same charges of barbarism against the indigenous Celts as Spenser, Stanyhurst, and other "New English" colonists leveled against their own descendants.[6] In much the same way, sixteenth-century apologists for the Saxons, generally regarded as the principal (though by no means the sole) ancestors of the English, noted how the Holy Roman Empire had come to center itself upon the "wyld" outlands of its unholy predecessor among the descendants of tribes deemed barbaric by

---

[4] Raphael Holinshed, *Chronicles of England, Scotland and Ireland* (London, 1808), 6: 4. Hereafter *Chronicles*. Stanyhurst writes in the tradition of Giraldus Cambrensis, according to whom the Irish were "a barbarous people, literally barbarous ... since conventions are formed from living together in society, and since they are so removed in these distant parts from the ordinary world of men ... they know only of the barbarous habits in which they were born and brought up, and embrace them as another nature." See Gerald of Wales, *The History and Topography of Ireland*, trans. John J. O'Meara (Harmondsworth, 1982), pp. 102-3.

[5] See Richard A. McCabe, "Edmund Spenser: Poet of Exile," *Proceedings of the British Academy*, 1991 Lectures and Memoirs, 80 (1993), 84-9.

[6] See Nicholas Canny, *The Formation of the Old English Elite in Ireland* (Dublin, 1975), pp. 18-29; Ciaran Brady, "The Road to the *View*: On the Decline of Reform Thought in Tudor Ireland," in *Spenser and Ireland: An Interdisciplinary Perspective*, ed. Patricia Coughlan (Cork, 1989), 32-6.

classical authors such as Tacitus.[7] Taken in conjunction, such instances indicate an alarming tendency for the marginal to displace the central and for the center to decline into "barbarity."

The rise of vernacular languages throughout the fifteenth and sixteenth centuries casts the issue of linguistic difference into high prominence. In *The Defence and Illustration of the French Language* (1534?), for example, Joachim Du Bellay fulminates against "this Greek arrogance [which], admiring only its own inventions, had neither law nor privilege to legitimise its own nation and bastardise all the others ... the Scythians were barbarians among the Greeks, but the Athenians were also barbarians among the Scythians."[8] The passage is of particular interest because of Spenser's reliance throughout much of *A View* upon the alleged Scythian ancestry of the Irish to bolster his claim that sixteenth-century Celtic society is, of racial necessity, "salvage" (pp. 107-8). In making this claim he employs the common ethnographic technique of argumentation by analogy, as demonstrated, for example, in Joannes Boemus's *The Fardle of Facions* (1555), one of the principal sources of Spenser's Scythian lore.[9] If a contemporary Celtic custom can be shown to resemble a practice recorded as "barbaric" by any ancient commentator or modern anthologist, the assumption is not merely that the contemporary must derive from the ancient but, more often than not, that the contemporary is the ancient. "I reasonablie Conclude," Spenser asserts, "that the Irishe are discended from the *Scythyans* for that they use even to this daie some of the same ceremonies which the *Scythyans* auncientlye used" (p. 107). This is tantamount to saying that Gaelic civilization exists at an earlier stage of development than that of contemporary English culture because savagery was regarded as the state antecedent to proper civilization.[10] Irish customs are held to preserve more of "antiquitye" than any other (p. 82), "for it is the manner of all barbarous nacions to be verye superstitious and dilligent observers of olde Customes and Antiquities which they receave by Continuall tradicion from theire parentes by recordinge of theire bardes and Cronicles in theire songes and by dailye use and ensample of theire elders" (pp. 109-10). Hence the notion that assimilation into Celtic culture constitutes social and even psychological regression or degeneracy rather than simple alteration.[11] In the case of the ancient Britons (whose relationship to the Irish is recognized in *A View*), Roman conquest was frequently seen as the instrument of civilization and, by direct analogy,

---

[7] Richard Verstegan, *A Restitution of Decayed Intelligence* (Antwerp, 1605), p. 53.

[8] Joachim Du Bellay, *The Defence and Illustration of the French Language*, trans. Gladys M. Turquet (London, 1939), p. 23.

[9] See Margaret T. Hodgen, *Early Anthropology in the Sixteenth and Seventeenth Centuries* (Philadelphia, 1964), pp. 194-99, 391. For Boemus's account of the Scythians, see *The Fardle of Facions* (London, 1555), "Asie," ch. 9.

[10] Hodgen, p. 308.

[11] Hodgen, p. 377.

Camden represented English conquest as serving precisely the same function for the Celts.[12]

The thrust of Spenser's cultural analysis is pervasively semantic and he relies very heavily upon highly politicized exercises in "etymology" to support his arguments. Thus, the practice of "tanistry" or elective leadership, which he identifies as the major stumbling-block to the Tudor policy of "surrender and regrant," is denigrated by association with "those Barbarous nacions that overranne the worlde which possessed those dominions whereof they are now so Called, And so it maye well be That from thence the firste originall of this worde *Tanist and Tanistry* came And the Custome theareof hathe sithence As manye others bene Contynewed" (p. 51).[13] To Spenser's way of thinking, the semantic evidence suggests that the practice of "tanistry" is an unwelcome survival from an earlier, primitive age, from a time when properly managed and enclosed lands were "overrun" by "salvage" nomads. Similarly, the contemporary war-cries of the Irish are analyzed etymologically to afford, with the support of standard authorities such as Diodorus Siculus and Herodotus, "verye manifest profe that the Irishe be Scithes" (p. 103).[14] Because speech was regarded as "the instrument of society," it was supposed that the users of a savage language could not but produce a barbarous culture.[15]

As Umberto Eco has demonstrated, Renaissance commentators were unanimous in positing the existence of a primeval or "natural" language spoken in Eden and common to all men until the confounding of tongues at the Tower of Babel.[16] This language was regarded as superior to its successors because it was believed to have afforded an absolute correspondence between signifier and signified. The names ascribed by Adam to the various creatures somehow encapsulated their true natures, thereby establishing a unique coherence between language and reality (Genesis 2.19-20).[17] The fragmentation of this primal language was held to have ushered in the phenomenon of linguistic degeneracy and to have facilitated racial conflict. In *A Restitution of Decayed Intelligence* (1605), for example, Richard Verstegan suggests that the origin of racial diversity was itself linguistic, for following the disaster at Babel,

---

[12] *Britain, or a Chorographicall Description of the most flourishing Kingdomes, England, Scotland, and Ireland*, trans. Philemon Holland (London, 1610), "Ireland," p. 66.

[13] For the policy of "surrender and regrant," see Colm Lennon, *Sixteenth-Century Ireland: The Incomplete Conquest* (Dublin, 1994), pp. 155-9.

[14] For this use of classical authorities, see Hodgen, pp. 182-4, 296-7.

[15] Ben Jonson, *Timber: or Discoveries* in *The Complete Poems*, ed. George Parfitt (Harmondsworth, 1975), p. 430.

[16] Umberto Eco, *The Search for the Perfect Language*, trans. James Fentress (London, 1997; first pub. 1993), pp. 73-116.

[17] Platonic theory lent support to the biblical notion. See Norman Kretzmann, "Plato on the Correctness of Names," *American Philosophical Quarterly* 8 (1971), 126-38; Gail Fine, "Plato on Naming," *Philosophical Quarterly* 27 (1977), 289-301; Bernard Williams, "Cratylus' Theory of Names and its Refutation," in *Language and Logos: Studies in Ancient Greek Philosophy presented to G.E.L. Owen*, ed. Malcolm Schofield and Martha C. Nussbaum (Cambridge, 1982), pp. 83-95.

many new distinct and different nations were begun, even of such as a litle before, were all one nation, and used all one language, and each troop (as in reason it followeth) having a naturall desyre to remain by it self, seperated from the others whose language it understood not, caused that they all resolved to departe divers wayes to seek themselves new and severall habitations, whereby such as but a litle before used all one language and were all one nation, were now become meer strangers the one unto the other, and thenceforward dayly grew unto more and more alienation.[18]

In effect, the concept of "otherness" is here seen to originate in linguistic difference. The title page to Verstegan's work shows the various peoples of the world dispersing in different directions towards the margins of the picture in order to establish new nations that will be linguistically distinct and geographically separate from one another. The central space, occupied by the incomplete and abandoned tower, has come to represent the insuperable problem of cultural diversity, the point at which unity of purpose and universality of co-operation necessarily break down through linguistic diversity, through the sheer failure of mutual comprehension (figure 4.1). Hence Du Bellay's contention that linguistic diversity articulates diversity of political will, "for languages are not born of themselves after the fashion of herbs, roots, or trees ... but all their virtue is born in the world of the desire and will of mortals."[19]

Du Bellay concludes that no vernacular language should be deemed superior or inferior to any other, but such tolerant relativism had little place in colonial discourse. Rather, it was assumed that some languages preserved more of the primeval purity than others. Thus Richard Verstegan makes high claims for "Teutonic," of which English was held to be a variant, on the grounds that the etymology of so many of its words revealed them to be, like those of the primary tongue, singularly appropriate to the things they signified.[20] Although the Celtic language was itself commonly regarded as one of the seventy-two mother tongues deriving from Babel—as even Stanyhurst admitted—the common association between cultural degeneracy and geographical marginality could be used to diminish its prestige.[21] Stanyhurst comments upon its inherent "obscuritie," the "strangenesse of the phrase, and the curious featnes of the pronuntiation" so that "scarse one in five hundred can either read, write, or understand it."[22] As the language spoken beyond the borders of civility, by a race Spenser accuses of being congenitally prone to lying (pp. 67-8), it was by definition a "barbarous tongue." Stanyhurst cites the alleged

---

[18] *A Restitution*, p. 6.

[19] *Defence and Illustration*, p. 21.

[20] *A Restitution*, pp. 191-4.

[21] Holinshed, *Chronicles*, 6: 6.

[22] Holinshed, *Chronicles*, 6: 7. See also Michael Neill, "Broken English and Broken Irish: Nation, Language, and the Optic of Power in Shakespeare's Histories," *Shakespeare Quarterly* 45 (1994), 19.

A
RESTITVTION
of
DECAYED INTELLIGENCE:
In antiquities.

Concerning the moſt noble and renovv-
med English nation.

By the ſtudie and trauaile of R. V.

Dedicated vnto the Kings moſt excellent Maieſtie.

Nationum Origo.

Printed at Antvverp by Robert Bruney.
1605.

And to be ſold at London *in* Paules-Churchyeard,
by Iohn Norton *and* Iohn Bill.

Figure 4.1
Title page
Richard Verstegan, *A Restitution of Decayed Intelligence in Antiquities*
(Antwerp, 1605)

absence of a word for "knave" as indicative of the moral values it encodes.[23] Whereas Goropius Becanus, a Dutch contemporary of Spenser, attempted to demonstrate by etymological means that some version of "Teutonic" was spoken in Eden, Spenser employs equivalent techniques to prove that the Celtic tongue derives from that spoken by the barbarous hordes that overran the Roman empire.[24] For him, the ethnographic argument from linguistic analogy is invariably negative—as necessitated by the politics of the colonial enterprise and, perhaps even more profoundly, by its psychology. Within living memory English itself, as an emergent vernacular, had struggled to throw off imputations of "barbarity," of being, in Thomas Heywood's description, "the most harsh, uneven, and broken language of the world, part *Dutch*, part *Irish*, *Saxon*, *Scotch*, *Welsh*, and indeed a gallimafrey of many, but perfect in none."[25] To denigrate the Celtic language in such circumstances was tantamount to appropriating "classical" status for English, and civilized status for English speakers. It was to suppress the disconcerting fact of linguistic hybridity in favor of a myth of ethnic cohesion. Edmund Campion suggested that "babes from their cradells should be enured under learned schoolemasters with a pure Englishe tonge, habite, fasshion, discipline" so that they might "in time utterlie forgett the affinitie of their unbroken borderers."[26] It was precisely this "affinitie" with "borderers," however, that threatened to unravel the entire ideology of the Pale.

The ultimate expression of the tendency towards linguistic denigration is the denial that the sounds uttered by some of the indigenous populations of Africa and America (regarded as the most extreme cases of geographical marginality) qualify as human language but rather partake of the nature of animal communication.[27] But this, too, has its origins in the ancient world for, as Anthony Pagden argues, "a close association in the Greek mind between intelligible speech and reason made it possible to take the view that those who were devoid of *logos* in one sense might also be devoid of it in another ... non-Greek speakers ... lived, by definition, outside the Greek family of man, the *oikumene*, and thus had no share in the collective cultural values of the Hellenic community."[28] The matter is relevant here in view of the common Elizabethan comparison between the Celtic and American frontiers and the "savagery" allegedly endemic to both.[29] Of the savage man of the sixth book of *The Faerie Queene*, we learn that:

---

[23] Holinshed, *Chronicles*, 6: 7-8.

[24] For Becanus's theories, see Verstegan, *A Restitution*, pp. 190-91.

[25] Thomas Heywood, *An Apology for Actors* (London, 1612), sig. F3r.

[26] Edmund Campion, *Two Bokes of the Histories of Ireland*, ed. A.F. Vossen (Assen, 1963), p. 144.

[27] Hodgen, pp. 411-12.

[28] Anthony Pagden, *The Fall of Natural Man: The American Indian and the Origins of Comparative Ethnology* (Cambridge, 1982), p. 16

[29] Of the new Irish plantations Moryson observes that "no lesse Cautions were to be observed for uniting them and keeping them from mixing with the other, then if these newe Colonyes were to be ledd to inhabitt among the barbarous Indians" (p. 249). See also D.B.

> other language had he none nor speach,
> But a soft murmure, and confused sound
> Of senselesse words, which nature did him teach,
> T'expresse his passions, which his reason did empeach.
>   (6.4.11)

It is noteworthy that "natural" expression is here seen to impede rational discourse rather than to facilitate a return to Edenic eloquence, and the connotations of "naturall" vary throughout *A View* from the pejorative to the favorable depending upon whether English or Irish customs are in question. The savage man's appearance in *The Legende of Courtesie* is significant in view of Stanyhurst's assertion that "the courtesie of the English language is cleane contrarie" to the self-centered values encoded in such Irish constructions as "I and you" (rather than "you and I").[30] The Gaelic language, he suggests, impedes the cultivation of social courtesy and consequently of civility itself. It was therefore easy for Spenser to represent English as the pure mother tongue from which the Old English families (whose French-speaking, Norman ancestry is tactfully overlooked) had degenerated owing to geographical marginality and intermarriage with the "salvage" peoples of the borderland. The "Englishe pale" had been preserved "in reasonable Civillitye" only "thoroughe nearenesse of the State" (p. 115). For those "planted" further off, the result was increasing alienation from the mother tongue and those who spoke it. This process proved fatal to the colonial project for, according to Fynes Moryson, "communion or difference of language, hath allwayes beene observed, a spetiall motive to unite or allienate the myndes of all nations, so as the wise Romans as they inlarged theire Conquests, so they did spreade theire language ... and in generall all nations have thought nothing more powerfull to unite myndes then the Community of language."[31] By contrast with the ancient Romans, Spenser argued, the Old English families had subverted their conquest by abandoning their language. As a result, vanquished territories had been "aliened" to the Irish (p. 118).

In the "epistle" to *The Shepheardes Calender*, E.K. warns against the contamination of "the good and naturall English" of "our Mother tonge" by the importation of foreign words owing to the danger that Englishmen may eventually become "straungers" and "alienes" in their own language. In his view the practice of indiscriminate borrowing from foreign languages had, as Heywood noted, "made our English tongue, a gallimaufray or hodgepodge of

---

Quinn, *The Elizabethans and the Irish* (Ithaca, 1966), pp. 21-7, 106-22; Nicholas Canny, *Kingdom and Colony: Ireland in the Atlantic World, 1560-1800* (Baltimore, 1988), pp. 7-13, 35.

[30] Holinshed, *Chronicles*, 6: 67. Stanyhurst's views were vigorously contested by Irish commentators such as Geoffrey Keating. See Brendan Bradshaw, "Geoffrey Keating: Apologist of Irish Ireland," in *Representing Ireland: Literature and the Origins of Conflict, 1534-1660*, ed. Brendan Bradshaw, Andrew Hadfield and Willy Maley (Cambridge, 1993), pp. 166-90.

[31] Moryson, p. 213.

al other speches." This closely corresponds to Stanyhurst's complaint that the Old English "have so acquainted themselves with the Irish, as they have made a mingle mangle or gallimaufreie of both the languages, and have in such medleie or checkerwise so crabbedlie iumbled them both togither, as commonlie the inhabitants of the meaner sort speake neither good English nor good Irish."[32] As perceived by Spenser, the Old English families represent extreme examples of linguistic estrangement and alienation to the point at which they "quite forgett theire Countrie and theire owne names" (p. 115). In so doing they derogate not only from civility but from the avowed colonial ideal of civilizing others, "for it hathe bene ever the use of the Conquerour to despise the Language of the Conquered and to force him by all meanes to learne his. So did the Romaines allwaies use in soe muche that there is allmoste no nacion in the worlde but is sprinckled with theire language" (pp. 118-19).[33]

As the origin of nations was commonly held to be linguistic, the Old English families were perceived to have adopted the Irish political outlook along with the Irish tongue. Stanyhurst illustrates the imagined stages of such declension into political apostasy quite graphically: "they were invironed and compassed with evill neighbours. Neighbourhood bred acquaintance, acquaintance waffed in the Irish toong, the Irish hooked with it attire, attire haled rudenesse, rudenesse ingendered ignorance, ignorance brought contempt of lawes, the contempt of lawes bred rebellion."[34] According to Spenser's less schematic account of affairs, geographical proximity encouraged practices of fosterage and intermarriage which precipitated the process of cultural degeneration by promoting the dangerous sexual influence of "salvage" women as wet-nurses and mothers,

> for firste the Childe that suckethe the milke of the nurse muste of necessitye learne his firste speache of her, the which beinge the firste that is enured to his tongue is ever after moste pleasinge unto him In so muche as thoughe he afterwardes be taughte Englishe yeat the smacke of the firste will allwaies abide with him and not onelye of the speche but allsoe of the manners and Condicions for besides that younge Children be like Apes which will affecte and ymitate what they see done before them speciallye by theire nurses whom they love so well, they moreover drawe into themselves togeather witn theire sucke even the nature and disposicion of theire nurses ffor the minde followethe much the Temperature of the bodye. (p. 119)

The term "mother tongue" is here interpreted in a very literal sense to create the impression that the child somehow "sucks" his allegiance with his

---

[32] Holinshed, *Chronicles*, 6: 5. See Paula Blank, *Broken English: Dialects and the Politics of Language in Renaissance Writings* (London, 1996), pp. 144-53.

[33] For the politics of linguistic colonialism, see Stephen Greenblatt, *Learning to Curse: Essays in Early Modern Culture* (New York, 1990), pp. 16-39.

[34] Holinshed, *Chronicles*, 6: 5.

milk, that political and cultural inclinations are inbred even though the logic of the argument implies that they are artificially inculcated. But whereas bonds of fosterage are regarded as occasioning shifts in political sympathy, the practice of intermarriage was seen to confound the very distinction between the two races by obscuring the bloodline: "for how cane suche matchinge but bringe forthe an evill race seinge that Comonlye the Childe takethe moste of his nature of the mother besides speache manners inclynacion which are for the moste parte agreable to the Condicions of theire mothers for by them they are firste framed and fashioned" (p. 120).[35] Thus, the Spenserian purpose of "fashioning" gentlemen "in vertuous and gentle discipline" is undone by what he regards as the evils of miscegenation. As one of Spenser's fellow planters asserted, "the blood of theire Irishe mothers, hathe wasted away the naturall love they bare to theire mother England."[36] Fynes Moryson expressed the matter even more bluntly when he observed that "children of mingled race could not but degenerate from theire English Parents."[37] The desire for linguistic purity demonized the racial hybrid, the problematic category of the "Englishe Irishe" whom Spenser alleged to be "more malitious to the Englishe then the verye Irishe themselves" (pp. 96, 210). Sexual intercourse and what Stanyhurst refers to as the "intercourse of languages" were seen to facilitate one another.[38] Since both fell into the moral category of the "licentious," Spenser issued a dual warning against "licentious Conversinge with the Irishe or marryinge and fosteringe with them" (p. 117). From this viewpoint, cultural assimilation is a form of moral seduction.

For Spenser, the ultimate linguistic sign of cultural degeneracy is the adoption of an Irish patronym in place of an English one. As his evident pride in his own surname suggests, to name oneself is to invoke a lineage and assert a loyalty.[39] During the events that led to the Battle of Kinsale (1601), Sir John Harington recalled the official anxiety that Hugh O'Neill should style himself "Hugh Tyrone" after the fashion of the English peerage rather than simply "O'Neill" in the traditional Gaelic manner.[40] The issue was significant because "Hugh Tyrone" was an English invention designed to frustrate the "barbarous" and "Scythian" custom of "tanistry" by substituting the English system of primogeniture, whereas O'Neill, despite his enforced upbringing in England, remained very much a part of the Celtic world. With the abolition of Irish surnames, however, Spenser predicts that the clansmen "shall not onelye not

---

[35] For fosterage, see Sir John Davies, *A Discoverie of the True Causes why Ireland was never Entirely Subdued* (London, 1612), pp. 178-80.

[36] *The Supplication of the blood of the English most lamentably murdred in Ireland, Cryeng out of the yearth for revenge*, ed. Willy Maley, *Analecta Hibernica* 36 (1995), 33.

[37] Moryson, p. 212.

[38] Holinshed, *Chronicles*, 6: 6.

[39] Spenser claims kinship with the Spencers of Althorp in the dedications to *The Teares of the Muses, Mother Hubberds Tale, Muiopotmos*, and in *Colin Clouts Come Home Againe* (536-9).

[40] See *Strangers to that Land: British Perceptions of Ireland from the Reformation to the Famine*, ed. Andrew Hadfield and John McVeagh (London, 1994), p. 93.

depende uppon the heade of theire septe as now they doe but allso shall in shorte time learne quite to forgett his Irishe nacion" (p. 215). Those who derived their new names from their "trades" or "facultyes" would simultaneously redefine both their nationality and their social class. In most cases racial inferiority would be translated into social inferiority.

Among the Old English families that Spenser accounts as degenerate were the Fitz Ursulas, now allegedly calling themselves the "MacMahons," who "did quite caste of theire Englishe name and Allegeance since which time they have ever soe remayned and have still sithens bene Counted mere Irishe" (p. 116). Spenser associates the two surnames by means of a questionable etymology whereby MacMahon is rendered as "the bear's son" in correspondence with Fitz Ursula.[41] This accords with the views of John Derricke who asserts in *The Image of Ireland* (1581) that the country was capable of transforming civil persons into animals.[42] One recalls the episode in the sixth book of *The Faerie Queene* when Sir Calepine rescues an infant from the clutches of a marauding bear in the midst of trackless woodland but manages to regain the "plain champion" (6.4.26) where he consigns the child to the care of Sir Bruin and Matilda to "traine in chevalry, / Or noursle up in lore of learn'd Philosophy" (6.4.35). Clearly, Sir Bruin and the bear represent twin aspects of the one persona, the latter indicative of the savage otherness latent within the civil knight, just as Fitz Ursula and MacMahon *mean* the same thing but *signify* contrary things. The reclamation of the child from wild woodlands to the "plain champion" of civility may be seen to reflect the hope that the Old English families might similarly be reclaimed. Chancellor Gerrard argued that the government must attempt to evoke the residual "instincte of Englishe nature" within such families in order to reclaim them from Celtic corruption. Force was unequal to such a task: "for can the swoord teache theim to speake Englishe, to use Englishe apparrell ... and to shonne all the manners and orders of the Irishe?"[43] By way of direct response, the Irish historian Geoffrey Keating expertly demonstrates the falsity of Spenser's etymologies and expresses astonishment that anyone ignorant of the Irish language should undertake the interpretation of genealogies recorded solely in Irish sources. His intervention caustically exposes colonial etymology as "poetic licence."[44]

In Gerrard's opinion, those who spoke Irish were likely to follow the dictates of the Brehon Law which Spenser and Fynes Moryson erroneously

---

[41] See Roland M. Smith, "The Irish Background of Spenser's *View*," *Journal of English and Germanic Philology* 42 (1943), 507-8.

[42] *The Image of Irelande with a Discoverie of Woodkarne*, ed. D.B. Quinn (Belfast, 1985), p. 29.

[43] *Lord Chancellor Gerrard's Notes of his Report on Ireland (1577-8)*, ed. C. McNeill, *Analecta Hibernica* 2 (1931), 96. Hereafter Gerrard.

[44] Geoffrey Keating, *The History of Ireland*, ed. and trans. David Comyn (London, 1902–14), 1: 25-31. See Clare Carroll, "Spenser and the Irish Language: The Sons of Milesio in *A View of the Present State of Ireland*, *The Faerie Queene*, Book V, and the Leabhar Gabhála," *Irish University Review*, special issue, *Spenser in Ireland, 1596-1996* 26 (1996), 281-90.

held to be a matter of verbal tradition rather than a written code (p. 47).[45] Thus, the Irish language was seen as the exclusive medium of a legal system which was, according to Spenser, "in manye thinges repugninge quite to godes lawe and mans" (p. 47). In effect, the adoption of an Irish surname signaled adherence to this "barbarous" code. Even in areas which seemed to acknowledge "subieccion" to English law, Spenser alleges, "the same *Brehon* lawe is privilye practiced amongeste themselves, By reason that dwellinge as they doe whole nacions and septes of the Irishe togeather without anye Inglishman amongest them they maye doe what they liste and Compounde or alltogeather Conceale amongest themselves theire owne Crimes" (p. 48). The Irish "community of language" is hereby represented as a criminal confraternity: Irish is the language of the outlaw. Hence the persistent fear of "greate assemblies" of Celts at which "they maye frelye mete and Conferr of what they liste" (pp. 128-9) or "practize or Conspire what they will" (p. 179). In the new order of affairs envisaged by Spenser, however, "they should not be able once to sturr or to murmure" uncensored (pp. 179-80)—a notable testament to the paranoia that finds poetic expression in the culture of suspicion and distrust that pervades the "waste" woodlands of *The Faerie Queene*.

For Spenser, as for many other Elizabethan commentators, the danger posed by the brehons, or judges, was exceeded only by that of the bards.[46] Here there could be no doubt that a written as well as an oral culture was involved, but since it would be inconsistent for Spenser to admit to reading or speaking Irish, he has recourse to the tactic of translation as a means of simultaneously appropriating and distancing bardic literature. He therefore explains his familiarity with certain Gaelic poems with considerable circumspection when he asserts that, "I have Cawsed diverse of them to be translated unto me that I mighte understande them" (p. 127). Not surprisingly, the politics of translation prove to be as relentlessly polemical as those of etymology.[47] George Steiner has observed that "the translator invades, extracts and brings home" and this is precisely what Spenser's translations, or paraphrases, tend to do.[48] Even in the best of circumstances, as Lawrence Venuti contends, "the ethnocentric violence of translation is inevitable: in the translating process, foreign languages, texts, and cultures will always undergo some degree and form of

---

[45] Moryson, p. 224.

[46] "The wilde or meere Irish have a generation of Poets, or rather Rymers vulgarly called Bardes, who in their songs used to extoll the most bloudy licentious men, and no others, and to allure the hearers, not to the love of religion and Civill manners, but to outrages Robberies living as outlawes, and Contempt of the Magistrates and the kings lawes." Moryson, p. 199. For Spenser and the bards, see Christopher Highley, *Shakespeare, Spenser and the Crisis in Ireland* (Cambridge, 1997), pp. 20-39.

[47] For the political uses of translation, see Cheyfitz, *The Poetics of Imperialism*, pp. 59-103; John Gillies, *Shakespeare and the Geography of Difference* (Cambridge, 1994), pp. 121-2.

[48] George Steiner, *After Babel: Aspects of Language and Translation* (Oxford, 1975), p. 298.

reduction, exclusion, inscription."[49] For Spenser's purposes, translation is a reductive mode, converting distinctive Gaelic virtues into familiar English vices through the common ethnographic technique of negative analogy. As François Hartog has argued in *The Mirror of Herodotus*, "a rhetoric of otherness is basically an operation of translation ... it is a conveyer of what is different," and the translator always has at his disposal "the handy figure of inversion, whereby otherness is transcribed as anti-sameness."[50] As Herodotus "translated" the Scythians, Spenser "translates" their supposed Celtic descendants. As a result, the traditional martial virtues praised by the bards as a matter of poetic convention are for him varieties of "lewdnes" adorned with encomiums "borrowed even from the prayses which are proper unto vertue it selfe" (p. 126). He cites the example of "a moste notorious Thiefe and wicked outlawe which had lived all his lief time of spoiles and Robberies," of whom one of the bards is alleged to have said,

> that he was none of those Idle milkesopps that was broughte up by the fire side but that moste of his daies he spente in armes and valiante enterprises that he did never eate his meate before he had wonne it with his sword that he laye not slugginge all nighte in a Cabbyn under his mantle But used Comonlye to kepe others wakinge to defende theire lives ... that his musicke was not the harpe nor layes of love but the Cryes of people and Clashinge of Armour, and that finallye he died not bewaylled of manye but made manye waile when he died that dearely boughte his deathe. (p. 126)

Whereas many extant bardic poems conform to the general pattern of this description, none coincides directly in proffering a senseless encouragement to violence for its own sake.[51] Rather, the bards evoke and inculcate, within a standard matrix of received literary conventions, traditions of martial endeavour stretching back to the heroes of ancient Celtic saga. Each poem is addressed to a specific individual or family, since the bards were expected to cultivate the genealogy of their patrons as assiduously as Spenser cultivates that of Elizabeth Tudor. By omitting the proper name, and replacing it with the terms "thiefe" and "outlawe," Spenser translates an exercise in heroic particularity into a general *exemplum* of cultural inferiority and represents the standard conventions of bardic encomium as irresponsible encouragements to various forms of "barbarity." Thus an apparently genuine act of quotation, designed to illustrate the nature of a foreign literature, functions as a weapon of racial polemic. Quotation becomes interpretation. The reader is given no access to the actual sentiments of the bard, any more than to his actual

---

[49] Lawrence Venuti, *The Translator's Invisibility: A History of Translation* (London, 1995), p. 310.

[50] François Hartog, *The Mirror of Herodotus: The Representation of the Other in the Writing of History*, trans. Janet Lloyd (Berkeley, 1988), pp. 213, 237.

[51] See Osborn Bergin, ed., *Irish Bardic Poetry* (Dublin, 1970), pp. 3-22; Michelle O'Riordan, *The Gaelic Mind and the Collapse of the Gaelic World* (Cork, 1990), pp. 62-118.

language. The paraphrase constitutes a translation not just into the English language but into the English value-system. Hence the deletion of all of the dense mythological allusion and genealogical detail that form the staple of bardic poetry but would quite literally "mean nothing" to readers unfamiliar with its cultural frame of reference. Furthermore, because it is virtually impossible to capture the complexity of bardic vocabulary, or the intricacy of bardic metres, in any language other than Gaelic, the act of translation strips away the artistry of the poems so thoroughly that one of the most highly-wrought and consciously rhetorical forms of European poetry is made to appear as though it were the artless expression of an unsophisticated and "salvage" culture.[52] Through various effects of rhythm and alliteration the paraphrase preserves something of the vigor and energy of the original, but only at the level of parody.[53] It is as though we are allowed to hear the voice of the bard through that of a highly gifted, satiric impressionist who replicates and caricatures simultaneously. Accordingly, Spenser finds that the poems translated for him "savored of swete witt and good invencion but skilled not of the goodlie ornaments of Poetrye yet weare they sprinkled with some prettie flowers of theire owne naturall devise which gave good grace and Comlinesse unto them The which it is great pittye to see so abused to the gracinge of wickednes and vice" (p. 127). If not overtly pejorative in this context, the term "naturall" is at least patronizing. As Eric Cheyfitz observes in relation to the New World, "the native's eloquence is always conceptualized as 'natural,' whereas the European's eloquence is nature 'aided and amended by art'"—an interesting counter-example being supplied by Montaigne's appreciative translation of native American poetry in his essay "Of the Caniballes."[54] Ironically, it seems, the bards can achieve their aesthetic potential only when they cease to be "bards" and become English-speaking, and English-thinking, poets. In Ben Jonson's *Irish Masque at Court*, for example, a reformed Celtic bard, introduced by "a civill gentleman of the nation," sings—in English—a paean of praise to James I as the man destined to redeem Ireland from "barbarisme."[55] In the meantime, suggested Sir William Herbert, "there should be set before the people songs in the Irish language which will encourage them to virtue and entice them to moderation and tranquillity of spirit."[56] As Andrew Hadfield points out, however, this apparent gesture of linguistic tolerance is

---

[52] For an account of bardic artistry, see Eleanor Knott, *Irish Classical Poetry* (Dublin, 1957).

[53] I discuss Spenser's use of parody in the forthcoming *Cambridge Companion to Spenser*, ed. Andrew Hadfield.

[54] *The Poetics of Imperialism*, pp. 121, 145-57.

[55] Ben Jonson, *Works*, ed. C.H. Herford and P. and E.M. Simpson (Oxford, 1925-52), 7: 403-5.

[56] Sir William Herbert, *Croftus sive de Hibernia Liber*, ed. A. Keaveney and J.A. Madden (Dublin, 1992), p. 115.

occasioned solely by Herbert's confidence that "the message can survive the medium," that translation can promote infiltration.[57]

Spenser's reading of bardic poetry typifies his attitude towards Celtic society in general, where all evidence of complex social organization is dismissed as residual primitivism by application of the simple axiom that "all barbarous nacions are Comonlye greate observours of Ceremonyes and Supersticious rites" (p. 50). Paradoxically, therefore, both the presence and the absence of various forms of "ceremony" are interpreted as indicative of cultural inferiority. What Spenser refers to as "myne owne readinge" of Celtic history "togeather with comparison of times likenes of manners and Customes Affinytie of wordes and names ... and manie other like circumstances" amounts to little less than a systematic deconstruction of Celtic historiography (pp. 84-5).[58] What gets lost in such "translation" is cultural autonomy. Yet the procedure achieves Spenser's immediate purpose in that it allows him to "understand" Celtic society within an English frame of reference by translating some of the more complex facets of cultural difference into simple categories of moral perversity. An act of translation rewrites bardic literature as the poetry of the borderland and Spenser wishes to subject all other aspects of Gaelic life—social, political, and religious—to a similar sort of "translation," thereby suggesting that the Irish will fulfill their potential only when they cease to be Irish. His cultural analysis moves to the point at which the terms "Irishe like" and "lewdelye" become synonymous (p. 73). The potential of the other is assessed solely in terms of its capacity to become the self—an attitude unconsciously informed by the lurking fear that the self may just as easily become the other.

Perceiving the association between the Celtic clans and their ancestral homelands, the almost symbiotic relationship between culture and place, Spenser would destroy this sustaining link by uprooting the entire population or, as he terms it, by "translating" clans from place to place: "I will translate all that remaine of them [of Leinster] into the places of the other in Ulster" (p. 179). The entire Celtic population is to be "translated" out of its geographical context so that it may be translated in cultural terms as well. Similarly, in the anonymous tract *A Discourse of Ireland* (1599), we encounter an even more radical plan for "all the race of them [the Irish] to be translated out of Ireland, and English with some Flemmings to be onely planted in their Roomes because the Flemming is a People of more propinquity to our Nature." As a result of such "translation," Ireland would become "mearely a West

---

[57] Andrew Hadfield, *Spenser's Irish Experience: Wilde Fruit and Salvage Soyl* (Cambridge, 1997), p. 38. For the contemporary debate as to whether meaning was immanent in language or created by it, see Richard Waswo, *Language and Meaning in the Renaissance* (Princeton, 1987), pp. 150-56.

[58] For Spenser's knowledge of Gaelic chronicles, see Roland M. Smith, "Spenser's Tale of the Two Sons of Milesio," *Modern Language Quarterly* 3 (1942), 547-57; "Spenser, Holinshed, and the *Leabhar Gabhála*," *Journal of English and Germanic Philology* 43 (1944), 390-401.

England."[59] The act of translation is, in a very real sense, an act of *translatio imperii*. Ireland's destiny is to be "translated" into England. While Spenser realized the obvious impracticability of the plan outlined in *A Discourse of Ireland*, his ultimate intention remained very similar. He argues that

> since Irelande is full of her owne nacion that maye not be roted out and somewhat stored with Englishe allreadye and more to be, I thinke it best by an union of manners and Conformitye of mindes to bringe them to be one people, and to put awaie the dislikefull Conceite bothe of thone and thother which wilbe by no meanes better then by there enterminglinge of them, that neither all the Irishe maye dwell togeather, nor all the Englishe, but by translatinge of them and scatteringe them in smalle nombers amonge the Englishe. (pp. 211-12)[60]

This directly contradicts the earlier insistence upon segregation deriving from the general colonial principle that "the fewer will followe the more" with the result that, as matters stand, "the Englishe sooner drawe to the Irishe then the Irishe to the Englishe" (p. 211). The ensuing dichotomy reveals the ambivalence of the colonial enterprise since it is agreed to be "unnaturall that anye people shoulde love anothers language more then theire owne" (p. 118). By implication, therefore, a conquered people must be forced to adopt an "unnatural" state in order to preserve the "natural" condition of the conqueror.

In *Enquiries touching the Diversity of Languages and Religions* (1614), Edward Brerewood analyzed the difficulties involved in realizing a cultural program such as Spenser's. "How hard a matter it is," he observed,

> utterly to abolish a vulgar language, in a populous country, where the Conquerers are in number farre inferiour to the native inhabitants, whatsoever act bee practized to bring it about, may well appeare by the vaine attempt of our *Norman* Conquerour: who although he compelled the *English*, to teach their young children in the Schooles nothing but *French*, and inforced all pleadings at the Law to be performed in that language ... purposing thereby to have conquered the language together with the land, and to have made all *French*: yet, the number of *English* farre exceeding the *Normans*, all was but labour lost, and obtained no further effect, then the mingling of a few *French* words with the *English*.

Complete linguistic transformation had occurred, Brerewood asserts, only in those countries

---

[59] The full text is published in David B. Quinn, "*A Discourse of Ireland* (circa 1599): A Sidelight on English Colonial Policy," *Publications of the Royal Irish Academy* 47, section C, no. 3 (1942), 151-66 (quotations taken from pp. 164, 166).

[60] For Gaelic suspicions that Tudor policy involved total suppression or even annihilation, see Richard A. McCabe, "The Fate of Irena: Spenser and Political Violence," in *Spenser and Ireland*, ed. Coughlan, pp. 119-20.

where either the ancient inhabitants have beene destroyed or driven forth, as wee see in our Country to have followed of the Saxons victories, against the Brittains, or else at least in such sort diminished, that in number they remained inferior, or but little superior to the Conquerors, whose reputation and authority might prevaile more then a small excesse of multitude.[61]

The force of the Saxon precedent was not lost upon Gaelic observers. Commenting upon Stanyhurst's opinions, for example, Geoffrey Keating remarks that "it is a pagan conquest which Hengist, the chief of the Saxons, made over the Britons, since he swept them from the soil of Britain, and sent people from himself into their places; and having altogether banished everyone, he banished their language with them. And it is the same way Stanihurst would desire to act by the Irish; for it is not possible to banish the language without banishing the folk whose language it is."[62]

Although conscious of the problems outlined by Brerewood, Spenser relied upon the panacea of total military conquest to bring about a situation comparable to that which obtained amongst the Britons and the Saxons. Under existing conditions, however, he realized that only reverse examples of "translation," in all senses of the term, were likely to occur. Thus, he deplored the manner in which "Irishe Captaines of Countries have encroched uppon the Quenes freholders and Tennantes how they have translated the Tenures of them from Englishe houldinge unto Irishe *Tanistrye* And defeated her maiestie of all her rightes and dewties" (p. 208). For Spenser, as for Sir John Davies, the proper business of translation would be accomplished only when a complete absence of Gaelic speakers rendered the practice redundant. Davies believed that through the enforced adoption of the English language the next generation of the Irish would "in tongue and heart, and every way else, becom *English*."[63] In other words, to return to our point of departure, if the tongue be English the heart must needs be English. At that stage, it was assumed, political opposition would cease not merely for lack of expression but, more profoundly, for lack of motivation because "wordes are the Image of the minde" (p. 119)—an idea which, as we shall see, optimistically ignores the sense of political alienation evident in the writings of even such staunchly "English" writers as Spenser himself. Holinshed records the opinion that Hugh O'Neill "would not frame himselfe to speake English" on the grounds that it was dishonorable to a high-born Celt to "writh his mouth" in so "clattering" a tongue, but in John Derricke's *Image of Ireland*, his close kinsman Turlough O'Neill, whose assimilation was regarded as imminent, is endowed with a 'civil' English

---

[61] Edward Brerewood, *Enquiries Touching the Diversity of Languages and Religions* (London, 1614), pp. 22-3. In the light of such criteria, Brerewood proceeds to cite Ireland as an example of the failure of linguistic colonialism (p. 29).

[62] *The History of Ireland*, 1: 37. Sir William Herbert entertained the possibility of extirpation. See *Croftus sive de Hibernia Liber*, pp. 85-7.

[63] *A Discoverie*, p. 272.

voice.[64] By contrast, the "outlaw" Rory Og O'More is made to confesse his crimes "in plaine Irishe"—which is actually plain English, the received medium of moral awareness.[65]

In this respect *A View of the Present State of Ireland* constitutes a rhetorical paradigm of the English-speaking state envisaged by Spenser, for whereas the form of the work suggests an exchange of views, a dialectical argument logically "rehearsed" as "the verie matter it selfe offereth" (p. 45), the medium necessarily excludes the Celtic voice from any possibility of participation. It is heard only in garbled translation or hostile paraphrase, or when quoted as etymological evidence of racial barbarity. Like the bardic poems it is translated not to be understood, but to ensure that the reasons for its suppression are understood. *A View of the Present State of Ireland* becomes a proper dialogue only when read in conjunction with the Gaelic response, as exemplified in works such as Geoffrey Keating's *Foras Feasa ar Eirinn* (1633).[66] Within the dialogue itself the impression of rational dialectic works to the exclusion of those voices deemed too barbarous to participate in such an exchange, much as, in *The Faerie Queene*, the savage man's "natural" tongue excludes him so effectively from rational discourse that others must speak for him (6.5.30). The destiny of Ireland must be decided by those who speak English because English is defined a priori as the medium of civility, just as Latin or Greek was similarly defined in the ancient world. In so far as metaphor may be regarded as "a translation of wordes from their propre sygnifycation," Spenser employs the metaphor of barbarity to translate the culturally different into the morally reprehensible, into "the evill that is of it selfe evill" and which must be destroyed because it "will never become good" (p. 148)—which is to say that it can never be assimilated.[67]

Yet ironizing, and to a large extent undermining, the desired business of translation and assimilation are some odd effects detectable in the transformation of Spenser's own language. Stanyhurst describes how the speech of the Old English preserved "the dregs of old ancient Chaucer English," including the sort of archaism that Spenser had labored to introduce into *The Shepheardes Calender* and *The Faerie Queene* and which led Ben Jonson to complain that he "writ no language"—as they might be said to speak none.[68] Willy Maley has even suggested that Spenser's use of archaism was initially inspired by contact with "the Irish colonial milieu," if only at second-hand through the Sidneys.[69] It might therefore appear that aesthetic sophistication and linguistic degeneracy display a disconcerting similarity. It is

---

[64] Holinshed, *Chronicles*, 6: 6; Derricke, *Image of Irelande*, pp. 83, 88-9.

[65] *Image of Irelande*, p. 92.

[66] *The History of Ireland*, 1: 5, 25-31, 65-7.

[67] *The Dictionary of syr Thomas Eliot knyght* (London, 1538), sig. N5r.

[68] Holinshed, *Chronicles*, 6: 4; Jonson, *Timber: or Discoveries* in *Complete Poems*, ed. Parfitt, p. 428.

[69] Willy Maley, *Salvaging Spenser: Colonialism, Culture and Identity* (London, 1997), pp. 34-47.

important to recognize, however, that Spenser objected not to the retention of Chaucerian words in Old English diction but to the intrusion of Celtic words. E.K.'s epistle to *The Shepheardes Calender* defends the new poet's practice of attempting "to restore, as to theyr rightfull heritage such good and naturall English words, as have ben long time out of use and almost cleare disherited." Maley's argument suffers from a failure to distinguish between words of Anglo-Saxon and words of Celtic origin. There is no reason to believe, for example, that Spenser would regard a word such as "churl" as "a peculiarly Irish expression," as Maley claims, since it originates in Anglo-Saxon and remained current in sixteenth-century England.[70]

Spenser's usage of the word "kernes" at *Julye* (l. 199) is more significant. "Kerne" is an Anglicization of the Celtic "ceithearnach" or "ceithern," meaning foot-soldier or band of foot-soldiers, and its occurrence demonstrates the chimerical nature of the search for absolute linguistic purity. Yet the matter is a good deal more complex than may at first appear for, as E.K.'s gloss recognizes, the primary Celtic sense cannot have been intended in the context in which it is employed. Rather the word is being used, as the *Oxford English Dictionary* indicates it sometimes was, in a derivative sense. One might even argue that it was only Spenser's subsequent experience of colonial life in Ireland, and possible contact with genuine "kernes," that transformed a loose derivative usage into a more semantically accurate, if polemically aggressive, one: in *A View of the Present State of Ireland* kerns are perceived not as E.K.'s pastoral "churles" or "farmers" but as "Cruell and bloddye full of revenge and delightinge in deadlye execucion licentious swearers and blasphemours Comon ravishers of weomen and murderers of Children" (p. 123). The use of loan words in English was countenanced by Spenser's schoolmaster, Richard Mulcaster, provided that they obeyed the rules of "enfranchisment" or naturalization by which they "becom bond to the rules of our writing ... as the stranger denisons be to the lawes of our cuntrie."[71] The simile is particularly apt in that it demonstrates the perceived relationship between language and sovereignty. As naturalized aliens become subject to English law, naturalized words must become subject to the laws of English grammar and pronunciation. A "kerne" who became a "farmer"— legally and linguistically—was quite acceptable; a kern who remained a foot-soldier, adhered to the Brehon Law, and "corrupted" both the speech and the loyalty of his Old English neighbors was not. The kerns of *The Shepheardes Calender* have been "civilized," those of *A View* remain "salvage." What Spenser and Stanyhurst condemn is not the "enfranchisment" of foreign words envisaged by Mulcaster, but the insidious alienation of English itself. "Why a Gods name," Spenser asked in the *Familiar Letters* of 1580, "may not we, as

---

[70] Ibid., p. 42. For a further discussion of this point, see my review essay "Embarrassing Spenser," forthcoming in *Bullán: An Irish Studies Journal*.

[71] Richard Mulcaster, *The First Part of the Elementarie which Entreateth Chefelie of the Right Writing of our English Tung* (London, 1582), pp. 154-5.

else the Greekes, haue the kingdome of our owne Language?"[72] The appeal to
the Greek *exemplum* is telling, but in the coming years Ireland would supply an
unsettling answer to Spenser's question.

When describing what he perceived as the process of linguistic
degeneracy in Ireland, Stanyhurst speaks of "meere Irish word[s] that crept
unwares into the English, through the dailie intercourse of the English and Irish
inhabitants."[73] Although Spenser agreed with this sentiment, one of the most
surprising features of *A View of the Present State of Ireland*, considered as a
dialogue, is the repeated necessity for Irenius to explain elements of his
vocabulary to Eudoxus, an Englishman who has not been to Ireland. At the
outset, for example, Eudoxus enquires, "what is that which youe call the
Brehon lawe it is a worde to us alltogeather unknowen" (p. 47). For a brief
moment, the distinction between "you" and "us" locates Irenius with the Irish
rather than the English, revealing him as someone whose association with
Ireland has already begun to influence his vocabulary in such a way as to
render comprehension difficult. "Brehon" is an everyday component of the
colonists' language, but is "alltogeather unknowen" to Eudoxus. Already, the
English "community of language" so highly extolled by Fynes Moryson is
showing signs of strain under the pressure of the colonial enterprise. Similarly,
a little further on, we find Eudoxus asking "what is this youe call *Tanist* and
Tanistrye? They be names and tenures never harde of or knowen to us" (p. 50).
Here the distinction between "you" and "us" appears to have grown more
acute. Eudoxus has not understood the tenor of Irenius's remarks and the
burden of exposition grows exponentially. The following paragraphs are
necessarily devoted to lengthy explanation and semantic analysis of the terms
Eudoxus has failed to understand. Almost imperceptibly, but surely, the
language of the colonist, and by implication his political interests, are
beginning to diverge from those of his fellow countrymen.

Despite E.K.'s insistence upon preserving the purity of the "mother
tongue" by excluding foreign words, within *A View of the Present State of
Ireland* the "well of [Chaucerian] English" is considerably "defyled" and the
effect extends beyond the mere use of vocabulary to the creation of an
imaginative frame of reference that is not English.[74] We are told, for example,
that those who "have degendred from theire antiente dignities" have grown to
be "as Irishe as Ohanlans breeche (as the proverbe theare is)" (p. 117).
Although the phrase in parentheses functions to distance the expression from
Irenius both linguistically and geographically, the proverb has effectively
become his own. At the outset we are given to understand that Irenius has
"latelye come" from Ireland to England (p. 43), and thereafter that the dialogue

---

[72] *The Prose Works*, 9: 16.

[73] Holinshed, *Chronicles*, 6: 4.

[74] For the influence of Irish on Spenser's vocabulary, see Roland M. Smith, "The Irish
Background of Spenser's *View*," pp. 501-6 and "More Irish Words in Spenser," *Modern
Language Notes* 59 (1944), 472-7. For Chaucer as the "well of English undefyled," see *The
Faerie Queene*, 4.2.32.

is conducted "here" in England rather than "there" (pp. 44, 68, 229). The language, however, tells a different story. It is not only the Celts, and the Old English they have assimilated, who speak a different political language to the English but the new colonists as well. Writing of this phenomenon in the twelfth century, at the very outset of England's military intervention in Ireland, Giraldus Cambrensis perfectly encapsulates the dilemma when he has a Norman warrior remark that "just as we are English ["Angli"] as far as the Irish are concerned, likewise to the English we are Irish ["Hibernici"]."[75] Similarly, in the sixteenth century, Edmund Campion distinguished between the conflicting political interests of "the Englishe of birthe and th'englishe of bloude."[76]

When Colin Clout visits the court of Gloriana in *Colin Clouts Come Home Againe*, he does so as a stranger, an outsider who detects sufficient corruption at the heart of "civil" society to send him scurrying back to Ireland despite the "griesly famine" and "nightly bodrags" which apparently characterize life there (ll. 314-15). But what is a "bodrag"? The word, which recurs in *The Faerie Queene* (2.10.63), is uncommon outside Spenser except in texts dealing with Ireland. Holinshed attributes a complaint about Irish "bodrages" to Spenser's fellow planter, Sir Walter Ralegh, and the word is used in similar contexts in the state papers.[77] It appears to be a corruption of some Gaelic word, possibly "buaidhreach" or "buadre" (meaning disturbance or uproar). Its occurrence in such a context as though it were an indigenious English word, without any perceived need for gloss or explanation, is indicative of the growing influence of Spenser's experience upon his vocabulary and the political attitude it articulates.

At the heart of the matter lies the disturbing awareness, often expressed in *A View*, that "civil" England was once like Ireland, "annoyed greatly with Robbers and outlawes which troubled the wholle state of the Realme, everie Corner havinge a Robin hoode in it that kepte the woodes and spoilled all passengers and inhabitantes as Irelande now hathe" (pp. 202-3). In chronological terms, "it is but even the other daye since Englande grewe Civill" (p. 118). The fragility of England's civility is exacerbated by its relative novelty: like Spenser's youthful St. George it is largely untried. In the case of many of the allegedly evil customs obtaining amongst the Old English, Spenser concedes, it is impossible to ascertain "wheather the beginninge theareof weare Englishe or Irishe" (p. 118). Similarly, he alleges that the term "kincongish" (actually a corruption of the Celtic "cin cómfhocais" or liability of kindred) is "a worde mingled of Englishe and Irishe togeather so as I ame partelye led to thinke that the Custome thearof was firste Englishe and after warde made Irishe" (p. 81). Linguistically, socially, and ethnically supposed polar opposites have become impossible to distinguish. This fact, combined

---

[75] Giraldus Cambrensis, *Expugnatio Hibernica: The Conquest of Ireland*, ed. and trans. A.B. Scott and F.X. Martin (Dublin, 1978), p. 81.

[76] Campion, *Two Bokes of the Histories of Ireland*, p. 98.

[77] Holinshed, *Chronicles*, 6: 440.

with the somewhat grudging perception of the common ancestry (through the ancient Britons) of so many Irish and "English" families (including the Tudors), lends urgency to the problem of assimilation (pp. 94-5).

To Spenser's way of thinking, assimilation represents regression to a sort of primeval, savage state. For the English colonist, Ireland was, in the words of Nicholas Canny, a "permissive frontier," free from many of the legal and social restrictions obtaining in the homeland.[78] Recognizing this danger, Spenser observed that "as it is the nature of all men to love libertye So they become Libertines and fall to all Licentiousnes of the Irishe, more boldlie daringe to disobaie the lawe thoroughe presumpcion of favour and freindeshippe then anye Irishe dareth" (p. 211). As a testing ground for English "civility," Ireland exposes the inherent fragility of Elizabethan culture, a phenomenon implicitly recognized in the perception of "degenerate" colonists as worse than the indigenous population "whiche beinge verie wilde at the firste are now become somwhat more Civill when as these from Civillitye are growne to be wilde and mere Irishe" (p. 209). Whatever the theoretical insistence upon segregation and difference, colonial experience tends to find the other in the self and, more often than not, to resent or fear the discovery.[79] The subtle change in Spenser's language, the infiltration of his "mother tongue" by words derived from the language of the other, bears witness to an unconscious process of assimilation of which his conscious polemic fights shy. It remains quite unclear where, if anywhere, Colin Clout and Irenius may identify as "home" when even the rhetorical structures they inhabit are infused with foreign or "alien" elements.

---

[78] Nicholas Canny, "The Permissive Frontier: Social Control in English Settlements in Ireland and Virginia, 1560-1650," in *The Westward Enterprise: English Activities in Ireland, the Atlantic, and America 1480-1650*, ed. K.R. Andrews, N.P. Canny and P.E.H. Hair (Liverpool, 1978), pp. 17-44.

[79] See Richard A. McCabe, *The Pillars of Eternity: Time and Providence in* The Faerie Queene (Dublin, 1989), pp. 46-7.

5

Colonials Write the Nation:
Spenser, Milton, and England
on the Margins

Linda Gregerson

Benedict Anderson has pointed out to us that the conceptual relationship between empire and nation is one of "fundamental contradiction";[1] history would seem to argue that it is precisely this foundational contradiction that produces the modern nation. The internal tension between a bounded community of fixed parameters and an expansionary community of unbounded mandate is immeasurably intensified when the community identifies itself, a priori or after the fact, as one of faith. In Reformation England we may behold the modern nation in the full force of its conceptual paradox, a politically and ideologically bounded bastion for an inherently universalist and transnational religion. As apologists for the English colonial venture in Ireland and as the latterday cultural subjects of a nation that has itself been formed by multiple waves of invasion and conquest, Edmund Spenser and John Milton negotiate the concept of nation from both sides of the colonial divide.

I consult that divide, and the colonial periphery in which it most sharply manifests itself, as part of an effort to learn more about the early modern nation and how it is perceived by those who claim to constitute it. In this I borrow a methodological commonplace of late twentieth-century ethnography. The texts upon which I focus here—Edmund Spenser's *View of the Present State of Ireland* and John Milton's *History of Britain*—do not share a common literary genre. The one, written as fictive dialogue, purports to offer a program for the present (that is, the immediate, as well as the Protestant, "New English") subjugation of an Ireland whose earlier subjugation (by the pre-Reformation "Old English") has left that unfortunate nation in the throes of an aggravated, cross-bred barbarity. The other, composed by Milton over some quarter century of violent reversals in national and personal affairs and published ten years after the Stuart Restoration, purports to offer the English nation a consolidated narrative of its past, culminating with its own subjugation by the Normans. What the *View* and the *History* do share, and, to my mind, in remarkable depth, is cognitive method:

---

[1] Benedict Anderson, *Imagined Communities: Reflections on the Origin and Spread of Nationalism*, rev. ed. (London, 1991), p. 93.

both reveal, both discursively produce, the modern nation as a back-formation, part of the retroactive logic of empire.

That Milton was well acquainted with Spenser's treatise on Ireland and in accord with its underlying logic is apparent in his own *Observations upon the Articles of Peace*. In this early defense of Cromwell's aggressive expedition into Ireland, Milton deliberately echoes Spenser's account of national identity and imperial mandate in the *View*: the Irish, writes Milton, reveal "their true Barbarisme" by "rejecting the ingenuity of all other Nations to improve and waxe more civill by a civilizing Conquest";[2] the civilizing English have thus been forced to use harsh measures. The vocabularies of nineteenth-century colonialism have led us to expect dominant powers to justify the colonial project by construing inherent racial and cultural differentials: the peoples and the culture of the metropole are understood as self-evidently superior to those of the backward or debased colony. The persistent and discomfiting correlation to this premise is a fear of contamination at the colonial periphery: for the French and Dutch in Indonesia, the British in India, for European powers, or at least the Northern European powers, in the New World, the great administrative and conceptual dilemma is how to maintain the purity and bounded identity of the race and civilization whose benefits are being conferred upon less enlightened sectors of the globe. The colonial project is chronically shadowed by the fear that its agents may in one way or another "go native," that bloodlines and cultures will succumb to mongrelization.

In contrast to their nineteenth-century heirs, Spenser and Milton make their crucial distinction not between the pure and the mongrel but between apt and recalcitrant learners. According to the logic of sixteenth- and seventeenth-century English colonialism, in other words, the only salient difference is that between good colonials and bad. The bad ones simply require more severe colonization. Enforceable distinctions between the colonizing English and the as yet imperfectly colonized Irish have always been notoriously difficult to describe and maintain: Milton, following Spenser, sought a way out of ideological impasse by acknowledging that Englishness itself was a highly permeable construct, and "England" an import economy in the radical sense.

I

This ideological solution is not seamlessly achieved within the confines of the *View*: "Of all nacions vnder heaven," Irenius expostulates at one point, "I suppose the Spaniarde is the moste mingled moste vncertaine and moste bastardlie, wherefore moste foolishelye do the Irishe thinke to enoble themselues by wrestinge theire ancestrye from the Spaniarde."[3] When Eudoxus mildly suggests

---

[2] *Observations upon the Articles of Peace*, in John Milton, *Complete Prose Words*, ed. Don M. Wolfe, et al. (New Haven, 1953-82), 3: 259-334; passage cited, p. 304.

[3] *A View of the Present State of Ireland*, in *The Works of Edmund Spenser*, ed. Edwin

that the Spanish are in some quarters more positively regarded, Irenius hastens to "clarify": "[I]n that I saide he is a mingled people is noe dispraise for ... theare is no nacion now in Christendome ... but is mingled and Compounded with others" (p. 92). And prompted perhaps by the continuing dissonance between this "no dispraise" and the former charge of "bastardy," Irenius goes further, patching up a fractured vista with a sweeping appeal to providential design. "[F]or it was a singuler providence of god and a moste admirable purpose of his wisdome to drawe those Northerne heathen nacions downe into these Cristian partes wheare they mighte receaue Christianitye and to mingle nacions so remote so mira-culouslye to make as it weare one kindred and bloud of all people and eache to haue knowledge of him" (p. 92). The mingling of races in this account is not just the colonist's headache or the metropole's embarrassment but is divinity's scheme for progressive revelation, the godhead's self-unfolding.

But while the forward march of international Protestantism is arguably one of the principal underlying political and cultural imperatives of the *View*, and is certainly an organizing principal for the English identity whose consolidation the *View* records, the details of religious reform are conspicuously subordinated to other concerns in Spenser's treatise. Despite repeated promptings from Eudoxus, Irenius again and again defers the question of religious reform: I am not "muche ... conuersante in that Callinge" (p. 136), he says; the particular abuses of Irish Catholicism "are to manye to be reckoned" (p. 142); and, crucially, "it is ill time to preache amongst swordes" "for instruccion in religion nedethe quiett times" (p. 138). On the surface at least, religion gives way to conquest as the "present" order of business.

In the service of conquest, the *View* sets forth an analytical survey, whose conceptual and rhetorical divisions it repeatedly announces. Irenius describes in three parts the evils that threaten and afflict colonial Ireland: 1) the abuses of the laws, 2) the abuses of custom, and 3) the abuses (much abridged) of religion. Then, he unfolds a three-part plan for remedy: 1) subjection by the sword (including the establishment of garrisons, starvation and dispersal of the native inhabitants, confiscation of lands, and plantation of New English colonists), 2) reformation of laws, customs, and religion (chiefly to be effected by a reconstituted parliament), and 3) the administrative ordering of a pacified (and decimated) colony.

My interest for the moment is in the first half of the dialogue, the inventory of abuses, for it is here that we enter the fascinating realm we have since come to think of as colonial ethnography. Properly to survey the customs of the Irish, those customs it is his business to eradicate, Irenius proposes to analyze them according to origin: Scythian, Spanish, Gaulish, British. This genealogical project in turn prompts discourses on the historical patterns of European conquest and migration, a linguistic atlas of Celtic and Germanic peoples, and so forth, until the instrumental ordering process threatens to exceed its boundaries as

---

Greenlaw, et al. (Baltimore, 1932-57), 10: 39-231; passage cited, p. 91. Subsequent citations from this edition will be noted parenthetically.

prolifically as ever barbarous hordes poured over the Alps. Under the rubric of Scythian abuses marked for reform Irenius notes: 1) itinerant herding and grazing, signified by the shepherd's hut or boolie, 2) the Irish mantle, 3) the glibe, or "thicke Curled bushe of haire" (p. 99), and 4) the hubbub. Now itinerant habitation, like the mantle and the glibe, can plausibly be cast as inimical to settlement and orderly surveillance.[4] But the hubbub, like the wailing lamentation and other forms of vocal excess, though it may be construed as a self-evident barbarity, is a matter of relative indifference to the reformer. "I did not rehearse it," admits Irenius, "as one of the Abuses I thoughte moste worthie of reformacion" (p. 105). Why, then, does Irenius devote nearly as much space to its ancestry and derivation as to the presumably much more urgent matter of religion? Because—and here his logic begins to go circular—the hubbub testifies so strongly to the Scythian ancestry of the Irish: "ffor by these oulde Customes and other like Coniecturall circumstances the discentes of nacions canne onelye be proued whear other monimentes of wrightinges be not remaining" (p. 105).

At this point Irenius's interlocutor might well demur: weren't these Scythian and Gallic and Spanish genealogies undertaken for the explicit purpose of ordering and expediting reform? But far from protesting the manifest superfluousness of "oulde Customes" and "Coniecturall circumstances" that have no practical bearing on imperial policy, Eudoxus exclaims with greatest enthusiasm: "Then I praye youe whensoeuer in your discourse youe mete with them by the waye doe not shunn but bouldlye tuche them for besides theire great pleasure and delighte for theire Antiquitye they bringe allsoe great proffitte and helpe vnto Civilytye" (pp. 105-6).[5]

It is the explicit argument of *A View* that the colonial project in Ireland requires radical expediting, that it ought ruthlessly to abandon its digressive half measures and cut to the bone, as ultimately the kinder surgery. "Pleasure" and "delighte" are not, on the face of it, the central business of a program for ethnic and cultural cleansing. But Eudoxus will repeatedly measure Irenius's disquisition

---

[4] On the mantle and the glibe, see Ann R. Jones and Peter Stallybrass, "Dismantling Irena: The Sexualizing of Ireland in Early Modern England," in *Nationalisms and Sexualities*, ed. Andrew Parker, Mary Russo, Doris Sommer, and Patricia Yaeger (New York, 1992), pp. 157-71.

[5] Willy Maley has recently argued that Spenser's preoccupation with Scythian origins and Scythian barbarity in the *View* "was structured by an underlying fear of Spanish and Scottish intervention in Ireland," (p. 15). "The Irish customs that Irenius abhors, and which critics often read as evidence of anti-Irish sentiment, are Scythian, which for Spenser's purposes means Scottish" (p. 13), Ireneus cites Buchanan (George Buchanan, *Rerum Scoticarum Historia*, 1583) to prove that the Scythians are Scots (*View*, 83), and the Spanish, Scythians (*View*, 91; *Commentary* on the *View*, 310-11, 319); from the perspective of an English colonial administrator, twin specters of hostile invasion thus shadow one another and shadow earlier, pan-European invasions as well. Maley's local emphases sometimes differ from my own, but his larger argument is one with which I emphatically agree, to wit, that Spenser "is preoccupied with using the complexities of the Irish colonial milieu as a means of refiguring metropolitan identities" (pp. 2-3). Willy Maley, "'So farre from all knowledge': The Ethnographic Present in Spenser's *A View of the State of Ireland*," in *Renaissance Knowing and Knowing the Renaissance: Cultural Difference and Critical Method*, ed. Philippa Berry and Margaret Tudeau-Clayton (Cambridge, forthcoming); passages cited from manuscript pages.

according to the delight it affords. "This rippinge vp of Ancestries is verye pleasinge vnto me and indede savorethe of good conceite and some readinge withall. I see hearebye howe profitable travell and experience of forren nacions is to him that will applie them to good purpose" (p. 95). One might well argue that Eudoxus's phraseology ("savorethe," "rippinge vp") betrays the shadowy pre-dation that links even the most "disinterested" colonial ethnography to more explicit deployments of force. But one might also profitably linger over the categories of "profitable ... experience" and "good purpose."

In the context of the colonial regime, what "good purpose" is it that the hubbub, for instance, furthers or illuminates? The boolie, or shepherd's hut, the mantle, and the glibe are deplored by the colonist on account of their very indigenous efficacy: they offer shelter from the elements and from surveillance; they are admirably suited to material employment, climate, and topography; they work so well that they must be done away with. But the adaptive or subversive function, the Irish function, of the hubbub goes largely unremarked and unexamined in the *View*. Spenser's readers may well imagine or recall from other sources that terrible yells on the battlefield will tend to dismay troops who conform to different martial protocols. But it is the function of the hubbub for epistemology that brings it to such prominence in Spenser's Irish treatise. That is, Irenius and Eudoxus and their analytic survey of Irish custom find the hubbub pleasurable and serviceable as the cultural trace that testifies to their own capacity for knowing. The hubbub and numberless distillations of its kind go into the making of a cultural inventory that has two inseparable faces: that of the colonial subject and that of civil administration. This ongoing, reciprocal production is what Spenser invites his readers to "view."

II

When Milton wrote *Paradise Lost* in the wake of the Stuart Restoration that ended his hopes for a Reformed secular state, he was not abandoning the idea of the commonwealth but contriving to pursue it by other means. The poem proposes, and is designed to produce, a reading subject whose essence is political, a subject whose foundational logic is the community organized by faith. Epic has always been an instrument of corporate imagination; in his revisionary and archeologizing appropriation of the form, Milton radicalizes an old idea.

Between the first and second editions of *Paradise Lost*, Milton also presented to the English public another kind of archeology: a six-book *History of Britain*, from its "first traditional beginning" to the Norman Conquest. Milton's *History* was begun during the English Civil War, interrupted by the author's recruitment for service to the commonwealth, resumed at an unknown date or dates, and published in 1670, ten years after the first major anti-royalist experiment in modern Europe had decisively collapsed. How does a national history composed over twenty-five years of violent reversals in national and personal affairs construe its "place"? Where does the nation reside when those who claim to embody it are at war with one another? How does the history of a nation incessantly invaded, contested, cross-bred, and reconstituted negotiate point of view? What kinds of amnesia does coherent memory require? What is the relationship between the history purporting to be "of Britain" and the providential history recounted by the Archangel Michael in *Paradise Lost*? What is the relationship between the *History*'s largely celebratory account of Roman conquest and the Son's sweeping rejection of empire, nation, and all things Roman in *Paradise Regained*? And how might a new, revisionary nation find its shape? These are the questions, I would argue, that make this too often neglected prose history a document of major historical and conceptual interest.

"[I]f it be a high point of wisdom," writes Milton, "in every private man, much more is it in a Nation to know it self,"[6] and he offers his *History* as a kind of glass in which the present "intereign" (p. 129) may contemplate its own motions.[7] But how exactly is the nation's "self" to be recognized? The Britain whose history Milton records is dependent in every realm—civic, military, doctrinal, linguistic—upon patterns brought in from elsewhere, by means of conquest, intermarriage, voluntary conversion, forced conversion, superior example, corrupting fashion. The instabilities of "we" and "them," "native" and "foreign," "friend" and "enemy" are chronically aggravated by incursion from without, factionalism and civil, even familial, dissension within. Most maddening of all, the historiographer who wishes to tell the nation the coherent story of its own emergence and providential instrumentality must make his way through a bewildering cacophony of unevenly reliable sources: for every sober chronicler who attempts to tell a proportioned and a linear tale, there are a score of "shallow and unskilfull Writers" who can convey no more than "the indistinct noise of many Battels, and devastations, of many Kingdoms over-run and lost" (p. 40). For the earliest history of his nation, "from the first peopling of the Iland to the coming of *Julius Caesar*" (p. 2), Milton can do no more than produce a skeptical redaction of fabling, obscure, distractable, and sometimes downright bungled accounts, for "nothing certain, either by Tradition, History, or Ancient Fame hath hitherto bin left us" (p. 2). "Nor have I stood," our author writes, "with others computing, or collating years and Chronologies, lest I should be vainly curious about the time and circumstance of things whereof the substance is so much in doubt" (p. 37). Dependent throughout the first book of his *History* upon the

---

[6] *The History of Britain, That Part especially now call'd England; Continu'd to the Norman Conquest*, in John Milton, *Complete Prose Works*, ed. Don M. Wolfe, et al. (New Haven, 1953-82), 5: xix-457; passage cited, p. 130. Subsequent citations from this edition will be noted parenthetically.

[7] "Intereign": one assumes at first that Milton is referring to the English Commonwealth, the "interregnum" between two periods of Stuart monarchy. If so, the term suggests a late composition or revision date for this portion of the *History*, since this particular acknowledgment of interim status can only be the product of (post-Restoration) hindsight. From a theological perspective, however, the term applies to any secular nation as well as another: all are mounted in the interim between two earthly reigns of the divine, the one that has been lost, and the one that is to come.

exclusive or dubiously corroborated authority of Geoffrey of Monmouth, Milton can only invoke the principle of *caveat lector*: "I ... have thought it not beneath my purpose, to relate what I found," he writes, but "I neither oblige the belief of other person, nor over-hastily subscribe my own" (p. 37).

For the Anglo-Saxon period, Milton's sources increase in number and density but not, to his mind, in quality. "[W]hat labour is to be endur'd, turning over [these] Volumes of Rubbish ... is a penance to think" (p. 230). "[S]o many bare and reasonless Actions, so many names of Kings one after another, acting little more then mute persons in a Scene" (p. 239), "how [the Danes] wallow'd up and down to every particular place" (p. 337), "such bickerings to recount ... what more worth is it then to Chronicle the Wars of Kites, or Crows, flocking and fighting in the Air?" (p. 249). Milton's impatience with his early medieval sources extends to the field of action they record, nor is the sorry reciprocity of action and chronicle accidental, to his mind, for if "worthy deeds are not often destitute of worthy relators" (p. 39), as Milton routinely asseverates, the obverse principle also obtains. From the fifth century to the Norman invasion, the student of British history must "stear by ... Authors ... in expression barbarous ... in civil matters ... dubious Relaters ... in ... matters of Religion, blind, astonish'd, and strook with superstition as with a Planet; in one word, Monks" (pp. 127-8). Learning retires to the cloister in Anglo-Saxon Britain, as do those persons who had done better to tend to their own business, and that of the kingdom, by light of day: "Kings one after another leaving thir Kingly Charge, to run thir heads fondly into a Monks Cowle," "Clerks and Laics, Men and Woeman, hasting to *Rome* in Herds" (pp. 230, 229). Even Bede, who is better than most, can relay only "a scatterd story pickt out heer and there ... from among his many Legends of Visions and Miracles," "superstition and monastical affectation" (pp. 229-30). And all this benightedness derives from a single cause. For the grim truth is that Rome in this period is no longer Rome; the culture that had been a beacon has become, with the waning of empire, a source of darkness and delusion and remains so to the present day, as the author expects his readers to be painfully aware.

III

Britain is a very tenuous proposition throughout most of the story Milton relates, but under imperial Rome, from the first coming of Julius Caesar in 53 BC to the final withdrawal of Roman jurisdiction in the year 409,[8] Britain gives some nascent sign of becoming itself. And in his account of Britain under the Roman occupation, Milton gives us the sharpest indications of what he takes to be the

---

[8] A marginal note in the first edition (1670-71) of Milton's *History* refers the reader to Calvisius, whose *Opus Chronologicum* (Frankfurt, 1629) identifies 409 AD as the year in which the Emperor Flavius Honorius advised the Britons by letter that Rome could no longer come to their aid militarily and thus officially reliquished imperial jurisdiction. *Complete Prose* 5: 127, fn. 87.

distinguishing nature and conduct of the corporate entity whose history he writes. In the author's simultaneous skepticisms and credulities, in his alternating praise and condemnation, in his unstable pronouns and vacillating point of view, we may catch the scent if not the frontal visage[9] of the nation in whose latter-day service he had publicly labored, a nation in the vanguard of universal Reform, the nation as a vessel for human hopefulness, the nation as an idea made real, made nearly real.

"[L]ike one who had set out on his way by night, and travail'd through a Region of smooth or idle Dreams, our History now arrivs on the Confines, where day-light and truth meet us with a cleer dawn" (p. 37). Thus writes Milton on the threshold of the Roman occupation. He invites his readers to understand, that is, that Caesar's arrival on British soil inaugurates not only the first real civilization of the British Isles but also the first reliable narrative of the British past. Worthy deeds find worthy relators. The ancient Britons discovered and described by their Roman conquerors were a people of some courage and considerable hardiness (pp. 58-9), a people plain-dealing for the most part and of little fraud (p. 60), but a people hopelessly divided among themselves (p. 60) and lacking the barest rudiments of practical and cultural amenity: "the makeing of Cheese they ... knew not, Woole or Flax they spun not, gard'ning and planting many of them knew not; clothing they had none, but what the skins of Beasts afforded them" (p. 59). The decisive measure of their backwardness is twofold: the likeness of these Britons to a barbarous people of Milton's own time—to the Irish—and also their lamentable proneness to the sovereignty of women.

Rather than meeting their Roman invaders in approved and manly battle formation (the textbook formation so fiercely invoked by a colonial Welshman in Shakespeare's *Henry V*),[10] the ancient Britons habitually ran "into Bogs, worse then *wild Irish* up to the Neck" (p. 59). Rather than conforming to other nations in the "liberty not unnatural for one man to have many Wives" (p. 103), the Britons "absurdly against nature" (p. 61) allowed a single wife to have many husbands, "Progenitors not to be glori'd in" (p. 61). These Britons were even known to endure outright "uncomel[y] ... Subjection" to a woman monarch (p. 74) and a woman commander-in-chief (p. 79).

The story of the woman warrior Boadicea, in particular, so exceeds the bounds of propriety that it prompts Milton to take issue for once with the Greek and Roman historians of Britain, who put into this woman's mouth such "a deal of ... fondness ... not worth recital; how she was lash'd, how her Daughters were

---

[9] The figure is Dante's. In *De Vulgari Eloquentia*, the poet searches with an exile's urgency not for the nation *per se* but for its language: the vernacular that will delineate the nation. *De Vulgari Eloquentia: Dante's Book of Exile*, ed. and trans. Marianne Shapiro (Lincoln, Neb., 1990), p. 64.

[10] Moreover, it is an Irishman—Macmorris—whose inaptitude for classical militarism drives the Welsh Fluellen to distraction: "By Chesu, he is an ass, as in the world; I will verify as much in his beard. He has no more directions in the true disciplines of the wars, look you, of the Roman disciplines, than is a puppy-dog" (*Henry V*, 3.2.70-73). Citation from *The Riverside Shakespeare*, ed. G. Blakemore Evans, et al. (Boston, 1974).

handl'd, things worthier silence, retirment, and a Vail, then for a Woeman to repeat, as don to hir own person, or to hear repeated before an host of men" (p. 79). That is, the atrocities committed against women in the course of warfare are too unseemly to bear repetition, and the taint of this unseemliness—the narrative unseemliness rather than the actual or purported physical violence—produces something of a crux in Milton's text. On the one hand, he seems to blame both his historiographers and their female subjects for the abuse of decorum. On the other hand, he registers an uncharacteristic suspicion of his Roman authors' motives and veracity: they write thus, he ventures, "out of a vanity, hoping to embellish and set out thir Historie with the strangness of our manners, not caring in the mean while to brand us with the rankest note of Barbarism, as if in *Britain* Woemen were Men, and Men Woemen" (p. 79). The insult to gender decorum hits home: the "us" and "our" in this passage are among the very rare deployments of the first-person plural in Milton's text, a text whose business it is after all to tell the story of "us" and "ours." But having contemplated the unreliability of his Greek and Roman sources, and having registered the constitutive force of the insult they deliver, Milton then proceeds as if a biased scribe were no great impediment to understanding after all. "[T]he truth is," he writes in summation, reverting again to the grammatical third person, "the *Britans*" under Boadicea observed "no rule, no foresight, no forecast, experience or estimation" but exhibited "such confusion, such impotence, as seem'd likest … to the wild hurrey of a distracted Woeman, with as mad a Crew at her heeles" (p. 80). And throughout these pages, the author renders women as woe-to-men, "Woemen."

In his largely approving account of the benefits conferred upon Britain by the Roman occupation, Milton acknowledges, and with some acerbity, that Roman tactics were not always of the noblest order. Even as they planted colonies to teach the conquered natives Roman law and Roman civility, they secured their conquest by conveying "certain cities" to a pliable native king, "a haughtie craft, which the *Romans* us'd, to make Kings also the servile agents of enslaving others" (p. 70). But for the most part in Milton's account, it is the colonized who are responsible for their own abjection. Agricola, the Roman governor of Britain under Vespasian, persuades the British to genuine cultural advances, "to build Houses, Temples, and Seats of Justice," and under the guise of a kind of paternalistic nativism ("preferring the Witts of *Britain*, before the Studies of *Gallia*") effects a salutary colonization of learning, causing "the Noblemens sons to be bred up in liberal Arts … and [bringing] them to affect the Latine Eloquence, who before hated the Language" (p. 85). If the British succumbed to cultural enslavement rather than cultural enlightenment, it was the consequence of their own inconstancy, their inability to distinguish good models from bad, the exemplary and durable patterns of cultural value from the allurements of fashion. "Then were the *Roman* fashions imitated, and the Gown; after a while the incitements also and materials of Vice, and voluptuous life, proud Buildings, Baths, and the elegance of Banqueting; which the foolisher sort call'd civilitie, but was indeed a secret Art to prepare them for bondage" (p. 85). In the *History*'s contempt for indigenous barbarism and indigenous failures of retention, in its tendency to identify with the Roman occupiers, in unstable pronouns and an ambivalent or vacillating point of view, Milton's readers may encounter in its early modern instance the habit of mind we have come to call "colonial." The Romans are not quite "us" in Milton's narrative, but neither—and this is worth emphasizing—are the Britons; gravitating toward the Roman point of view, Milton identifies his British forebears more than once as "the Enemie" (pp. 85, 101).

After the withdrawal of its Roman governors in the fifth century, Milton reports, Britons at first took freedom from empire to be freedom indeed. Later Britons have congratulated themselves on launching Rome's decline when they became the first of the subjected nations to throw off the Roman yoke (pp. 130-1). But Rome's decline, according to Milton, was neither a local nor a general triumph. For "with the Empire fell also what before in this Western World was chiefly *Roman*; Learning, Valour, Eloquence, History, Civility, and eev'n Language it self" (p. 127). True liberty, as Milton will also argue in his epic poems, is referential rather than absolute, and is less to be found in arbitrary severance than in submission to a worthy master. "Of the *Romans*," he writes, "we have cause not to say much worse, then that they beate us into some civilitie" (p. 61).

What constitutes the nation? It must have some substance and some boundedness, some "us not them," some "here not there." But it is not to be found, Milton's *History* makes clear, in unmixed genealogy or "race," nor in the providential insularity of symbolic geography. The first-person plural is not in this book secured by dynasty or bloodline or mappable topography. Even the sea-girt island setting of the nation, so prominent a feature of Elizabethan triumphalism, is in Milton's account the complex apprehension and discovery of strangers. A cohort of mutinous Germans, he reports, having slain their centurion and fled, are carried by tide and weather around the British coast during the second century of Roman rule and come back to report to their Roman masters that the empire's furthest outpost is an island. It is strangers conscripted by strangers, in other words, who locate a boundary for Britain. And tellingly, they find no outside to empire: even in rebellion, these Germans are agents of Rome (p. 88). Earlier, when Caesar had first sent imperial troops to Britain, those troops are reported to have "murmured," protesting that the place was "beyond the World's end" (p. 65). It is presumably with some irony that Milton, himself a native of this outlandish place, reports the murmuring some seventeen centuries later. Richard Helgerson has traced in some detail the nation nascently imagined in Tudor chorography,[11] the peculiar mixed genre that narrativizes topographical survey and finds history inscribed in space, but Milton has no more patience for the babble of place-names[12] than for the "Bead-roll" of abbotts and abbesses (p. 239) or the

---

[11] Richard Helgerson, *Forms of Nationhood: The Elizabethan Writing of England* (Chicago, 1992).

[12] "Neither do I care," he writes, "to wrincle the smoothness of History with rugged

genealogies of kings. No reified nor apostrophized "land" can ground the identity he cares to delineate.

IV

One scant year after Milton published *The History of Britain*, he published a poem in which all versions of earthly empire, including that of Rome, are sweepingly rejected. In order to understand how the Son's position in *Paradise Regained* might accord with the painstaking constructions of national identity and imperial mandate rehearsed above, we must look more closely at the central temptation in that poem, the temptation of the kingdoms.[13]

In a sequence that turns out to be not one thing after another but a complex, mutually dependent whole, Satan sets before the Son the embodied nations of Judea, Parthia, Rome, and ancient Greece. Judea constitutes the simplest appeal to patriotic pride: "[F]ree / Thy Country from her Heathen servitude" (3.175-6) the Tempter urges; behold "*Judaea* now and all the promis'd land / Reduc't a Province under Roman yoke" (3.157-8). But the Son refuses to recognize the captive nation as his own:

> themselves were they
> Who wrought their own captivity, fell off
> From God to worship Calves ...
> ... distinguishable scarce
> From Gentiles but by Circumcision vain ...
> Should I of these the liberty regard,
> Who freed, as to their ancient Patrimony,
> Unhumbl'd, unrepentant, unreform'd,
> Headlong would follow, and to their Gods perhaps
> of *Bethel* and of *Dan*? No, let them serve
> Thir enemies, who serve Idols with God. (3.414-32)

---

names of places unknown, better harp'd at in *Camden*, and other Chorographers" (pp. 239-40). For other examples of Milton's irreverence on the subject of British place names, see p. 337 ("it were an endless work to relate how they wallow'd up and down to every particular place") and p. 342 ("thence to *Ashdune*, and other places thereabout, neither known nor of tolerable pronuntiation").

[13] The number and structure of the Son's temptations in *Paradise Regained* have been the subject of extensive critical debate. I concur with Merritt Hughes, however, in finding a broad conceptual deference to the three-part temptation in Luke: the temptation of bread, the temptation of the kingdoms, and the temptation of the tower. I take the second of these to comprise nearly half the poem (2.302 to 4.397) and to begin with the banquet scene, whose unfolding of appetite has very little to do with the body's need for nourishment (the temptation of bread) and very much to do with "regal mode" (2.340). Parenthetical citations to book and line numbers here and in the main body of this essay are drawn from the Merritt Hughes edition of *Paradise Regained*, John Milton, *Complete Poems and Major Prose* (Indianapolis, 1957).

It is not just Israel in its lapses that the Son rejects; it is Israel as an ideal. It is not merely that the Old Testament nation falls repeatedly into idolatry, but that the Old Testament nation as an ultimate value and goal is itself an idol.

The Parthian instance is less direct. Satan unfolds an animated spectacle of the Parthians in all their military glory, troops "In Rhombs and wedges, and half-moons, and wings" (3.309), as though their power to organize vision extended beyond the landscape and martial strategy to epistemology itself. The Son is invited to construe and cultivate the Parthian kingdom as an ally in the ongoing struggle to secure the throne of David. For how can you hope, says Satan, to enjoy a lasting reign "Between two such enclosing enemies / *Roman* and *Parthian*? ... [O]ne of these / Thou must make sure thy own" (3.361-3). The temptation is as much a temptation to sovereign "policy" (3.391) as to Parthia per se, as the Son unblinkingly discerns. In deference to "due time and providence" (3.440), he rejects strategic "Means" (3.394).

But the Tempter must affect to believe that the differences among nations are still of moment. Having tried Rome once as enemy, he tries it again as bait:

> All Nations now to *Rome* obedience pay,
> To *Rome*'s great Emperor, whose wide domain
> In ample Territory, wealth and power,
> Civility of Manners, Arts, and Arms,
> And long Renown thou justly mayst prefer
> Before the *Parthian*; these two Thrones except,
> The rest are barbarous, and scarce worth the sight. (4.80-6)

As we have seen, the opposition between Roman civility and far-flung barbarism, between center and colonial periphery, was not a hollow opposition to the poet of *Paradise Regained*, or not, at least, when he authored *The History of Britain*. In Rome, the Tempter implies, the Son may unite ambition and pity, self-seeking and selflessness. Supplanting Tiberius on the imperial throne, the Son would free a "victor people" from a "servile yoke" (4.102). Satan's tactical reversal is so frictionless as to be partly comic: You don't want to ally with the Parthians against Rome? How about with Rome against the Parthians? You don't want to be King of the Jews? How about Emperor of Rome? What the reversal exposes, of course, is Satan's opportunism, but also, and perhaps more seriously, the relativism of all nationalistic perspectives. Milton had hoped for a time that one nation in particular, a nation of the elect, might hold a place for universal reform. But historical vehicles of transhistorical hope must always be a strained proposition: how can endemic partiality (my nation, not yours, though yours may be "mine" to you) serve as a proper route to transcendence?

> Know therefore when my season comes to sit
> On *David*'s Throne, it shall be like a tree
> Spreading and overshadowing all the Earth,
> Or as a stone that shall to pieces dash
> All Monarchies besides throughout the world ...

Means there shall be to this, but what the means,
Is not for thee to know, nor me to tell. (4.146-53)

Satan's final, most pernicious, kingly offering takes Athens as its symbol. "Conversation with the Gentiles" affords an alternate version of community, with much to recommend it. "Without thir learning how wilt thou with them, / Or they with thee hold conversation meet? / How wilt thou reason with them, how refute / Thir Idolisms …?" (4.231-4). The Son is invited to embrace pagan wisdom as a means of overcoming pagan idolatry. The extramural stroll beside the Illisus, the intramural academy: the Son is invited to imagine he can have it all. "These rules will render thee a King complete / Within thy self" (4.283-4). Is this not where temptation began, in the Garden as in the wilderness? "Would'st thou not eat?" the Tempter asked (2.321). "Thereafter as I like / The giver, answer'd Jesus" (2.321-2). The salient distinction is not between inner and outer kingdom: either may be idolatry. The salient question is to whom the kingdom refers. "[R]elation stands" (4.519).

Many critics have understood the Son to be making the same choice they ascribe to Restoration Milton: inwardness and private virtue as opposed to common weal. "[H]e who reigns within himself," the Son avers, "is more a King" than he "who wears the Regal Diadem" (2.466-7, 461). But, crucially, the Son continues:

> But to guide Nations in the way of truth
> By saving Doctrine, and from error lead
> To know, and knowing worship God aright,
> Is yet more Kingly; this attracts the Soul,
> Governs the inner man, the nobler part;
> That other o're the body only reigns,
> And oft by force, which to a generous mind
> So reigning can be no sincere delight. (2.473-80)

As the sequence of clauses makes clear, the "inner man" in question is not merely the self, a kingdom of one, but the soul and inwardness of nations. The "body" Satan has invited the Son to rule is not the merely private body (Satan's campaign is not on behalf of austerity) but the body of others. In so far as the soul the Son opposes to this body is private rather than collective (and grammar tells us this is so), it is a soul "governed" by the thought of guiding nations in the way of truth. The Son's ambitions are not narrower than those Satan advocates but, on the contrary, more "generous," that is, both deeper and broader. The grammatical circularity of the passage cited above (the eight lines constitute an independent period) is symptomatic of its epideictic function. Like the exemplary Savior, the inward semantic turning (the private soul, the inner man) moves outward again to constitute, and rescue, a collective.

When, in book 12 of *Paradise Lost*, the archangel Michael describes the Israelites' forty years of wandering in the wilderness, he explains both the practical advantage of their indirection (they avoid sudden war with the

Canaanites) and also a further sort of "gain" (*PL* 12.223),[14] for in the wilderness the tribes "shall found / Thir government, and thir great Senate choose" (*PL* 12.224-5), shall receive their laws, shall found both civil and religious ceremony, shall constitute themselves, in other words, and for the first time, as a nation. David Quint persuasively argues that the desert wandering so construed is the closest model in *Paradise Lost* to the republican experiment Milton had devoutly served during the interregnum.[15] I would only add that the vision of the nation without an earthly homeland might well have had intensified rather than diminished appeal for a republican once the commonwealth had collapsed. Nation was always for Milton an interim measure, a means of structuring hope and performing fidelity during the interval between two Comings. The conceptual and practical problem, both before and after the Restoration, was how to inhabit the meantime. It is not nation the poet rejects in *Paradise Regained*; it is nation for its own sake.

V

In Spenser's account, the Normans receive more credit than does Rome for imposing civility upon an earlier, barbarous Britain. Irenius credits the Normans (incorrectly) for the importation into Britain of the "Comon Lawe ... that which *William of Normandy* brought in with his Conquest and laied vpon the necke of Englande" (p. 46). But the paradigm of imposition and emulation is very much like that which Milton will celebrate more than half a century later in *The History of Britain*. "[F]for the Inglishe," says Eudoxus, "weare at firste as stoute and warlike a people as ever weare the Irishe," but "by the discipline of the Lawes ... are now broughte vnto that Civilytie that no nacion in the worlde excelleth them in all goodlye Conuersacion and all the studies of knowledge and hvmanitye" (p. 54). If Edmund Spenser's national self-portraits appear at times to be more sanguine than those John Milton saw fit to produce, this is more likely the sign of differing rhetorical and literary strategies than the straightforward symptom of greater complaisance. In their structural account of nations and nation-making, our two colonial informants, the Elizabethan and the Cromwellian, tell highly coincident tales.

"Nation," as Spenser again and again describes it in the mirroring progress of Faeryland and England, as Milton construes it in the commemorative, community-constituting narration of Eden and Eden's loss, is mimetically produced. Its measure lies not in self-sufficiency, immunity to outside influence, nor unchangeable contour over time, but in a collective aptitude for retentive imitation, an absorption of good example, a shrugging-off of the bad, and in a

---

[14] Citations are drawn from the Merritt Hughes edition of *Paradise Lost*, John Milton, *Complete Poems and Major Prose* (Indianapolis, 1957).

[15] David Quint, *Epic and Empire: Politics and Generic Form from Virgil to Milton* (Princeton, 1993), p. 306.

complex machinery of pleasure and delight. It is this final measure—we may call it the esthetic—that proves most disconcerting to twentieth-century retrospection. At the conclusion of their dialogue, Eudoxus extracts from Irenius the promise of a sequel: "that which ye haue formerlye halfe promised that heareafter when we shall mete againe ... ye will declare vnto vs those your observacions which ye haue gathered of the Antiquities of Ireland" (pp. 230-1). That is, the absorbing textures and delightful prospects of the delineated colonial field—its antiquity, its complexity, its implicit testimony to the prowess of the administrative mind— repeatedly waylay the expedient "remedy" it is the ostensible business of the *View* to promote. The eradication, root and branch, of matters Irish must be preceded by commemorative and analytical "gathering," a process Steven Mullaney delineated some years ago in the Welsh case and dubbed "the rehearsal of cultures."[16] Ireland constituted as a field of knowledge and as a field for the production and advancement of Englishness competes with Ireland effectively subdued.

Let me be perfectly clear: I do not adduce these internal fault lines as mitigating evidence, part of some effort to show that Irenius's (and Spenser's) proposals for the systematic eradication of culture and populations were somehow less savage than at first appears. On the contrary. The poet of *The Faerie Queene* is quite explicit about the relationship between force and civilization:

> Who so vpon him selfe will take the skill
> True Iustice vnto people to *diuide,*
> Had neede haue mightie hands, for to fulfill
> That, which he doth with righteous doom decide,
> And for to maister wrong and puissant pride.
> For vaine it is to deeme of things aright,
> And makes wrong doers iustice to deride,
> Vnlesse it be perform'd with dreadlesse might.
> For powre is the right hand of Iustice truely hight.[17] (italics mine)

Note the fascinating infinitive at the beginning of this passage. Arthegall, and the English colonists in Ireland, are there to "divide" justice: to apportion, to assign severally, to allocate among differently vested and often opposed interests, but also to analyze, to divide into constitutive parts, to study, and to understand. The justice Spenser propounds and wishes to advance (a justice explicitly premised on genocide),[18] the administration that was his daily labor as a planter and civil

---

[16] Steven Mullaney, *The Place of the Stage: License, Play, and Power in Renaissance England* (Chicago, 1988; rpt. Ann Arbor, 1995), pp. 60-87.

[17] *The Faerie Queene* (5.4.1) in *The Works of Edmund Spenser,* ed. Edwin Greenlaw, et al., vol. 5.

[18] On this point, and this point only, I disagree with Debora Shuger's fascinating argument in "Irishmen, Aristocrats, and Other White Barbarians," *Renaissance Quarterly* 50 (1997), 494-525; see esp. p. 515. In an eight-page section of the *View* (pp. 151-8), Irenius sets forth his plan for the systematic eradication of all non-submissive populations in Ireland. His method of choice is starvation: "the enemye ... shall finde no wheare safe to kepe his crete [his cattle] nor hide him selfe but flyinge from the fire into the water and out of one daunger into

servant, the ethnographic and linguistic survey it is our own delight to correct and continue, and the exquisite divisions of the epic poem are all aspects of a single intellectual, imperial, and esthetic adventure, profitable for civility.

Sir Philip Sidney, whose father had been for a time, and to the ruin of his private and financial affairs, Lord Deputy in Ireland, wrote as follows in his "Discourse of Irish Affairs" (1577): "For untill by time [the Irish] fynde the sweetnesse of dew subjection, it is impossible that any gentle meanes shoolde putt owt the freshe remembrance of their loste lyberty."[19] When we turn to Milton, it is immensely important to realize that, despite his status as a defender of regicide and political revolution, this "sweetness of dew subjection" will be a key concept in his political thinking as well as in his epic poems. It is an "ingenuity" in any nation "to improve and waxe more civill by a civilizing conquest."[20] As ideologue and propagandist for Britain's own most chronically contested colonial venture, the venture in Ireland, Milton invokes the same import–export measure of cultural progress and the same mimetic account of national identity he formulates at greater length in his account of Britain's earlier colonization by Rome. The nation may be ruthless because it is provisional. The recurrent course of nation-making confesses our common provisionality on earth.

Britain's own record of cultural, political, and religious fitness is profoundly mixed in Milton's account, as its cyclic conversions, redemptions, and fallings-off amply testify. Like the prophetic history Michael narrates in *Paradise Lost* and like the Old Testament history upon which Michael's is based, the *History of Britain* is the lamentable and exemplary history of a nation chosen by Providence to be the vehicle for human Reformation after the Fall, the instrument whose conspicuous fallibility is inseparable from its aptitude.

"Nation" implies both a structure of hope and a means of construing the past. The corporate unit, whose authority and coherence are always precarious, requires a history. Milton endeavored to write that history twice: once in a prose tract, where the chronic precariousness frequently exceeds authorial control, and

---

another that in shorte space ... he shall haue no harte nor habilitye to endure his wretchednes .... The ende will I assure me be verye shorte ... Allthoughe theare should none of them fall by the sworde nor be slaine by the soldiour, yeat ... by this harde restrainte they woulde quicklye Consume themselues and devour one another" (pp. 154, 158). Irenius's notorious description of the defeated Irish in Munster ("Out of euerie Corner of the woods and glinnes they Came Crepinge forthe vppon theire handes for theire Leggs Coulde not beare them, they loked like Anotomies of deathe, they spake like ghostes Cryinge out of theire graues, they did eate the dead Carrions, happie wheare they Coulde finde them ...," [p. 158]) is presented as evidence for the feasibility of his policy recommendations. I do not argue for a simple conflation of Edmund Spenser and his fictional interlocutor Irenius, but it is worth reminding ourselves that the course of those "late warrs of mounster" (p. 158) are emphatically defended in both *The Faerie Queene* and the *View*.

[19] Sir Philip Sidney, "A Discourse on Irish Affairs," in *The Prose Works of Sir Philip Sidney*, ed. Albert Feuillerat (Cambridge, 1912), 4: 46-50; passage cited, p. 49.

[20] John Milton, *Observations upon the Articles of Peace*, 304. For recent analyses of this tract, see Thomas N. Corns, "Milton's *Observations upon the Articles of Peace*: Ireland under English Eyes," in *Politics, Poetics, and Hermeneutics in Milton's Prose*, ed. David Loewenstein and James Grantham Turner (Cambridge, 1990), and Willy Maley, "Rebels and Redshanks: Milton and the British Problem," *Irish Studies Review* 6 (Spring 1994), 7-11.

once in a poem, which makes our collective precariousness part of its argument for Providence. Symptomatically in the prose tract, and with full deliberation in the poem, Milton anticipates a precept recorded in a later century by the French sociologist Ernest Renan: "Getting its history wrong," said Renan in 1882, "is part of what it means to become a nation."[21]

---

[21] "L'oubli et je dirai même l'erreur historique, sont un facteur essentiel de la formation d'une nation," cited in E.J. Hobsbawm, *Nations and Nationalism Since 1780: Programme, Myth, Reality*, 2nd ed. (Cambridge, 1992), p. 12. Renan's "Qu'est-ce qu'une nation?" was originally delivered as a lecture at the Sorbonne, 11 March 1882, and subsequently published in *Oeuvres Complètes* (Paris, 1947-61), 1: 887-906. For a readily available English version of this essay, see the translation by Martin Thom in Homi K. Bhabha, ed., *Nation and Narration* (London, 1990), pp. 8-22.

Portions of the present essay were delivered at the Fifth International Milton Symposium in Bangor, Wales; at a conference on *The Faerie Queene in the World: 1596-1996*, sponsored by the Yale Center for British Art; at meetings of the Modern Language Association, the Renaissance Society of America, and the Newberry Milton Seminar. My thanks to the organizers of these events. Thanks also to the editors of *Prose Studies*, in which an earlier version of the *History of Britain* materials appeared (*Prose Studies* 19 [December 1996], 247-54).

6

The Social and Political Thought of Spenser in his Maturity

Nicholas Canny

The "mature" Spenser whom I propose to consider within the spectrum of English social and political thought is the man of no more than forty-four years who, in 1596, had overseen the publication of the only six books of *The Faerie Queene* that he would ever complete, and who in that same year, or in the months preceding it, sat down to compose *A Viewe of the Present State of Ireland*. We will be comparing him with the Edmund Spenser who appears as a character in Ludowick Bryskett's *A Discourse of Civill Life*, probably completed in 1584, and also with the actual Edmund Spenser who, in 1590, published the first three of a projected twelve (or twenty-four) books of *The Faerie Queene*, and whose status as a major epic poet was then signaled by his reception at court. This comparison is justified because much scholarship on Spenser has identified sharp differences between a younger humane person and an older sour man, embittered by the disappointments of his life. Attention will be devoted to Spenser's social and political priorities because these have not been systematically examined by previous scholars even though Spenser identified himself as a moral guide and decided to become a poet only because verse provided him with the best vehicle for his moral purpose.

Spenser, the character in Bryskett's *Discourse*, seemed to be in accord with all the parties to that discussion on the efficacy of education in promoting reform, and their only difference seemed to be over whether the prime object of their educational efforts should be all English-speaking subjects of Queen Elizabeth or only those in the Anglicized areas of Ireland where the *Discourse* was taking place. If we ignore that difference, we find that the participants in the *Discourse* were of one mind that reform should proceed from the top downwards and should begin with the instruction of the sons of the prominent members of society in the rules of good behavior. This could be effected through formal schooling, where the principles of good conduct would be encouraged while the pupils were mastering the basic skills of literacy in the English language. Then the pupils would become acquainted with the moral principles expounded in the classical texts that provided the best guides to good behavior, although, because time was pressing, these were to be made available to them in English translation, rather than in the original classical languages or in Italian. Bryskett, who valued education as an end in itself, did not anticipate difficulty in winning for his scheme the co-operation of the parents of his potential pupils, whom he believed (and here he might have been summarizing the pragmatic ambitions of the Old English in Ireland) would be willing to "spend their wealth to purchase them learning and knowledge" out of a "desire to make them able to be employed, and a hope to see them raised to credit and dignity in the commonwealth."[1]

We might consider education of this kind, described by Bryskett as "teaching by rule," to have been derived from the Latin verb *educo, educare*, meaning to pour in, while the purer form of education, favored by the character Spenser, and described by him as "teaching by example," certainly had its origin in the Latin verb *educo, educere*, meaning to lead forth. While there probably was, as there still is, a fundamental philosophical difference between the two concepts of education, the characters in the *Discourse* did not consider them to be necessarily incompatible. Rather, it seems that Spenser accepted that his "teaching by example" could become effective only after the initial instruction had taken place, by which time people would be sufficiently informed to read (or listen to) and appreciate his poetry, which was designed to provide that moral guidance which was most appropriate for the subjects of Queen Elizabeth. Spenser was therefore seeking to update, and make relevant to his own generation, the moral teaching of the classical authors, and all parties to Bryskett's *Discourse* accepted that these teachings needed thus to be recast, and that this would best be undertaken by English humanists for the benefit of English-speaking pupils, just as it had been done for Italian speakers by the Renaissance scholars whose work formed the model for Bryskett's *Discourse of Civill Life*.[2] Again, it becomes clear that there was no inconsistency in the two approaches to education advocated by the different members of the company. For example, when Bryskett himself praised the "reading of histories" which he likened to "mirrors or looking glasses for every man to see the good and evil actions of all ages, the better to square his life to the rule of virtue, by the examples of others,"[3] he was anticipating, both in

---

[1] Bryskett, *A Discourse of Civill Life: Containing the Ethike Part of Morall Philosophie Fit for the instructing of a Gentleman in the course of a vertuous life* (London, 1606); the text cited here is Ludowick Bryskett, *A Discourse of Civill Life*, ed. Thomas E. Wright (Northridge, Ca., 1970), p. 9; for general details on the career of Bryskett, see H.R. Plomer and T.P. Cross, *The Life and Correspondence of Ludowick Bryskett* (Chicago, 1927); Deborah Jones, "Ludowick Bryskett and his Family," in C.J. Sisson, ed. *Thomas Lodge and Other Elizabethans* (Cambridge, Mass., 1933), pp. 243-362; *The Spenser Encyclopedia*, ed. A.C. Hamilton, et al. (Toronto, 1990), p. 119; the subject of this essay will be treated in a more straightforward chronological fashion in "Spenser sets his Agenda," ch. 1 of Nicholas Canny, *Making Ireland British, 1580s-1650s* (Oxford, forthcoming); and the context of Spenser's involvement with Ireland is developed in the first two chapters of that book and in Andrew Hadfield, *Spenser's Irish Experience: Wilde Fruit and Salvage Soyl* (Oxford, 1997).

[2] The principal treatises employed by Bryskett were Giambattista Giraldi, "Tre dialoghi della vita civile," in *De gli hecatommithi* (1565); Alessandro Piccolomini, *Della institutione morale* (1560); and Stefano Guazzo, *La civil conversazione* (1574).

[3] Bryskett, *Discourse*, pp. 15-16.

vocabulary and sentiment, what Spenser would have to say on the purpose of poetry in his open letter to Ralegh of 1590, published as an introduction to the first three books of *The Faerie Queene*. Here, Spenser proclaimed that his "general intention and meaning" was moral, and that he strove, by the examples he set before his readers, "to fashion a gentleman or noble person in virtuous and gentle discipline," while, at the same time, he entertained his audience with stories relating to the life of King Arthur.[4] In thus undertaking what he described as "a historical fiction," Spenser likened his endeavor to that of the ancient authors Homer and Virgil, and that of the Renaissance writers Ariosto and Tasso, who all chose to compose poetic works "for examples sake." Spenser also expressed particular admiration for Tasso because he had drawn the clearest distinction between "the virtues of a private man," "which they in philosophy call Ethic," and the public achievements of that same man, "named politic." In line with this, Spenser set out in *The Faerie Queene* to dwell upon the formation of the character of King Arthur before he became king, presenting him "in the image of a brave knight, perfected in the twelve private moral virtues" as these had been defined by Aristotle, after which he proposed to treat, in a further series of books, of the "politicke virtues in his person, after that he came to be king."[5]

We can see therefore that Bryskett and the other members of the company who had had a preview of sections of the poem and agreed with its purpose, accepted that Spenser's agenda complemented rather than conflicted with their own, and they would have recognized that *The Faerie Queene* was especially useful for teaching by example because it had been designed as a historical fiction. What comes as a surprise, and what we have not been prepared for in the *Discourse*, is that by approving *The Faerie Queene* this seeming Erasmian group was silently endorsing the use of violence to promote reform. That they were doing so becomes clear when we come to appreciate that the essential "lesson by example" which Spenser wished to convey through the medium of *The Faerie Queene* was that even persons of the highest rank and virtue would remain on the path of righteousness only so long as the temptations that lured them from that path were systematically destroyed. Nor did Spenser conceal this from Bryskett's company, because as well as providing them with passages from the poem, and possibly the overall plan which he was to unveil in 1590, he explained that it was "not unknown" to them that in his work "in heroical verse, under the title of a *Faerie Queene*," he would seek to represent all the moral virtues, "assigning to every knight to be the patron and defender of the same: in whose actions and *feats of arms and chivalry*, the operations of that virtue, whereof he is the protector, are to be

---

[4] Open letter to Ralegh, 23 January 1590, and published with the first three books of *The Faerie Queene*, in Edmund Spenser, *The Faerie Queene*, ed. A.C. Hamilton (London, 1977), pp. 737-8; this edition of *The Faerie Queene* will be referred to throughout as *FQ*, with relevant book, canto and stanza numbers.

[5] Ibid.

expressed, and the vices & unruly appetites that oppose themselves against the same to be *beaten down & overcome*."[6]

Most commentators have acknowledged that Spenser the poet, as well as Spenser the author of the prose text *A View of the Present State of Ireland*,[7] advocated the use of violence to achieve higher ends, but they tend to associate his ruthlessness with the second series of three books of *The Faerie Queene*, published in 1596. Moreover, they attribute what they regard as this coarsening of the character of Spenser either to his direct involvement with the wars in Ireland, or to his personal disappointment at not having won the favor he believed his talents deserved when he did gain access to the Queen in 1590 to present her with the first three books of the poem.[8] These assumptions lack credibility not only because they deny coherence both to *The Faerie Queene* as a poem and to Spenser as a social and political thinker, but more particularly because they disregard Spenser's most compelling point, which he made explicit from the outset in the examples he set before his readers, that even people from the upper reaches of society who had enjoyed the best possible educational advantages could not be trusted to follow a fixed moral purpose. The squires assigned to the knights in the earlier books might be considered the equivalent of humanist teachers, but their persistent nagging to divert their charges from false paths, and the knights' persistent meandering from these paths once they eluded their mentors, suggests that Spenser, while accepting that education could prove efficacious in guiding people towards better behavior, did not believe that it alone would provide a guarantee of correct conduct. And, as also becomes clear from the very outset of the poem, once Spenser's knights set out on their assigned tasks they were active not only in protecting the virtues they had been directed to defend, but they also lived up to their responsibility to root out and destroy the "vices & unruly appetites" that were opposed to those virtues. Indeed, as if to establish these priorities from the outset, Spenser began in Book I with a story that reached its happy conclusion of a betrothal between Una and the Redcross Knight only after three gruesome encounters with dragons, and the defeat in single combat of three Saracen knights. Each of these battles is depicted in pen pictures whose shocking vividness has not been surpassed even by Hollywood at its most graphic, and it can justly be said that Book I, no less than Book V or any other book of *The Faerie Queene*, is steeped in gore. Besides the six bloody conflicts already mentioned, Book I features several other violent acts such as the stripping of the witch Duessa undertaken by Arthur at the request of Una, the personification of Holiness, the virtue to which the book is dedicated. As we contemplate this passage we must remember that stripping, as it was practised in the wars of early modern Europe (and most notoriously in the Irish

---

[6] Bryskett, *Discourse*, p. 22, italics mine.
[7] The edition used here is Edmund Spenser, *A Viewe of the Present State of Ireland,* [1596], ed. W.L. Renwick (Oxford, 1970), referred to hereafter as *Viewe.*
[8] The most recent, in a long line of scholars, to articulate this opinion is Richard Rambuss, *Spenser's Secret Career* (Cambridge, 1993).

insurrection of 1641), was a tactic designed not only to deprive the victims of status and dignity, but also to put them in danger of death from exposure[9]:

> To do her dye (quoth *Una*) were despight,
> And shame t'auenge so weake an enimy;
> But spoile her of her scarlot robe, and let her fly.
>
> So as she bad, that witch they disaraid,
> And robd of royall robes, and purple pall,
> And ornaments that richly were displaid;
> Ne spared they to strip her naked all.
> Then when they had despoild her tire and call,
> Such as she was, their eyes might her behold,
> That her misshaped parts did them appall,
> A loathly, wrinckled hag ill fauoured, old,
> Whose secret filth good manners biddeth not be told.
>
> Her craftie head was altogether bald,
> And as in hate of honorable eld,
> Was ouergrowne with scurfe and filthy scalde;
> Her teeth out of her rotten gummes were feld,
> And her sowre breath abhominably smeld;
> Her dried dugs, like bladders lacking wind,
> Hong downe, and filthy matter from them weld;
> Her wrizled skin as rough, as maple rind,
> So scabby was, that would haue loathd all womankind. (1.8.45-7)

It is doubtful if the privileged members of Bryskett's *Discourse* had been given a preview of this or other equally vivid passages from *The Faerie Queene*, and they certainly did not address themselves to the apparent contradiction of recommending the use of violence to advance reform. However, it is obvious that anybody who was conscious of Christian teaching on the fall of humanity from God's favor would have seen no such contradiction, and would have agreed with Spenser that the source of temptation had always to be sought out and destroyed if people were to remain true to their moral principles. And when his allegorized message was translated into the world of reality, it would have been evident that it was only the power of the state that could be called upon to support the educational drive for reform. This interpretation suggests that Spenser, like all humanists who had lived through the experiences of the Reformation and the Counter-Reformation in Europe, had arrived at the conclusion that moral reform, as this had been conceived in a secular sense by the ancients and their imitators in Renaissance Italy, could not be divorced from religious considerations. Therefore, for Spenser and his associates, reform always had to include religious reform, and they accepted

---

[9] On the practice of stripping in Irish revolt, see Nicholas Canny, "What Really Happened in Ireland in 1641?" in Jane Ohlmeyer, ed., *Ireland: From Occupation to Independence, 1641-1660* (Cambridge, 1995), pp. 24-42, and ch. 8 of Canny, *Making Ireland British*.

that the promotion of reform through education and evangelization would prove illusory unless it was supported by the authority and rigor of the state. Again, Spenser was entirely consistent when he showed concern for the integrity and moral purpose of the royal court, because it was only a morally upright state that could keep its subjects on the path of righteousness. His criticism of English government policy, including his criticism of life at court which is explicit in his later verse, was present from the outset, and its later manifestation should therefore not be taken as evidence of a dawning disillusionment or a nascent disloyalty on the part of one who had previously been fawning in his loyalty to the Queen. Those who have identified a shift in allegiance have failed to recognize that Spenser was a consistent critic of government policy, and their contentions also lack weight because some of the evidence they cite in support of their case for a change of attitude by Spenser after his visit to court in 1590 had been written by him, although not published, before that date.

The most unambigious of Spenser's many denunciations of the court was contained in *Prosopopoia or Mother Hubbard's Tale*, presented for publication with his other *Complaints* in 1591. This was admittedly subsequent to the suggested watershed date of 1590 when he was supposedly disenchanted by his visit to the court, but we have it on Spenser's own authority that these particular lines had been "long since composed in the raw conceit of [his] youth" and had been rescued by him from his papers at the request of "others" who "liked the same" and "moved" him "to set them forth."[10] Even if we acknowledge this explanation as no more than a judicious shield against the wrath of people in power who were likely to be offended by the verses, we must still take account of Spenser's unvarnished statement on the responsibility of the poet to serve as a social and political critic. This took the form of a sonnet, presented in 1586 to his friend Gabriel Harvey, whom Spenser clearly considered a role model for himself:

> Harvey, thee happy above happiest men
> I rede; that sitting like a looker on
> Of this world's stage, dost note with critic pen
> The sharp dislikes of each condition:
> And as one careless of suspicion,
> Ne fawnest for the favour of the great;
> Ne fearest foolish reprehension
> Of faulty men, which danger to thee threat:
> But freely dost, of what thee list, entreat,
> Like a great lord of peerless liberty;
> Lifting the Good up to the honour's seat,
> And the Evil damning evermore to die:

---

[10] For Spenser's minor poems, I have used Edmund Spenser, *The Shepherd's Calendar and Other Poems*, ed. Philip Henderson (London, 1932), referred to throughout as *Shepherd's Calendar*; see pp. 159-91, esp. p. 159.

> For Life, and Death, is in thy doomful writing!
> So thy renown lives ever by inditing. [11]

Although Spenser did not formally articulate this role for the poet as social critic until 1586, he had been practising this part ever since he had won recognition as a literary figure with the publication, in 1579, of *The Shepherd's Calendar*. Each of the twelve aeglogues in this collection was based on a classical or Renaissance model, and Spenser acknowledged Theocritus, Virgil, and Clement Marot, among others, as the authors of the poems he was imitating. He was attracted by the aeglogue as a vehicle for his ideas both because it provided him with the opportunity to demonstrate that poetry in English could match the best in the classical languages, and because it allowed him to treat of subjects that varied from the "plaintive" to the "recreative" to the "moral." The greater number of his twelve aeglogues (each called after a month in the year) fell into the moral category and these "for the most part [were] mixed with some satirical bitterness."[12] In these moral poems Spenser treated of subjects that were to remain his concern throughout his working life as a poet: these included the insatiable greed of the church of Rome, the continuing corrupting influence of Catholicism even after the success of the Reformation, the seductions that were put in the way of poets by tyrants who aspired to be immortalized in verse, and the countervailing disrespect for those who remained true to their vocations. Side by side with these concerns was the aeglogue for April which was devoted to Spenser's most enduring theme, being "intended to the honour and praise of our most gracious sovereign Queen Elizabeth."[13] Spenser was further convinced that the form of the aeglogue was appropriate to his purpose because, as originally invented by Theocritus, aeglogues had been "goatherds' tales" and had been modified by Virgil only to the extent that the speakers were "more shepherds than goatherds."[14] This pastoral setting was attractive to Spenser because it enabled him to reflect on the great affairs of the world from an idealized rural setting, and through the eyes of the simple but perspicacious shepherd, Colin Clout. This character had originally been created by John Skelton,[15] and this association was important for Spenser because it enabled him to trace his social criticism backwards through Skelton to Chaucer and Langland. For Spenser, Chaucer was the English counterpart of Virgil and for this reason he referred to him as Tityrus (the pen-name used by Virgil),[16] but association with the English tradition of country criticism of life at court was equally important to him, and to achieve

---

[11] Ibid, p. 366.

[12] *Shepherd's Calendar*, pp. 9-11.

[13] Ibid., pp. 13-101, esp. pp. 31-9.

[14] Ibid., p. 9.

[15] John Skelton, *The Complete English Poems*, ed. John Scattergood (London, 1983), pp. 246-78; *Shepherd's Calendar*, p. 15.

[16] *Shepherd's Calendar*, pp. 53, 55-6.

this Spenser deliberately introduced archaisms into the speech of the rustic savants who feature as spokesmen in *The Shepherd's Calendar*.[17]

When account is taken of these commitments of Spenser, it is logical that he should have returned briefly to his pastoral mode after the publication in 1590 of the first installment of *The Faerie Queene* and his visit to court, if only to provide proof that he was, as Chaucer—and Harvey—had been, still the same fearless indicter. However, the satire and criticism in *Colin Clouts Come Home Againe*, to which the scholars who argue for a bifurcation in Spenser's career make reference, is balanced by an unqualified admiration for the Queen which surpasses anything he had previously written.[18] Spenser also seemed genuinely flattered that Queen Elizabeth had taken an interest in his verse, even if she had done so at the behest of Ralegh (the Shepherd of the Ocean), and out of affection for the memory of Philip Sidney (Astrophel), whom he believed had apprised her of his talents. He also seemed moved by the attentions he received from the ladies at court, especially that from Sidney's sister, and Spenser's frequently cited reference to the falseness and superficiality of life at court, notably in *Prothalamion*, where he spoke of his "fruitless stay in Prince's court, and expectation vain of idle hope" was a stock complaint in the pastoral tradition and was no more severe than what he (or Skelton for that matter) had previously made.[19] Indeed, the satirical passages in *Colin Clouts* would seem to have been introduced by Spenser only to explain his decision to return to Ireland rather than remain at court where he might have enjoyed the continued patronage of the Queen. This issue was raised in the poem by the character Thestylis (who is thought to represent Ludowick Bryskett) when he asked why, since he had found "such grace with Cynthia and all her noble crew," he should

> ever leave that happy place,
> In which such wealth might unto thee accrue;
> And back returnedst to this barren soil,
> Where cold and care and penury do dwell,
> Here to keep sheep, with hunger and with toil?[20]

This query had been anticipated and an appropriate answer already provided by Cuddy, the voice of rustic common sense, when he had suggested that the height to which Colin had mounted was not appropriate for a "base shepherd,"[21] but Colin endorsed this sentiment in his considered reply to Thestylis when he acknowledged that he, a

---

[17] The question of language, both the merits of English as opposed to the classical languages and Italian, and the appropriateness of antique usage, were discussed in Spenser's letter to Gabriel Harvey of April 1579, which served as an introduction to the collection "The Shepherd's Calendar," in *Shepherd's Calendar*, pp. 3-8.

[18] The entire poem appears in *Shepherd's Calendar*, pp. 247-69.

[19] *Shepherd's Calendar*, p. 361.

[20] Ibid., p. 262.

[21] Ibid., p. 261.

silly man, whose former days
Had in rude fields been altogether spent,
Durst not adventure such unknowen ways,
Nor trust the guile of fortunes blandishment;
But rather chose back to my sheep to turn,
Whose utmost hardness I before had tried,
Than, having learned repentance late, to mourn
Amongst those wretches which I there descried. [22]

This statement outweighs any countervailing evidence that Spenser was then aggrieved and had been alienated from the Queen because he had not got the preferment he expected. It is probably true that he, like everybody else who was received into the royal presence, had hoped for a more substantial reward than pleasant words, but we must remember that Spenser had already been well rewarded by the Queen with the grant of an estate in the Munster plantation. Many literary scholars have discounted or disregarded this, and Philip Henderson's assertion (made admittedly in 1938), that Spenser's only reward was "virtual exile among savages in Ireland, and a small pension that was not regularly paid," has been repeatedly reiterated even if not in the same unfortunate words.[23] The truth is that estates in Munster were keenly sought after by those who were in favor with the Queen, and Spenser was one of the very few English-born servants of the crown in Ireland who was favored in this way. Grants such as this, initially in Munster and later throughout Ireland, were always appreciated, but especially so by English people like Spenser who came from modest circumstances, because they provided them with the opportunity to achieve a social and economic uplift for themselves and their heirs that would have never come their way in England.[24] The fact that the benefits of the grant of Kilcolman were soon to be lost through insurrection, and that Spenser would die a refugee in England, could not have been anticipated in 1591, and there seems no justification to treat this year as a watershed in the loyalties of Edmund Spenser.

To summarize, therefore, Spenser was consistently a moralist both in the traditions of English pastoral verse and of the Renaissance. Some may look askance at his advocacy of violence in *The Faerie Queene*, but scholars like Dr. Brendan Bradshaw who assert that this places him outside, and opposed to, the traditions of Renaissance humanism are proceeding from a false premise that humanists were so hostile to war as to be almost pacifists.[25] It is true that

---

[22] Ibid., p. 263.

[23] *Shepherd's Calendar*, introduction, p. vii.

[24] M. MacCarthy-Morrogh, *The Munster Plantation: English Emigration to Southern Ireland, 1583-1641* (Oxford, 1986); Nicholas Canny, *The Upstart Earl: A Study of the Social and Mental World of Richard Boyle, first Earl of Cork* (Cambridge, 1982).

[25] Bradshaw, "Sword, Word and Strategy in the Reformation in Ireland," *Historical Journal* 21 (1978), 475-502; *idem*, "Robe and Sword in the Conquest of Ireland," *Essays on Tudor and Stuart Government in Honour of Geoffrey Elton*, ed. Claire Cross, et al. (Cambridge, 1978) pp. 139-62; *idem*, "Edmund Spenser on Justice and Mercy," *The Writer as*

the humanists of the generation of Erasmus did devote much of their writings to the castigation of Christian society because of its devotion to war, but the issues they isolated for particular criticism were dynastic wars of aggression, the existence of a plenitude of private armies that occasioned the impoverishment of the weakest members of society, and the preoccupation of supposedly Christian rulers with warlike pastimes whenever they were not actually engaged in war. At the same time, however, all humanists of all generations believed that Christians had an obligation to use force to defend and promote the truths of religion, to maintain order at times of popular insurrection, and (as is best exemplified in some passages of More's *Utopia*), to extend the boundaries of civility into "barbaric" regions.[26] It is also likely that Christian humanists would have accepted Spenser's Hobbesian notion, which he elaborated in Books II and V of *The Faerie Queene*, that civil society had first been established by force,[27] and while few humanists actually addressed the question of how the first civil society had come into being, they generally accepted that civility had been extended by force from its first narrow heartland. The humanist guidelines governing the justifications for war were rigidly adhered to in *The Faerie Queene*, and when we take account of such real episodes as the suppression of the Peasants' Revolt in Germany or the depredations of Parma in the Spanish Netherlands, it becomes clear that even the most revolting episodes conjured up by Spenser in his historical fiction did not surpass the horror of actual wars in sixteenth-century Europe, even when these conformed with the principles laid down by Christian humanists. In this respect Spenser might be regarded as a poetic counterpart of Pieter Bruegel the Younger who, like Spenser, represented the violence which he witnessed everywhere about him while accepting war as a necessary, if regrettable, facet of human existence.

Where Spenser did depart from the earlier generations of humanists was in his pessimism about the capacity of people to achieve self-improvement, and in his conviction that moral lapse and degeneration were little short of inevitable, even in the best-ordered societies. Brendan Bradshaw has attributed such notions in the writings of Spenser, and of other English officials in Ireland, to their adherence to the Calvinist doctrine of predestination, and he even contends that the issuance of statements to the effect that people were not amenable to reform is in itself proof that their authors were Calvinists.[28] This supposition collapses when account is taken of contemporaneous Catholic opinions on the reform of primitive or "depraved" peoples

---

Witness: Literature as Historical Evidence: Historical Studies XVI, ed. Tom Dunne (Cork, 1987), pp. 76-89.

[26] *The Yale Edition of the Complete Works of Saint Thomas More*, ed. E. Surtz and J.H. Hexter (New Haven, 1965), 4: 137.

[27] *FQ*, 5.1.1-2; 2.10.4-11.

[28] Bradshaw, "Sword, Word and Strategy"; see also Ciaran Brady, "Spenser's Irish Crisis: Humanism and Experience in the 1590s," *Past and Present* 111 (1986), 3-49, and the debate between Brady and Canny on how Spenser should be read in *Past and Present* 120 (1988), 201-15.

which were as diverse and sometimes as despairing as those articulated by Protestants.[29] In so far as religion had anything to do with the widespread pessimism that prevailed throughout European society of the 1590s—and not only in England—it is probably because the evangelization endeavors of both Protestant and Catholic reformers during the course of the sixteenth century would have made all people more aware than previously of the consequences of the Fall. However, a far more important influence in convincing people of the fragility of a moral and civil order would have been the experience of living through the conflicts of that century. This experience provided ample evidence that the optimistic notion that all social ills could be remedied simply by providing for the education of future leaders was illusory. Spenser's remedy for this problem, as we saw, was that leaders should be active against the corrupting influences that were pitted against the moral and civil principles that had been expounded to them during the course of their education. While Spenser's poetry alerted people to the likelihood of social degeneracy and moral decay, it was still truly humanist because it showed how these pitfalls could be evaded. His concerns and preoccupations therefore complemented those of his fellow discussants in Ludowick Bryskett's *Discourse*.

Thus, despite their apparent radicalism, the sentiments expressed by Spenser in his poetry were probably reflective of those fostered by a broad spectrum of his generation in England who had been nurtured on John Foxe's *Acts and Monuments* of 1563 (popularly known as the *Book of Martyrs*), even if these popular opinions were not articulated in any formal political text of the 1590s. More importantly for our present purposes, the study of the complete works of Spenser reveals that his political and social principles remained consistent throughout his career as a poet. There were, however, two aspects to his later poetry which rendered it controversial and pointed to the more extreme of the ideas that he was to expound more specifically in the *Viewe*. The controversy arose because of his close discussion, in Book V of *The Faerie Queene*, of the politics of the 1570s and 1580s, including the execution of Mary Queen of Scots, whom he depicted as Duessa. Here he made clear his identification with the rigid Protestant line advocated by Walsingham and Leicester while that episode was being played out and which led to the Queen of Scots being put to death.[30] Spenser's narrative of events would have been acceptable and even praiseworthy close to that time. Not so in 1596, however, when it was generally accepted that Mary's son, James VI of Scotland, would succeed Elizabeth on the throne of England. Spenser, for his efforts, earned a reprimand from James, and it is likely that he would have further provoked the royal ire if the King of Scots had looked more deeply into the poem and taken note of Spenser's "little-Englander" approach to any possible union of the

[29] Anthony Pagden, *The Fall of Natural Man: The American Indian and the Origins of Comparative Ethnology* (Cambridge, 1982); *idem, European Encounters with the New World* (New Haven, 1993).

[30] On the execution and the politics associated with it, see Jenny Wormald, *Mary Queen of Scots: A Study in Failure* (London, 1991).

crowns. Spenser's Faerie Queene, the "Great lady of the greatest isle,"[31] was a monarch whose authority held sway throughout Britain and not just England, and this dominion, which he represented as having been first achieved by Brutus through force of arms,[32] had resulted in a unitary state which made no allowance for cultural or religious diversity. Indeed, as if to reinforce his argument, Spenser insisted, when he came to speak of the compromised authority that that same monarch endured in Ireland, that cultural and religious diversity led inevitably to the degeneration of the central authority itself. This proposition, first made in *The Faerie Queene*,[33] pointed to what he would detail in the *Viewe*, but even as these two arguments were elaborated in his verse they enable us to situate Spenser within the spectrum of English political thought of the early modern period. His model of what the authority of the English monarchy should be was not unique to him nor did it originate with him. On the contrary, it had been clearly stated by Geoffrey of Monmouth in the twelfth century and became a matter of public policy when Somerset was in charge of the English government during the reign of Edward VI, as it was to become so again during the rule of Oliver Cromwell.[34] Many of his English contemporaries would have shared this opinion, but this narrowly English perspective was unfashionable at the English court in 1596, and those who wielded influence there would have appreciated neither folkloric reminders of the origin of Britain nor the rehearsal of the more recent events during Queen Elizabeth's reign when war between England and Scotland had seemed imminent. And courtiers who had lived through these events would have been especially discommoded by Spenser's rendition in Book V of *The Faerie Queene* of their roles in the trial and execution of the mother of their future king.

What all this amounts to is that the message which Spenser had to convey remained consistent throughout his life but that his manner of expressing those sentiments underwent a fundamental shift as he entered into his mature years. At all times he identified himself as an uncompromising champion of the achievements of the Protestant Reformation and he made it clear that it was worth fighting to maintain these gains since, as was clear from his earliest definitions in *The Shepherd's Calendar*, a civil society was a Protestant society. While thus convinced, Spenser made the deliberate decision as he embarked upon the composition of *The Faerie Queene* to advance his arguments obliquely under the guise of allegory, and always to support his

---

[31] *FQ*, 1. Proem. 4; the term "little-Englander" to describe this political position comes from Dr. John Morrill.

[32] *FQ*, 2.10.4-11.

[33] *FQ*, 4.11.40-44.

[34] Roger Mason, "Scotching the Brute: Politics, History and National Myth in Sixteenth-Century Britain," Roger A. Mason, ed., *Scotland and England, 1286-1815* (Edinburgh, 1987), pp. 60-84; *idem*, "The Scottish Reformation and the Origins of Anglo-British Imperialism," Roger Mason, ed., *Scots and Britons: Scottish Political Thought and the Union of 1603* (Cambridge, 1994), pp. 161-86; F.D. Dow, *Cromwellian Scotland, 1651-60* (Edinburgh, 1979).

controversial contentions by citation from experiences in King Arthur's rather than Queen Elizabeth's reign, thus remaining "furthest from the danger of envy, and suspition of present time."[35] As he did so, he remained confident that his audience would always divine his purpose if they followed "certain signs" that he had "set in sundry place" throughout the work. Those who pursued these leads, he claimed (and he likened their task to that of bloodhounds tracking a scent) would indeed come to know "Faerie Land," and he assured Queen Elizabeth, the "fairest Princess under sky," that she would, as in a "faire mirrhour," behold her "face" and her "owne realmes in lond of Faery" and would recognize her "great auncestry" in this "antique image."[36] Therefore, the later books of *The Faerie Queene* are novel not because of the messages they contain but because they display Spenser as having cast to the winds his self-denying ordinance when he began to support his propositions through citation from contemporary experience and in an allegorical form that was so thinly disguised as to leave no room for ambiguity. Our concern thus becomes one of explaining why the previously cautious Spenser engaged on a course that both contravened his own prescription and that exposed himself to considerable personal risk.

The answers to this question are the obvious ones because, as is always the case with Spenser, they lie close to the surface of his writing. There seems no doubt that, as he embarked upon his epic, he was satisfied that the propositions he was advancing and upholding were shared by all right-thinking English Protestants, including the Queen, and his epic, like all poems of that genre, was designed both to celebrate past achievements and to exhort people to ever more glorious deeds. However, experience was to convince him that the achievements of the Reformation were even less secure than he had believed at the outset, and he was to become ever more disillusioned as those who had championed the cause and stood in the breach had either gone without due reward or had suffered disgrace. This was all the more galling because these—Leicester, Ralegh, Philip Sidney, and Arthur Lord Grey de Wilton—were those who had been Spenser's principal supporters throughout his career. His casting aside of the mask, and his explicit abandonment of his epic—symbolized by the breaking of the bagpipes in Book VI[37]—combined, therefore, to make the point that there was no longer a glorious achievement to be celebrated, and his criticism of current policy and the aspersions he cast on Lord Burghley were with a view to reminding Burghley of the worthy path on which he had once directed government policy and from which he had strayed.[38]

---

[35] *FQ*, pp. 737-8.

[36] *FQ*, 2. Proem. 2-5.

[37] *FQ*, 6.10.18.

[38] It is interesting that Burghley was identified by Spanish diplomats as a Protestant hardliner both in the 1570s and the 1580s; see Xavier Gill, "Aragonese Constitutionalism and Habsburg Rule: the Varying Meanings of Liberty," and Geoffrey Parker, "David or Goliath? Philip II and his World in the 1580s," both in Richard Kagan and Geoffrey Parker, eds., *Spain,*

However, as we take account of Spenser's litany of disappointments, there is no doubt that what he believed to be the unwarranted disgrace of Lord Grey for the actions he had taken in Ireland surpassed all others. This therefore suggests that it was Spenser's own experiences in Ireland, as much as his integrity, which explains why his views were advanced explicitly in his later writings. His experience in Ireland also effected a change in his attitude towards that country, and hints in this change are evident in his later verse. We have already noted, in our discussion of *The Faerie Queene*, some hints of Spenser's misgivings over the progress of England's mission in Ireland, and these were put more emphatically in *Colin Clouts Come Home Againe*. Besides the suggestion that he had "banished" himself

> like wight forlorne,
> Into that waste, where I was quite forgot, [39]

there is the famous juxtaposition between social conditions in England and in Ireland which infers that Spenser felt constantly threatened in his rural retreat:

> "Both heaven and heavenly graces do much more"
> (Quoth he) "abound in that same land than this:
> For there all happy peace and plenteous store
> Conspire in one to make contented bliss.
> No wailing there nor wretchedness is heard,
> No bloody issues nor no leprosies,
> No grisly famine, nor no raging swerd,
> No nightly bordrags, nor no hue and cries;
> The shepherds there abroad may safely lie,
> On hills and downs, withouten dread or danger:
> No ravenous wolves the goodman's hope destroy,
> Nor outlaws fell affray the forest ranger.
> There learned arts do flourish in great honour,
> And poets' wits are had in peerless price:
> Religion hath lay power to rest upon her,
> Advancing virtue and suppressing vice.
> For end, all good, all grace there freely grows,
> Had people grace it gratefully to use:
> For God His gifts there plenteously bestows,
> But graceless men them greatly do abuse." [40]

This passage does not hold that English society was perfect, but it does suggest that it could readily be made into an ideal pastoral world if people had the grace to make it so. In Ireland, on the other hand, the very lives, as well as the livelihoods, of shepherds were under constant threat, so that while it was a rural society it was not a pastoral one, nor was it capable of being imagined as

---

Europe and the Atlantic World: Essays in Honour of Sir John Elliott (Cambridge, 1995), pp. 160-87, 245-66.

[39] *Shepherd's Calendar*, p. 251.

[40] Ibid., pp. 254-5.

such. This same point was again made by Spenser in *The Mutabilitie Cantos*, and there he offered an explanation for Ireland's unfortunate condition. The explanation was given in the context of his retelling of Ovid's tale of the naked Diana having been spied upon at her bath by Acteon. In Spenser's version, the event occurred in the vicinity of his own estate in Munster at the time when Ireland

> florished in fame
> Of wealths and goodnesse, far aboue the rest
> Of all that beare the *British* Islands name. [41]

However, this was all changed because Diana took her revenge not only by converting the transgressor into a deer who would henceforth be followed by his hounds, but out of "indignation" she also abandoned the fertile hunting-ground where her honor had been been besmirched, and then

> parting from the place,
> There-on an heauy haplesse curse did lay,
> To weet, that Wolues, where she was wont to space,
> Should harbour'd be, and all those Woods deface,
> And Thieues should rob and spoile that Coast around.
> Since which, those Woods and all that goodly Chase,
> Doth to this day with Wolues and Thieues abound:
> Which too-too true that lands in-dwellers since haue found. [42]

One of the "land's in-dwellers" was, of course, Edmund Spenser in his capacity as a planter, and the most pressing problem that confronted him at this time was to explain why the careful scheme that had been designed for the plantation in Munster had not created the perfect pastoral society that the resources of the province showed it was capable of sustaining. An answer to this question was urgently required because the collapse of the plantation, which Spenser and several of his fellow planters in Munster believed to be imminent, would have resulted in the cancellation of all the social and material gains he had made during his working life as an official and a poet. It was with the purpose of winning support for his answer to this question and to resolving the problem that Spenser all but discarded allegory in Book V of *The Faerie Queene* in his desperation to make the point that the struggle that was being fought in Ireland was a central—if not the central—element of the assault that was being launched by the blind forces of papal superstition against the light of the Reformation, and that those, like Lord Grey, who fought the good fight there were those most worthy of praise. That Spenser's obsession at this time was to advance universal principles based on his particular experience in

---

[41] *Mutabilitie Cantos*, 6.38; many critics treat the "Mutabilitie Cantos" as part of a seventh book of *The Faerie Queene*. I believe that Spenser did intend them for inclusion in the poem but we cannot establish where he intended to fit them within his grand scheme.

[42] Ibid., 6.55.

Ireland is further sustained by the fact that he not only abandoned his epic, and probably all poetic writing, in 1596, but he did so to facilitate Eudoxus and Irenius entering into their discussion on *A Viewe of the Present State of Ireland*. In the course of this exchange Spenser endeavored to show that his solution to the problem of managing Ireland was both attainable and reasonable and was the objective to which the government of Queen Elizabeth should direct its energies.

Part III

The Functions of Allegory

7

"Worke fit for an Herauld": Spenser in the '90s

Paul Alpers

My starting point is encoded in my title: interpretation of Spenser in the 1990s has been particularly interesting in respect to the works he wrote in the 1590s. Indeed, one of the effects of recent Spenser studies has been to recognize that "Spenser in the 1590s" is an important subject. It is now common to distinguish the 1590 *Faerie Queene* from the poem published in 1596, and to think of Spenser's writings in the 1590s as specifically belonging to the last decade of his career. One sign of the enabling effect of recent styles of criticism is that Book V has become newly interesting and consequential, and it is with it that I want to begin.

The difficulties Book V presented to critics of my generation can be seen in Roger Sale's *Reading Spenser*. The final chapter of this excellent book emphasizes the aspects of Book V that remind us of *A View of the Present State of Ireland* which, interestingly, Sale does not mention. What I want to draw to your attention is the title of his final chapter: "What Happened to *The Faerie Queene*." In his account, Spenser's attempt to use "Faerie Land as a means of rendering history" caused a permanent loss in the poem.[1] If this is so, then all the critic or reader can do is walk away from Book V. Of course, not all critics agreed with this view. But most of us, like Harry Berger and I, voted with our feet: we simply didn't write much about Book V. On the other hand, critics who took it up felt they had to claim it to be as good as the rest of the poem and on the same terms. In the words of Thomas P. Roche, "Until Book Five of *The Faerie Queene* is accepted as a successful part of the poem, we will not be able to see Spenser's achievement in its true greatness."[2] The monument to this critical endeavor is Angus Fletcher's *The Prophetic Moment*,[3] in which Book V is used to exemplify the magnificent opening account—in my view, the finest my generation produced—of the poetics of *The Faerie Queene*.

Recent modes of interpretation, with their alertness to impasses or contradictions in a piece of writing, have been more open to what is interesting

---

[1] *Reading Spenser: An Introduction to* The Faerie Queene (New York, 1968), p. 176.
[2] This statement appears on the dust jacket, of T.K. Dunseath, *Spenser's Allegory of Justice in Book Five of* The Faerie Queene (Princeton, 1968).
[3] *The Prophetic Moment: An Essay on Spenser* (Chicago, 1971).

and at times vital in Book V. Even passages that fail poetically are not occasions for apology or dismay, but are taken to be part of the evidence the book presents about its project. This is what various recent critical practices have taught me, and I hope this paper suggests how I have benefited. I want to begin with a line in Book V and show one way in which it can help us construe Spenser in the '90s.

I first encountered this line not in *The Faerie Queene* itself, but in C. S. Lewis's *The Allegory of Love*. "Even the innocent trappings of the courtly life do not attract [Spenser]," Lewis says; "he dismisses the externals of a tournament as contemptuously as Milton himself: to describe them, he says, 'Were worke fit for an Herauld, not for me.'"[4] Fifty years later, and without sharing Lewis's belief in the "exquisite health" of Spenser's imagination, Richard C. McCoy interpreted this line in similar terms. He calls it "a quiet but striking declaration of poetic independence, in which the writer asserts his freedom from the details of courtly pomp and pageantry and the demands of merely documentary accuracy."[5] The line is indeed striking. It occurs when the narrator is recounting the gathering "of Lords and Ladies infinite great store" for the wedding of Florimell and Marinell:

> To tell the glorie of the feast that day,
> The goodly seruice, the deuicefull sights,
> The bridegromes state, the brides most rich aray,
> The pride of Ladies, and the worth of knights,
> The royall banquets, and the rare delights
> Were worke fit for an Herauld, not for me. (5.3.3)[6]

This is better than the usual *praeteritio*: rather than saying it will not declare what it then declares, it lays out a lovely Spenserian listing, which it then renounces. As Lewis saw, it is a vigorous gesture of dismissal, but it is not as secure as he and McCoy take it to be.

The stanza concludes by stating the proper work of this canto:

> But for so much as to my lot here lights,
> That with this present treatise doth agree,
> True vertue to aduance, shall here recounted bee.

But the canto's purposes as a "treatise" of justice come into conflict with the romance narration the poet has just renounced.[7] The conflict is apparent in the two episodes of appearance and reality which occupy the middle of the canto.

---

[4] *Allegory of Love: A Study of Medieval Tradition* (London, 1936), p. 329.

[5] *The Rites of Knighthood: The Literature and Politics of Elizabethan Chivalry* (Berkeley and Los Angeles, 1989), p. 143.

[6] All quotations are from *The Faerie Queene*, ed. J.C. Smith (Oxford, 1909).

[7] To judge from the *Oxford English Dictionary*, the modern meaning of "treatise" was its dominant sense from the beginning. This is the only occurrence of the word in Spenser's poetry.

First, Artegall, berating Braggadocchio, exposes him as a pretender. This is immediately followed by the confrontation between Florimell and the false Florimell. Artegall calls for this as part of his endeavor to settle all accounts, and to him Braggadocchio's lady is "some fayre Franion, fit for such a fere" (5.3.22). But the actual confrontation of the two ladies is an occasion of wonderment and has an entirely different tone. Following Katherine Eggert's lead, we might say that the scenes are differently gendered.[8] Artegall's harsh masculine assertiveness, which includes displaying his wounds (5.3.22), is set against the feminine loveliness with which the false Florimell disappears:

> As when the daughter of *Thaumantes* faire,
> Hath in a watry cloud displayed wide
> Her goodly bow, which paints the liquid ayre ...
> So did this Ladies goodly forme decay. (5.3.25)

The contrast between the two episodes is so pointed that it seems intentional. But if so, this is an instance in which the poet's awareness does not guarantee expressive coherence or artistic control.

The end of canto 3 shows that the relation between chivalric romance and the treatise of justice is an uneasy one. After the ridiculous scene in which Guyon is proved to be the owner of the horse which Braggadocchio stole, Artegall, enraged when the pretender knight resents his judgment, moves to kill him. Guyon pacifies him in the following terms:

> Sir knight, it would dishonour bee
> To you, that are our iudge of equity,
> To wreake your wrath on such a carle as hee:
> It's punishment enough, that all his shame doe see. (5.3.36)

Artegall is calmed, but as in other cases, his impulses are played out by Talus, who administers a savage punishment. It is not enough to say that Spenser is aware, as he clearly is, of the distinction between social judgment and judicial punishment. His insistence on the punishment, which goes on for two stanzas (5.3.37-8), shows that he has confidence neither in the civility and adequacy of Guyon's words nor in the kind of episode we find in Guyon's own book of the poem—the witty correction of the hero at a moment of excess or impasse.

Spenser certainly recognizes a world in which ease and generosity of wit are at home. The penultimate stanza of the canto begins:

> Now when these counterfeits were thus vncased
> Out of the foreside of their forgerie,
> And in the sight of all men cleane disgraced ... (5.3.39)

---

[8] "'Changing all that forme of common weale': Genre and the Repeal of Queenship in *The Faerie Queene*, Book 5," *English Literary Renaissance* 26 (1996), 259-90.

The poet speaks of "these counterfeits" in the plural presumably to assimilate the exposé of the false Florimell to the judicial punishment of Braggadocchio's "forgerie." But in the rest of the stanza, the process is reversed and Braggadocchio's deception is assimilated to the false Florimell's:

> All gan to iest and gibe full merilie
> At the remembrance of their knauerie.
> Ladies can laugh at Ladies, Knights at Knights,
> To thinke with how great vaunt of brauerie
> He them abused, through his subtill slights,
> And what a glorious shew he made in all their sights. (5.3.39)

The easier, somewhat Chaucerian tone of these lines recalls the romance mode of Book IV, which is continually engaged with issues of plausible appearance and social reality. Book V is committed to treating them with Artegallian rigor, so the final stanza of this canto consciously bids farewell to "all deare delices and rare delights, / Fit for such Ladies and such louely knights." But these lines recall the world of romance even as the poem turns away from it. It is such recurrences of the romance mode in this canto, revealing at each moment what its exclusion will cost the poem, which shows the insufficiency of the initial renunciation.

But there is another sense, beyond the internal conflicts of canto 3, in which Spenser cannot disown "worke fit for an Herauld." Some of his finest poetry of the 1590s answers precisely to that description. The herald's task of blazoning forth noble personages and their accoutrements is at the heart of *Prothalamion* and is given extended scope in the poet's marshaling of local deities and human attendants in the ceremony of *Epithalamion*. The splendors of Spenserian listing, which occasioned the poet's gesture of renunciation in Book V, are on full display in these poems. One sees them too in another of the great late pieces, the procession of the seasons and the months in the *Mutability Cantos*. Heralds were minor officials and functionaries, and I am struck by the fact that it is just such a figure, Order, identified as "Natures Sergeant" (7.7.4), who brings in the procession of the seasons and the months. Order functions, to quote the *Oxford English Dictionary*'s definition of "sergeant," as "an officer whose duty is to enforce the judgements of a tribunal or the commands of a person in authority." His first act is to arrange the places of those who attend the trial, an act performed by Nature herself in Chaucer's *Parlement of Foules*; later, he obeys Nature's command to summon the seasons and months as evidence in the trial. Spenser's adding the figure of Order to his Chaucerian source brings out what Gordon Teskey reminds us of—that the testing of Mutability's claims is not merely a metaphysical contemplation, but a judicial and political process.[9]

---

[9] "Mutability, Genealogy, and the Authority of Forms," *Representations* 41 (1993), 104-22.

But how is the presence of this judicial officer connected with the poetic brilliance of the procession he ushers in?—for this is what I have suggested in associating his function with heraldic listing. Let us consider the relation between the poet and the figures who initiate two other processions in *The Faerie Queene*. The masque of Busyrane is introduced by the figure of Ease, who is initially represented as impressive and who bears a branch of laurel (3.12.3-4); but clearly if we are looking for the poet's self-representation in this episode it is Busyrane himself, the magician who conceives the masque as a whole and who uses the heart's blood of the tortured Amoret to write the "straunge characters of his art" (3.12.31). Busyrane is what Northrop Frye would call a "demonic parody" of the poet himself. Closer in substance to the procession of the seasons and months is the procession of rivers in Book IV. Here there is no figure like Ease or Order. The poet appears as "presenter" in his own person: he begins as narrator by stating his task, to represent all the earth's rivers, and then invokes the aid of the Muse, in an apostrophe that recalls the very beginnings of the poem (4.11.8-10). Where can we locate the figure of the poet in the procession of the seasons and months? The usual view is that the orderliness of the pageant refutes Mutability's case. If so, then the poet would seem to reverse the demonic parody of the Busyrane cantos and implicitly identify with Nature herself, the presiding intelligence at the trial. But any such possibility is blocked by the opening stanzas of canto 7, which emphasize Nature's inaccessibility to ordinary human and authorial comprehension. Following Teskey, I would say that we find the poet partly in the figure of Mutability herself—it is she, after all, who calls for the seasons and months—and partly in the figure of Order. Whatever his name suggests, he cannot provide a summary answer to Mutability; the summary answer, when it is given by Nature, is notoriously puzzling and represented as such. Order can only do what any minor offical does—his job. And this is what the poet himself does in filling out what the "invention" of the procession requires, a representation, one stanza apiece, of each season and month. "Worke fit for a sergeant" is not the whole of the poetic accomplishment of this episode, but it is part of it. If we think of the poet's imaginative allegiance with Mutability combined with an implicit self-representation as the officer charged with an orderly presentation, we can appreciate Teskey's fine sentence about this pageant: "Its beauty proceeds out of a deep and even bitter awareness of the painfulness of life, and ... its courage as art is in the energy, even the cheerfulness, with which the poet transforms this pain into beauty."[10]

This discussion of "worke fit for an Herauld, not for me" has tended to undo the line's negation, in order to suggest that the herald is one of the late Spenser's rhetorical roles. We can align this figure not only with Nature's sergeant Order, but also with direct self-representations which are notable for social diffidence. The most important of these figures, of course, is Colin Clout. But we should also recall the poet's appearance as a plowman, in both

---

[10] Ibid., p. 116.

Book V (3.40) and Book VI (9.1), and there is a question whether he is to be seen in the poet Bonfont, whom we meet, dreadfully punished, at Mercilla's court (5.9.25-6). One of the dedicatory sonnets to *Amoretti* addresses the poet as Colin, and the Petrarchan lover is certainly akin, in his humility and vulnerability, to his pastoral persona.

But I do not want to claim that all Spenser's appearances as a poet are tantamount to the moments in which he appears under one of the figures I have just mentioned. Rather than collapsing the distinction in "worke fit for an Herauld, not for me," I want to follow its lead and ask about the relation or interplay between these representative roles and the poetic first person. Let us recall that the canto in which Colin Clout appears in Book VI begins with the poet, in his own person, weighing the pros and cons of Sir Calidore's pastoral retreat. Furthermore, when Calidore comes upon Colin Clout, the poet as narrator does not disappear into his pastoral self-representation. He draws attention to himself when he asks "who knowes not Colin Clout?" and he concludes the stanza with four lines—beginning "Pype iolly shepheard, pype thou now apace"—in which vivid address gives the narrator a lyrical presence that is separate from the figure who represents him as a lyric poet (6.10.16). Similarly, in the great apostrophe to Gloriana, it is impossible to say whether we are to conceive the speaker of "Pardon thy shepheard, mongst so many layes, / As he hath sung of thee in all his dayes" as the fictional Colin Clout or as the poet himself, who in a literal apostrophe, turns aside from his narration to speak in his own voice (6.10.28).

"Worke fit for an Herauld, not for me" encourages us to heed the relation between the poet's speaking in the first person and his appearing in specific represented roles. *Prothalamion* is a striking example of this double aspect of the lyric Spenser, but I want to conclude by discussing it in the first stanza of *Epithalamion*. The poem begins:

> Ye learned sisters which haue oftentimes
> Beene to me ayding, others to adorne:
> Whom ye thought worthy of your gracefull rymes.[11]

This address to the Muses brings into play the interpenetration of first-person speech and represented poetic roles. "*Whom* ye thought worthy" has a double reference: it can refer both to those others whom the poet praised and to the poet himself, who is able to "adorn" others because he too is worthy of the Muses' "gracefull rhymes." This double syntax brings the Muses, goddesses petitioned by a merely human speaker, into the orbit of "my muse," a figure one frequently encounters in Elizabethan lyric as a representation of the first-person speaker. The next lines add the suggestion of a specific role to this suggestion of "my muse":

---

[11] *Minor Poems*, ed. Ernest de Sélincourt (Oxford, 1910).

> That euen the greatest did not greatly scorne
> To heare theyr names sung in your simple layes.

It would seem odd to call the lays of the learned sisters "simple," were it not
that we already feel the presence of the speaker, doubly dependent on the great
ones he praises and on whatever powers enable him to speak well. We can
accept the attribution of his own simplicity to the goddesses of song, because
behind "your simple layes" we sense the presence of *"my* simple layes."
Furthermore, "simple" is more than a gesture of humility, for it calls up the
poetic role which was Spenser's main explicit self-representation—the
shepherd as singer.

I am not saying that *Epithalamion* is a pastoral, and I don't want to say
simply that the shepherd–singer is one of the roles the poet assumes. Rather,
this role can underlie and inform first-person lyric speech. In the same way, it
is misleading to isolate "The woods shall to me answer and my Eccho ring" as
by itself a version of Virgil's famous line *formosam resonare doces
Amaryllida silvas* ("you teach the woods to resound lovely Amaryllis,"
Eclogues 1.5). It is when we trace the presence of that line throughout the first
stanza of *Epithalamion* that we see how Spenser's refrain is informed by
Virgil's representation of the woods responding to the shepherd in love.

> And when ye list your owne mishaps to mourne,
> Which death, or loue, or fortunes wreck did rayse,
> Your string could soone to sadder tenor turne,
> And teach the woods and waters to lament
> Your dolefull dreriment.

"Teach" is not a surprising word to use of the Muses (though its only use in
The Teares of the Muses [290] is of the pastoral Muse Euterpe). But what
indicates the Virgilian underpinning here is that like his line, Spenser's
suggests the singer's self-enclosure. "When ye list your owne mishaps to
mourne" may send us off in search of a mythological reference, but there
seems to be none. What this line calls up is the poet's own *The Teares of the
Muses* and perhaps other poems in the *Complaints* volume. Once again the
Muses overlap with *"my* muse." These muses of the poet's "teach the woods
and waters to lament," which is not the word in Virgil's line. But that word
emerges when the poet calls on his muses to "helpe me mine owne loues
prayses to *resound.*" Finally, the two lines preceding the refrain show why we
should recognize that these verbal echoes intimate, without specifying, a
particular poetic role:

> So Orpheus did for his owne bride,
> So I vnto my selfe alone will sing.

These lines show exactly the combination of elements we have been
discussing—a self-representation as another figure and a self-presentation in

the first person. The underlying figure of the passionate shepherd is implicated in both the allusion to Orpheus's love lament and the ambiguities of the poet's singing "alone."

What does it mean to have uncovered the herald in Spenser? One way of answering this question is along the lines of Louis Montrose's "Spenser's Domestic Domain."[12] This essay argues that in the years after the 1590 *Faerie Queene*, Spenser's increasing sense of Anglo-Irish identity and of his own cultural authority as a poet led him to resist London, the court, and "the symbolic personage of the Queen" and to represent "alternative centers of authority and ... alternative feminine subjects of celebration" (p. 120). However, Montrose resists construing Spenser's poetry in the '90s in terms of a "split between the public and private spheres of poetic and poetically represented experience" (p. 95). He is insistent that the apparently "private" poet, such as we might infer from his appearance as Colin Clout and as the first-person speaker of his own epithalamion, is very much a public presence, both because he appears in print (and with conspicuous reference to his other writings) and because so much of his identity is bound up with material social circumstances, chief among them his becoming a landowner in Kilcolman. Montrose equally resists viewing the poet—either the real person whose biography we construe or the figure who appears in his poems—as entirely determined by his society's structures of power. But he wants us to recognize that for Spenser, the claim of poetic authority is necessarily imagined as and profoundly complicated by a claim for social authority. We can thus find a considerable irony in Spenser's dismissing "worke fit for an Herauld." For what is that work? Heralds were experts in coats of arms and had originally functioned at tournaments to identify the participants and judge the performances; this is the role Spenser rejects as narrator of Book V. But expertise in coats of arms led to heraldry as professional knowledge, and in sixteenth-century England, where the crown sought to control social ranks and be the source of all honors, the College of Arms, staffed by heralds, determined who had a claim to coats of arms and to the various noble ranks.[13] If, as Montrose argues, "Spenser's motives were undoubtedly to affirm his status as a gentleman" (p. 97), the way to confirm this status was with a coat of arms. So Spenser's term comes back to bite him. Saying he is better than a herald, Montrose might argue, reveals his anxiety about the need to persuade the heralds of his merits. Though he does not take notice of this line, Montrose points out that in 1595, the year of *Colin Clouts Come Home Againe*, the Spencers of Althorp, the noble family with whom the poet regularly asserted his connection, had the Clarenceux King of Arms concoct a pedigree that would show the family's antiquity.

---

[12] "Spenser's Domestic Domain: Poetry, Property, and the Early Modern Subject," in *Subject and Object in Renaissance Culture*, ed. Margreta de Grazia, Maureen Quilligan and Peter Stallybrass (Cambridge, 1996), pp. 83-130.

[13] See Mervyn James, *Society, Politics, and Culture: Studies in Early Modern England* (Cambridge, 1986), pp. 327-9, 333-7.

Montrose's cultural and materialist critique of Spenser's career is differently inflected from, but not fundamentally at odds with, my own more formalist assessment of Spenser in the '90s. The conflicts we have traced in Book V, canto 3 are among the many signs that the epic–allegorical project of *The Faerie Queene* was coming apart. I entirely agree with Roger Sale that something happened to the poem: as I have argued elsewhere, the pastoral cantos of Book VI, precisely by their poetic distinction, reveal how unsatisfactory is the ensuing heroic narration.[14] Just as the pastoral episode—and particularly Colin Clout's discourse on the Graces—is set apart from heroic knighthood in Book VI, so Spenser's poems of the 1590s constitute an alternative body of work to further installments of his epic. In a sense, however, they continue the project of *The Faerie Queene*. They contain much—mythological representations, issues of political and courtly service, love as both human experience and cosmic force—that could have found a place in *The Faerie Queene*. Formally, these poems (all of them in genres that are new for Spenser) are what we might call "public lyrics." The poet speaks in the first person, but on public occasions (*Prothalamion*) or about public situations (in *Colin Clouts Come Home Againe*) or about love impersonally conceived as a cosmic reality (*Fowre Hymnes*). Spenser's innovation in *Epithalamion*—celebrating his own marriage in a genre which is character-istically employed on consequential occasions, often a royal or aristocratic wedding—suggests strong claims of authority and entitlement. Hence, we should not be surprised that *Epithalamion* recalls his epic pageants in its cosmic staging, its moral and symbolic scope, and its mythological personages, or that the poet constitutes the first-person speaker of the poem in ways that recall moments of authorial rhetoric and self-representation in *The Faerie Queene*. If *The Faerie Queene* itself is threatened with disintegration in its later books, each of these public lyrics can be regarded as what the poem's final installment, the *Two Cantos of Mutabilitie*, explicitly is—a coherent fragment of the original epic and allegorical project.

---

[14] "Spenser's Late Pastorals," *English Literary History* 56 (1989), 797-817.

8

The Enfolding Dragon:
Arthur and the Moral Economy of
The Faerie Queene

Susanne L. Wofford

To interpret the extended celebratory ecphrasis with which Prince Arthur enters the poem, the reader of Spenser's *Faerie Queene* (sixteenth- or twentieth-century) similarly must enter into a landscape characterized by peculiar and unexpected tensions between esthetic, religious, and political (national and courtly) meanings.[1] What is most striking about Arthur in his appearance is his resistance to allegorical meaning or intentionality. He remains Prince Arthur, a character described in an unusually consistent chivalric idiom from the moment of his appearance in Book I until his departure from the poem in Book VI. Some interpreters of the poem respond to the many possible meanings that may be attached to Arthur by choosing one as the primary or determining symbolism, and leave the matter there. Arthur, then, may be said to embody the virtue of magnificence (as Spenser tells us he is intended to do in the "Letter to Raleigh"), which itself may refer to Aristotle's concept of magnanimity, or may be a combination of aristocratic munificence, patronage, and another version of the Glory to which the poem in one aspect of itself may be devoted. But "magnificence" recedes from view in the course of the narrative, since Spenser seems to identify Arthur at the moment of his entry with "heavenly grace" (1.8.1). C.S. Lewis was perhaps one of the most honest of twentieth-century critics when he commented about Arthur in *Allegory of Love*: "It will be noticed that I have made no mention yet of Prince Arthur. The regrettable truth is that in the unfinished state of the

---

[1] As will become apparent, this essay relies on the excellent work of Kenneth Gross in his account of the poem's iconoclastic romance with idolatry (*Spenserian Poetics: Idolatry, Iconoclasm, and Magic* [Ithaca, 1985]), of Darryl Gless, in his rereading of the nature of Arthur's heroism (*Interpretation and Theology in Spenser* [Cambridge and New York, 1994]), of Michael Leslie in his studies of armor (*Spenser's 'Fierce warres and faithfull loves': Chivalry and Martial Symbolism in* The Faerie Queene [Cambridge and New Jersey, 1983]), and of Paul Alpers's study of Spenser's use of Ariosto (*The Poetry of* The Faerie Queene [Princeton, 1967]). For congruences and tensions between political and religious symbolisms of Arthur, see David Lee Miller, *The Poem's Two Bodies: The Poetics of the 1590* Faerie Queene (Princeton, 1988), esp. pp. 126-9 and 139-42. For the argument that the religious and political aims of the poem are not always reconcilable, see my argument in *The Choice of Achilles: The Ideology of Figure in the Epic* (Stanford, 1992), esp. pp. 256-62 and pp. 311-53.

poem we cannot interpret its hero at all."[2] This essay proposes that Arthur becomes a central figure—perhaps the central figure—through which Spenser attempts to work out the deeper implications of his poem's effort to unite religion, politics, and romance. What analogy pertains, in other words, between chivalric romance and the work of grace? Attempting to understand the role that Arthur plays in the poem, and the reasons that the imagery associated with him is overdetermined, is also to reconsider the place, in our readings of Spenser at the turn of the millennium, of theories of symbol and narrative that connect Spenser's methods to concerns of genre or figuration. One of the challenges that faces historicist readers of the poem is to explain why Spenser is so committed to the romance texture of his poem, and why chivalry might possibly be thought a vehicle with which to express the workings of grace.[3]

The Dragon in Spenser's Typology

The hero enters the poem in a long description that seems to incorporate all of the previous threats of the poem, now somehow purified, transformed or at least controlled or contained (see 1.7.29-36):

> At last she [Una] chaunced by good hap to meet
> A goodly knight, faire marching by the way
> Together with his Squire, arayed meet:
> His glitterand armour shined farre away,
> Like glauncing light of Phoebus brightest ray ...
>
> His haughtie helmet, horrid all with gold,
> Both glorious brightnesse, and great terrour bred;
> For all the crest a Dragon did enfold
> With greedie pawes, and ouer all did spred
> His golden wings: his dreadfull hideous hed
> Close couched on the beuer, seem'd to throw
> From flaming mouth bright sparkles fierie red,
> That suddeine horror to faint hearts did show;
> And scaly tayle was stretcht adowne his backe full low.
> (1.7.29, 31)[4]

---

[2] C.S. Lewis, *The Allegory of Love: A Study in Medieval Tradition* (Oxford, 1936), p. 336.

[3] For a political explanation of the attraction of chivalric romance to Spenser, see Richard Helgerson ("The Politics of Chivalric Romance," in *Forms of Nationhood: The Elizabethan Writing of England* [Chicago, 1992], pp. 40-59), who argues that romance as a genre can be associated with a late feudal formation of independent aristocratic power, which sought to resist or even rebel against the growing power and control of the absolutist monarchy.

[4] All citations of Spenser's *Faerie Queene* are taken from A.C. Hamilton's edition (London, 1977).

One of ways in which this return of past threats, now domesticated or estheticized, can be understood is through the language of typology: using the concept of "figura," and appropriating for Spenser, in other words, what David Miller has called the "New Testament's authoritative metalepsis, or reversal of priority over the Hebrew scriptures."[5] We are able to read Arthur's entry as presenting an extended anti-type to the earlier images, the "true" or life-giving version of what we now see as the dead letter of the prideful or otherwise corrupted versions of experience. Thus, just as Arthur's "glitterand" armour uncomfortably reflects the glittering palace of Lucifera, so the dragon which has weaved through the narrative from its partial incarnation in Errour's den to its appearance in a spot under Lucifera's throne now suddenly appears in the dragon crest on Arthur's helmet. Conversely, the "trembling leaves" used in the Almond tree simile to describe the "bunch of hairs discolord diversly" on Arthur's helm retrospectively refer to or "fulfill" (in the language of typology) the image of the trembling leaves of the Fradubio and Fraelissa metamorphosis (1.2.28). The structure of Book I seems to suggest a deep structural divide, whereby readers (and perhaps poet) meet first the evil or literal version of these much repeated images, and then need to learn to recognize the redemptive or restorative version. Thus, the dangerous wood of error and the imprisoning tree of Fradubio suggest that trees and woodiness—perhaps matter itself, as in Servius's glosses on the woods in Book VI of *The Aeneid*—might be said to find their redemptive version in the salvific tree that drips balm on Redcrosse in canto 11 (1.11.46), while the water associated with the threat of Duessa's sexuality (a threat expressed both in her bathing scene, and in the later moment when Redcrosse Knight, having drunk from the nymph's stream is "pourd out in loosnesse on the grassy grownd"[1.7.7]) and even more widely again with human experience in this world—"all that in the wide deepe wandring arre" (1.2.1)—is redeemed by the health-bringing water from the well of life that saves Redcrosse during the dragon fight (1.11.29). This typological structure is too familiar from close readings of Book I and of Dante's *Commedia* to need to be detailed any further here. Though this pattern may seem to be mostly characteristic of Book I, in fact it can be shown to run throughout *The Faerie Queene*, if in more disguised form. The moment of Arthur's appearance in canto 7 is the beginning of the turn, and the dragon crest, in particular, can serve as a means to test the theories of typology and symbolic structure that have directed our understanding of the episode and of the poem—theories of interpretation that accept as part of the cultural and religious meaning of the work the need to read according to the spirit and not the letter, the need to learn to read figuratively as a way of avoiding idolatry, as a way of discovering the hidden Christian meaning in the literalisms of in this case not the Old Testament but the fictions of chivalric romance.[6]

---

[5] Miller, *The Poem's Two Bodies*, p. 90.

[6] See also Ernest Gilman, *Iconoclasm and Poetry in the English Reformation* (Chicago, 1986), p. 31 and ch. 2; David Norbrook, *Poetry and Politics in the English*

   The difficulty with reading these doubles (threatening trees, restorative trees, and so on) simply as characteristic symbolic oppositions of romance or allegory is that if we follow the logic of such oppositions,[7] the Spenser who emerges seems to be able to find little goodness in the world, in "the wide deepe," in matter, in the body, or in the fallen human being: the poem begins to look resolutely dualistic, and the physical world can no longer be seen as the place of incarnation, a location of the merging of divine and human form. It appears to be not the place of redemption but the site of disgust and evil. C.S. Lewis again provided a still-useful commentary on a similar problem in the poem when he wrote about the very ending of *The Mutabilitie Cantos* that it represents "a magnificent instance of Spenser's last-minute withdrawal from dualism."[8] If we followed the symbolic oppositions to their logical conclusions, Redcrosse's battle with "That Old Dragon" would need to be read as a battle against the body itself, a desire to eradicate the physical from the self—a gesture that finally is tantamount to suicide (perhaps part of the dust to which Arthur's shield reduces his enemies). It would be to try to kill off the very imagery and matter that makes up the poem—to eradicate the glittering surface itself. I would argue, then, with Lewis, and with Ken Gross (who has written movingly about Spenser's anti-apocalyptics) and with Richard McCabe, who writes that Spenser cannot be seen as writing in an intensely apocalyptic manner in the context of the highly apocalyptic 1590s, that part of this poet's project is to articulate a Protestant vision that will also somehow avoid requiring an apocalyptically dualistic universe.[9] Revisiting these questions may allow us to redefine the kind of ambivalent articulations of meaning that seem characteristic not only of allegory as a mode but of this allegorical epic in its national and religious efforts at self-definition.

   The theory of typology helps us to step around the problem of dualism, by suggesting that the type—tree, water, glittering light, trembling leaves, dragon—is not negated but fulfilled by the anti-type. The literal trees—the wandering wood—would kill, would be only evil (or only Ovidian and Virgilian, or only a romance topos) if they were not cast into this larger temporal scheme according to which what comes first is reread and reunderstood following a paradigm applied retrospectively.[10]

Renaissance (London, 1984), p. 111; and John N. King, *Spenser's Poetry and the Reformation Tradition* (Princeton, 1990), pp. 66-9, on the way that Protestant attacks on idolatry could make the distrust of the image the first step in a constructive production of literature and art.

[7] On the dualistic structuring of allegory itself, see Angus Fletcher, *Allegory: The Theory of a Symbolic Mode* (Ithaca, 1964).

[8] Lewis, *Allegory of Love*, p. 356.

[9] Kenneth Gross, "'Each Heav'nly Close': Mythologies and Metrics in Spenser and the Early Poetry of Milton," *Publications of the Modern Language Association of America* 98 (1983), 21-36; Richard McCabe, *The Pillars of Eternity: Time and Providence in* The Faerie Queene (Dublin, 1989).

[10] See King, *Spenser's Poetry and the Reformation Tradition*, chs. 2 and 3, esp. pp. 79-93, for an excellent illustration of Book I's movement from Protestant iconoclasm through the typology of Revelations to locating a place for the non-toxic poetic image.

The Tree and the Well of canto 11 can clearly be best understood as both examples of Christian allegory and of a typological allegory that fulfills, explains and gives meaning to the earlier adventures set in the world. But these are examples that come directly out of the New Testament and its own transumptive schemes for self-authorization by means of appropriation of the Hebrew scriptures, reunderstood as the "Old" Testament. The matter becomes more difficult when we look more closely at images or ideas that come from the romance or epic origins of the poem, for to reconsider typology—to reconsider any kind of metaleptic system by which retrospectively we reread the past as pointing towards a *telos* already defined—is to reconsider the nature of origins, and specifically to question the position of etiology within the epic romance. Also, as the very structure of typology depends upon a retrospective appropriation of meaning that inverts cause and effect, origin and ending, to reconsider typology is to re-examine the use of prophecy in the poem.[11]

It is clear that, in terms of time scheme, a secular and political typology is at work in the general use of the Arthurian matter—a typology that has been well described by Richard McCabe in *The Pillars of Eternity*. By typology here I mean a temporal structure whereby Arthur is seen not only as the ancestor or forerunner of the Tudors, but as the prophetic prefiguration of them—*Rex Quondam Rexque Futurus*—thus reunderstanding the Tudors, and especially in this case Elizabeth herself, as part of a prophetic time scheme in which the current success of the monarchy should point to a greater glory to come. This use of prophecy, so evident in the poem, has generally been interpreted through the lens of Tudor propaganda and the Tudor myth of history, and therefore has been read only as a system by which the Tudors attempted to legitimize themselves, and, by extension, Spenser attempted to flatter them and to participate in that act of legitimation. This kind of analysis leads to a view of Spenser as essentially a brilliant propagandist. Both Andrew Hadfield and Richard McCabe have suggested in contrast a very different valuation to the poem's invocation of prophecy—McCabe reminding us that "the *Faerie Queene* is future-oriented in the sense that Arthurian heroism is as much an ideal towards which Britain must strive as an image of past glory."[12] In speaking about the abrupt breaking-off of Arthur's chronicle, the *Briton moniments*—"after him Vther, which Pendragon hight, / Succeeding There abruptly it did end, / Without full point, or other Cesure right" (2.10.68)—a dramatic breaking-off of ending matched only by the unfinished Merlin's unfinished epic catalogue of Britomart's ancestors ("But yet the end is not" [3.3.50]), Hadfield comments, "A clear warning is given that just as a book can

---

[11] For a brilliant account of the complexities of prophetic utterance, and for the political ambiguities and dangers of prophecy, see Howard Dobin, *Merlin's Disciples: Prophecy, Poetry and Power in Renaissance England* (Stanford, 1990), esp. pp. 1-8 and ch. 1. For a fuller account of the inversion of cause and effect in allegorical reasoning and for its relation to prophetic and metaleptic narratives, see my *The Choice of Achilles*, pp. 262-81.

[12] McCabe, *The Pillars of Eternity*, p. 51.

be torn so can a dynasty if it is not looked after properly."[13] "Prophecy," he adds a bit later, "serves as a radical and dangerous political discourse expressing current forebodings."[14] In this vision of the poem, readers are urged to recognize the dark guises through which Spenser's poem can speak with "a critical voice."[15] Hadfield argues that "the unfinished poem mirrors the split body politics; the *Faerie Queene* stands or falls on the hope for a national public sphere."[16] Hadfield's reasoning here helps to show how the nationalism of the poem is a more serious project than might be suggested by the notion that the poem either praises the monarch (flattery) or reincarnates a Tudor myth of legitimacy. In fact, by importing this secular prophetic dimension the poem is discovering an avenue by which it can articulate what are viewed as crucial failings in the Elizabethan body politic, beginning with the problem of the succession, but going beyond it to the broader articulation of nationalism with religion.

One convention of Spenser criticism has been to conjugate the romance and epic allegory with the religious allegory, to read the kind of secular prophetic structure by which the Arthurian matter is embedded in the poem as though it were seamlessly one with the use of biblical typology with which I have begun. This is a strategy I would like to question by turning now to the problem of Arthur's armor. It is more difficult than it might at first seem to read the ecphrasis of Arthur's armor as part of a biblical typological structure, because that organization of imagery implies that this dragon must somehow be the good, providential, or benevolent (or at least a conquered) version of the dragon, while many details of the dragon crest lead us to question this assertion. Here, again, is the description of the crest:

> His haughtie helmet, horrid all with gold,
> Both glorious brightnesse, and great terrour bred;
> For all the crest a Dragon did enfold
> With greedie pawes, and ouer all did spred
> His golden wings: his dreadfull hideous hed
> Close couched on the beuer, seem'd to throw
> From flaming mouth bright sparkles fierie red,
> That suddeine horror to faint hearts did show;
> And scaly tayle was stretcht adowne his backe full low.
> (1.7.32)

The dragon here seems surprisingly alive and powerful, in the way that he enfolds the crest with "greedie pawes." Although Spenser tells us that he has golden wings, it is easy to feel that this dragon is alive, not only a representation. Of course, some respond differently. Michael Leslie has written

---

[13] Andrew Hadfield, *Literature, Politics and National Identity: Reformation to Renaissance* (Cambridge, 1994), p. 195.
[14] Ibid., p. 198.
[15] Ibid., p. 200.
[16] Ibid., p. 201.

that "the impression of the dragon's submission is strengthened by Spenser's use of the word 'couched.' The poet avoids the normal heraldic term for this type of pose, 'couchant' ... and instead Spenser uses a form associated with real rather than symbolic animals. 'Couched' describes an animal crouching or cowering in obedience or fear ... Prince Arthur's dragon, its tail stretched down well out of the way, has also been mastered ..."[17] It is more difficult than Leslie allows, however, to conclude that Spenser's description of the dragon crest indicates an image that is domesticated and contained, because the word "enfold" suggests something very close to the state of being wrapped in the dragon's "traine," while the detail that the mouth "seems" to flame and to sparkle fiery red insists that we recognize that this image still threatens, if perhaps its power has been somehow harnessed by Arthur in ways that I will go on to discuss. Certainly, the image echoes specific problems with dragons that have beseiged the Redcrosse Knight earlier in Book I or will do so. Thus, danger from the dragon's flaming breath will threaten Redcrosse Knight severely in canto 11, stanza 26 and again in stanza 44. In the final dragon fight when the dragon attacks the shield itself, Redcrosse is for a while unable to free his shield from the grip of the dragon (1.11.41), as if the dragon had become a horrific and literalized version of a heraldic dragon on a shield.

The image of the tail stretched down his back is also disturbing after seven cantos' worth of images of characters being wrapped in different ways in the endless tails/tales of Errour and Pride. It also alludes proleptically to the power of the Dragon's tail in the final battle where Redcrosse's horse (perhaps symbolizing the passions) will be wrapped entirely in the real dragon's tail in a crucial moment of the battle (1.11.23). So, at least, we must conclude that Spenser is reminding us of the dangers of "That Old Dragon" even while he is representing the dragon as an image that may serve to enhance, not threaten, Arthur's power, both heroic and spiritual.

Kathleen Williams articulated the idea that the dragon symbolizes Arthur's power when commenting that "Arthur's dragon [on his crest] is now part of his strength, while Red Crosse's is still to fight."[18] This logic still assumes in some degree a typological pattern that connects Arthur's dragon crest with all the dragons throughout Book I, a pattern culminating in the great dragon beast of the Apocalypse, which the Redcrosse Knight has the good fortune to be able to fight in canto 11. Darryl Gless most recently and most persuasively has followed this line of argument and taken what I see as the anti-dualistic implications of the scriptural typology seriously. His is the best explanation of how to incorporate the dragon within a Christian framework, though Hamilton's notes on how to read the dragon as the scourge of God lead towards some similar insights. Gless is arguing, however, not that the dragon is the scourge of God, but rather that the presence of the dragon represents a kind

---

[17] Leslie, *Spenser's "Fierce warres and faithfull loves,"* p. 54.
[18] Kathleen Williams, *Spenser's World of Glass: A Reading of* The Faerie Queene (Berkeley, 1966), p. 22.

of strength in Arthur, a capacity that has to do with not simply turning the letter into the figure or by a process of transumption eliminating the body as a part of the moral equation. Here is the core of Gless's argument about the dragon crest:

> For readers prepared to assimilate the hero's armor to its Pauline antecedents, these lines present Arthur's 'helmet of salvation' in a shape that both surprises and potentially carries its own commentary. For interpreters thinking in generic terms—and I will do that in just a minute—of course, the dragon helmet might recall a variety of antecedents: the chimaerae on Turnus' shield in *Aeneid* 7, Arthur's helmet in Geoffrey of Monmouth, or the dragon on Soliman's helmet in *Jerusalem Delivered*. Literally, of course, all these express the military utility of fierce-looking armor when it is turned against faint hearts ... The likelihood is that the dragon-helmet expresses a terrifying aspect of the power that Arthur represents, a divine power which inherently inspires salutary terror. Embedded in, even crowning Arthur's helmet, the source of this terror can be seen as a salient part of the elect man's best defence and of his 'hope of salvation.' In a remarkably novel way, Arthur's helmet invites the recognition that the old serpent himself plays a necessary role in humankind's individual and collective salvation. The dragon must somehow belong to the spiritual equipment that believers put on when grace enables them to don the whole armor of God.[19]

Gless suggests also that we need to reunderstand Arthur as himself struggling and growing spiritually—as a figure in whom the Old Man and the New Man are still in tension, and therefore as a character who enacts the redemption brought by grace but not Grace itself.

In what sense can "That Olde Dragon" be a part of a Christian's armor unless we read the dragon, with Michael Leslie, as having been overcome? In comparable classical myths to which I will turn shortly, Perseus can use the Medusa head as an image because he has literally conquered and beheaded Medusa; has the artist conquered "That Olde Dragon" when he represents him? We remain fundamentally unsure how the dragon can serve as part of Arthur's armor. Gless rightly wants to read this image more profoundly as an attempt on Spenser's part to articulate a deeper sense in which the salvation of individual and nation will finally triumph uncompromised by the things about human and material life signified by that old dragon.

The Dragon, The Epic and the Medusa

The ambivalence of this description of Arthur is perhaps felt most keenly if we examine the epic sources for the dragon crest. It seems certain that Spenser was thinking both of Virgil's description of Turnus's helmet topped by the

---

[19] Gless, *Interpretation and Theology in Spenser*, p. 127.

Chimaera in *The Aeneid*, and Tasso's description of the Sultan's Helmet in *Jerusalem Delivered*. The Sultan's dragon is aggressive: it raises itself up on its legs and curves up in an arc its forked tail;[20] it also seems to be almost alive, as might seem appropriate for an image representing the enemy:

> Porta il Soldan su l'elmo orrido e grande
> serpe che si dilunga e il collo snoda,
> su le zampe s'inalza e l'ali spande
> e piega in arco la forcuta coda.
> Par che tre lingue vibri e che fuor mande
> livida spuma, a che 'l suo fischio s'oda.
> Ed or ch'arde la pugna, anch'ei s'infiamma
> nel moto, e fumo versa insieme e fiamma. (9.25)[21]

> High on the Soldan's helm enamell'd laid
> A hideous dragon, arm'd with many a scale,
> With iron paws, and leathern wings display'd,
> Which twisted in a knot her forked tale;
> With triple tongue it seem'd she hiss'd and bray'd;
> About her jaws the froth and venom trail,
> And as he stirr'd, and as his foes him hit,
> So flames to cast and fire she seem'd to spit.[22]

The sense of the mythic power of the represented monster is even stronger in the Chimaera on Turnus's helmet, which is exhaling fires and which roars and spreads terror in violence that matches and represents the battle.

> Ipse inter primos praestanti corpore Turnus
> vertitur arma tenens et toto vertice supra est.
> cui triplici crinita iuba galea alta Chimaeram
> sustinet Aetnaeos efflantem faucibus ignis;
> tam magis illa fremens et tristibus effera flammis
> quam magis effuso crudescunt sanguine pugnae. (7.783-8)[23]

> Turnus himself came on, a mighty figure
> Moving among the captains blade in hand
> And by a head the tallest. His high helm
> With triple plume bore a Chimaera's head
> Exhaling Aetnean fires—raging the more
> With savage heat the more blood flowed, the wilder
> Grew the battle. (7.1077-83)[24]

---

[20] I echo in this phrase Leslie's translation, p. 53.

[21] All citations of Torquato Tasso's *Gerusalemme liberata* are taken from Lanfranco Caretti's edition (Turino, 1971).

[22] *Jerusalem Delivered: The Edward Fairfax Translation* (1600), intro. by Roberto Weiss (Carbondale, Ill., 1962).

[23] Citations of Virgil's *Aeneid* are taken from R.D. Williams's two-volume edition with his commentary (London, 1972-3).

[24] *The Aeneid of Virgil*, trans. Robert Fitzgerald (New York, 1981).

R.D. Williams comments on this passage:

> This is a splendid piece of imaginative symbolism; on one level it
> can be rationalized into the hot passion of Turnus in battle, but on
> another it deliberately defies the limitations of the inanimate ... The
> Chimaera was amongst the monsters in the jaws of hell. Its
> significance as a symbol for Turnus is not only fierceness and
> strength, but also primitive and archaic violence; it is the kind of
> monster of which a Hercules would rid the world to everyone's
> benefit. The association with Aetna, with volcanic violence, with the
> giants, strengthens this concept.[25]

Spenser's Arthur is thus shown here to have a power that likens him to Turnus
and to the primitive and contaminating violences of this danger—and even to
the Sultan, the foreign other, the non-Christian enemy. Marlowe responded to
these images by adopting the description of Arthur's armor to describe
Tamburlaine, his heroic destroyer (to use Gross's words).[26] To put the situation
simply, these are representatives in their poems of the forces of evil. They are
great warriors, but destructive: why should Arthur be compared to them?
Kenneth Gross comments about this dense, and powerfully visual passage:

> ... that the poet should have located his emblem of his chief hero at a
> threshold where magical vision cannot quite be distinguished from
> idolatry, or a proper image of the knight's self separated from the
> manifestations of a power beyond that self, is part of the dragon's
> peculiar, perversely clarifying force. In the long run, the allegorical
> watcher constitutes a talismanic defense against the reductions (the
> 'evil eye') of allegorical reading ...[27]

Thus, for Gross, the threat to be warded off by this representation is two-fold:
on the one hand, the threat of the literal, of the idol, of the worship of image
(this passage certainly seems prominently to display an enjoyment of the
power of images), but on the other the threat of the reductions of allegorical
reading, the threat that the figure will somehow become not that which will
save us from the letter but a tyrannical reduction that enslaves.

An additional source for the crest is Achilles's armor as it appears in
some Renaissance paintings. Although not in *The Iliad*, the dragon crest is
given to Achilles in some visual representations of the Trojan legend, "as can
be seen," Michael Leslie comments, "in Giulio Romano's version of the hero
in the Palazzo Ducale in Mantua."[28] Achilles certainly seems a more
appropriate heroic comparison for Arthur than Turnus, and indeed a simile
used to describe the dragon's eyes resembles closely an epic simile involving
Achilles. Here the simile connects the dragon not with danger but with that

---

[25] Williams, op. cit., 2: 225.

[26] *Tamburlaine* II (4.4.115-21).

[27] Gross, *Spenserian Poetics*, p. 135.

[28] Leslie, *Spenser's "Fierce warres and faithfull loves,"* p. 55.

which would warn of danger—the good watchers who set warning beacons in fields:

> His blazing eyes, like two bright shining shields,
> Did burne with wrath, and sparkled liuing fyre;
> As two broad Beacons, set in open fields,
> Send forth their flames farre off to euery shyre,
> And warning giue, that enemies conspyre,
> With fire and sword the region to inuade;
> So flam'd his eyne with rage and rancorous yre:
> But farre within, as in a hollow glade,
> Those glaring lampes were set, that made a dreadfull shade.
> (1.11.14)

An analogy to a simile in the *Iliad* highlights this as an epic moment in Spenser's poem. Homer tells of how Athene holds the aegis with its representation of the Gorgon's head over Achilles, and a blaze shines out from Achilles's head, just as flares and signal fires can be set to warn and call for help from neighboring islanders.

> But Achilleus, the beloved of Zeus, rose up, and Athene
> swept about his powerful shoulders the fluttering aegis;
> and she, the divine among goddesses, about his head circled
> a golden cloud, and kindled from it a flame far shining.
> As when a flare goes up into the high air from a city
> from an island far away, with enemies fighting about it
> who all day long are in the hateful division of Ares
> fighting from their own city, but as the sun goes down signal
> fires blaze out one after another, so that the glare goes
> pulsing high for men of the neighboring islands to see it,
> in case they might come over in ships to beat off the enemy;
> so from the head of Achilleus the blaze shot into the bright air.
> (18.203-14)[29]

The dragon's eyes blaze with the light to warn of its own evil, yet it is odd that Spenser would want to describe that warning with a simile that would link the dragon to admirable defensive activity. In fact, the Spenserian version in 1.11.14 identifies a specifically political threat—enemies like the Spanish conspiring to invade. As Hamilton notes, and Kenneth Gross describes, these blazing eyes of the dragon unfold the etymological root of the word "dragon." Gross quotes Bruno Snell:

> *Drakon*, the snake, whose name is derived from *derkesthai*, owes his designation to the uncanny glint in his eye. He is called 'the seeing one' not because he can see particularly well ... but because his stare commands attention. By the same token, Homer's *derkesthai* refers

---

[29] Citations of Homer's *Iliad* are taken from Richmond Lattimore's translation, *The Iliad of Homer* (Chicago, 1951).

not so much to the function of the eye as to its gleam as noticed by someone else. The verb is used of the Gorgon, whose glance incites terror, and of the raging boar whose eyes radiate fire.[30]

The danger of watching the blazing eyes of the dragon, then, is that one will be perverted or petrified rather than warned. As Hamilton comments, the dragon serves both as the warning—here set into a heroic and a national context with the beacon fires and with the analogy to Achilles—and as the evil that is to be warned against. But these similes also suggest that Achilles himself, in his violence, in his anger, in his defilement, and even in the terror he invokes in others, is a figure whose ambivalence only complicates our efforts to sort out a way of understanding Arthur as a figure of purity or grace.[31]

Indeed, the issue here has more to do with apotropaic representation and the threat of the Gorgon than it does with specific heroic analogies for Arthur.[32] Probably the most conventional way of understanding epic ecphrases describing armor—the literary tradition in which Spenser sets his description of Arthur—is to suggest that the bearer increases his or her capacity to inspire fear by representing terrifying images on the armor. Certainly, this kind of power is implied in both the description of Zeus's aegis and of Agamemnon's shield in *The Iliad*:

> Now in turn Athene, daughter of Zeus of the aegis,
> beside the threshold of her father slipped off her elaborate
> dress which she herself had wrought with her hands' patience,
> and now assuming the war tunic of Zeus who gathers
> the clouds, she armed in her gear for the dismal fighting.
> And across her shoulders she threw the betasselled, terrible
> aegis, all about which Terror hangs like a garland,
> and Hatred is there, and Battle Strength, and heart-freezing Onslaught
> and thereon is set the head of the grim gigantic Gorgon,
> a thing of fear and horror, portent of Zeus of the aegis. (5.733-42)

> And he took up the man-enclosing elaborate stark shield,
> a thing of splendour. There were ten circles of bronze upon it,
> and set about it were twenty knobs of tin, pale-shining,
> and in the very centre another knob of dark cobalt.
> And circled in the midst of all was the blank-eyed face of the Gorgon
> with her stare of horror, and Fear was inscribed upon it, and Terror.
> The strap of the shield had silver upon it, and there also on it
> was coiled a cobalt snake, and there were three heads upon him
> twisted to look backward and grown from a single neck, all three.

---

[30] Gross, *Spenserian Poetics*, p. 134.

[31] On the ambivalent nature of Achilles's heroism and the status of the warrior as outside the boundaries of civilization, see James M. Redfield, *Nature and Culture in* The Iliad: *The Tragedy of Hector* (Chicago, 1975).

[32] I follow here the fine work of Kenneth Gross in *Spenserian Poetics* on this subject.

Upon his head he set the helmet, two-horned, four-sheeted,
with the horse-hair crest, and the plumes nodded terribly above it.
(11.32-42)

The idea behind representations of the Gorgon's head, more specifically, is to harness the power of this horror, and to make one's enemies fearful, or, more powerfully, actually to use the power of the Gorgon for one's own ends—thus, to petrify one's enemies with the image of the Gorgon. The use of the Gorgon as an apotropaic talisman reaches back into at least the seventh century BC, into the ancient mystery religions, and is perhaps most clearly exemplified in the temple of Artemis at Corcyra in the early sixth century where in the very center of both pediments of the goddess's temple stood a colossal Medusa, the chief ornament of the edifice.[33] This kind of apotropaic talisman is also associated with the evil eye, of which belief anthropologists have found evidence all over Europe and throughout the Mediterranean world.[34] Anthropologists and folklorists identify a belief in the efficacy of the evil eye particularly with moments of praise: if someone praises one's child, one must immediately dispraise the child to ward off the evil eye, which is the eye of envy expressed euphemistically as praise. Thus, to ward off the threat implied by praise, one oneself must criticize and defame the praised object or person— that is, one must perform verbally modified versions of the actions which one fears the evil eye would perform, as a protective device. Both the belief in the evil eye and the use of the *gorgoneion* on armor have in common an idea with unusual implications for art, whether verbal or visual: one protects against that which is feared by representing it. Precisely this tension is present in Arthur's dragon crest: Spenser's representation of a dragon crest thus may suggest that Arthur can ward off the evil of the dragon by representing it. Furthermore, the ability to represent the dragon in the first place may suggest that Arthur has gained a kind of control over the threats the dragon represents. Yet, since seeing or projecting an image of violence can itself be violating, this representation also poses the question of whether such control or containment of the dragon image threatens efforts to fashion a moral self in any way. We cannot be sure that the dragon's contagious powers do not threaten to contaminate the employer of such a representation.

---

[33] See Thalia Phillies-Howe, "The Origin and Function of the Gorgon-Head," *American Journal of Archaeology* 58 (1954), p. 215. Howe notes that there is some evidence that the *gorgoneion* existed before the figure of Medusa (the story of whom was created to explain the image, according to her theory) and suggests that this representation was involved in the process of hierarchizing the lower and the Olympian gods. See also Charles Segal, "The Gorgon and the Nightingale: The Voice of Female Lament and Pindar's Twelfth *Pythian Ode*" in *Embodied Voices: Representing Female Vocality in Western Culture*, ed. Leslie Dunn and Nancy Jones (Cambridge, 1994), pp. 24-5.

[34] See Lawrence Di Stasi, *Mal Occhio: The Underside of Vision* (San Francisco, 1981); Alan Dundes, ed., *The Evil Eye: A Folklore Casebook* (New York and London, 1981); Frederick Elworthy, *The Evil Eye: The Origins and Practices of Superstition* (London, 1958); Edward S. Gifford, *The Evil Eye: Studies in the Folklore of Vision* (New York, 1958); and R.C. Maclagan, *Evil Eye in the Western Highlands* (London, 1902).

The story of Perseus's use of the Medusa head as told by Ovid exemplifies both the capacity of images or reflections to protect by deflection, and the contagious or mimetic powers of the image. In Ovid's version, Perseus is able to kill Medusa for two reasons—partly because she is asleep, but also because he avoids looking directly at her face. His use of the reflecting shield at this moment—"But he ... looked at her ghastly head / Reflected in the bright bronze of the shield / In his left hand"—has often been glossed as an example of how art or a represented image can control violence (or the other threats represented by the Medusa).[35] The reflected image is not dangerous, though even a glance at the head itself would turn Perseus into a part of the landscape. His reflecting shield, then, presents an apotropaic image of the Medusa.

But once he has the head off the Gorgon's body, Perseus uses the head itself as a weapon—and everyone and everything that sees or touches the head of Medusa is transformed into stone. The first example, in the story of Perseus and Andromeda, demonstrates the contagious and mimetic power of the Gorgon's head—mimetic power in the sense that it enforces imitation. As Perseus flies over Libya with his winged shoes, the head of the Medusa drops blood:

> The blood-drops from the Gorgon's head dripped down.
> The spattered desert gave them life as snakes,
> Smooth snakes of many kinds, and so that land
> Still swarms with deadly serpents to this day. (4.618-20)

This is also, of course, an origin tale, as is the next example in Ovid's narrative, the petrification of Atlas. The giant Atlas had been told by an oracle to fear the theft of his golden apples by a son of Jove and in fear has walled his orchard and set an enormous dragon to guard them. He tries to send Perseus off as he has other strangers, but Perseus tricks him by pretending to offer him a gift. He "turned his face away, / And on his left hand held out the loathesome head, / Medusa's head. Atlas, so huge, became / A mountain, beard and hair were changed to forests ..." (4.657). Here, too, a story of Medusa's power provides an origin story, this time for the stone shoulders of Atlas, holding up the vault of heaven. As in this classical example of a powerful image that is simultaneously apotropaic and mimetic, Arthur's dragon crest also profoundly connects him to his origins—his is also an etiological myth of the origins of the poem, of the nation's origins, and of his own fictional beginnings, and yet he remains the hero ignorant of origins who cannot read the meaning in his own helmet.

The entire Perseus and Andromeda story is surprisingly rich in analogues to the account of St. George slaying the dragon as it appears in *The Golden Legend*. Indeed, it might be read as a classical version of this same narrative, with the result that Ovid's story seems filled with lessons relevant to

---

[35] Citations of Ovid's *Metamorphoses* are taken from Melville's translation, p. 98.

Book I of *The Faerie Queene,* as if the miraculous faith and consequent success of St. George had replaced the Gorgon's head (a connection echoed in the description of Arthur's shield). Here we might simply note one more case of contagious metonymy in the classical story. After winning the battle, Perseus places the Medusa head on a bed of soft seaweed to protect it from the hard rock. Here is Ovid's description of what happens to the seaweed:

> The fresh sea-weed, with living spongy cells,
> Absorbed the Gorgon's power and at its touch
> Hardened, its fronds and branches stiff and strange.
> The sea-nymphs tried the magic on more weed
> And found to their delight it worked the same,
> And sowed the changeling seeds back on the waves.
> Coral still keeps that nature, in the air
> It hardens, what beneath the sea has grown
> A swaying plant, above it, turns to stone. (4.740-52)

This extraordinary myth of origins reveals the petrification caused by the Medusa's head to be also a source of power—the seaweed is hardened but informed by a mimetic power transferred through touch—it retains the destructive (or is it creative?) power of the original. These examples will suffice to show why apotropaic images are so deeply ambivalent, serving to ward off a threat that they themselves may well be imitating if not embodying, employing the methods of petrification in scenes of creation.

The contagiousness or mimetic potential of the image of the dragon is made clearest in *The Faerie Queene* in Book I, canto 12, where the townspeople from Eden seem to have the power to reanimate the dead dragon as they look at its body and discuss its power. A similar threat is implicit in the dragon crest: can Arthur use the dragon as his symbol without in some fashion becoming himself like the dragon, as if his own puissance as a knight must somehow be connected to the forces of primitive violence symbolized by the dragon? The dragon can be read as pointing to a danger associated with the very chivalric apparatus of the poem (how can a knight fighting chivalric battles ever serve adequately to represent grace?); it can be seen as a reminder of the influence of original sin in human affairs ("That olde dragon"); or it can point to the ways in which a hero who personifies a nation will necessarily always stand apart, never fully integrated into the very community he makes possible (as is clearly the case with Achilles: all of these readings of the dragon on Arthur's crest raise questions about the extent to which Arthur can employ and yet distance himself from his symbol).

We feel some of this sense of danger in the description of the powers of Arthur's shield, for, in contrast to Perseus's shield, Arthur's shield is danger-ous to look upon:

> His warlike shield all closely couer'd was,
> Ne might of mortall eye be euer seene;

> Not made of steele, nor of enduring bras,
> Such earthly mettals soone consumed bene:
> But all of Diamond perfect pure and cleene
> It framed was ... (1.7.33)

Being made of diamond too, it seems to hint at a reflective surface, but this is not a protection or reflection that renders the image safe to look upon. Arthur's shield rather brings into the world a devastating absoluteness of vision, that turns anything that is merely appearance to stone or dust:

> But all that was not such, as seemd in sight,
> Before that shield did fade, and suddeine fall:
> And when him list the raskall routes appall,
> Men into stones therewith he could transmew,
> And stones to dust, and dust to nought at all;
> And when him list the prouder lookes subdew,
> He would them gazing blind, or turne to other hew. (1.7.35)

The effect of Arthur's shield sometimes resembles that of the Medusa head itself: to petrify, to turn the evil-doer or apparent evil-doer to stone. It is notable, again, that the shield, like the dragon helmet, seems to define both a destructive and a creative heroic dimension. The divided, doubled effect of the shield—it can conquer Orgoglio but it carries the threat that the power of the divine might turn all the human world of seeming and appearances to stone—matches the disturbing sense created by the dragon crest, that Arthur is both the conqueror of the forces represented by the dragon and somehow also the wielder of them.

Spenser's description of Arthur's armor, and especially of his helmet with its allusion to the many descriptions of inscribed armor in classical and Renaissance epic, brings us up a meta-step of abstraction to the question of Spenser's own representations of dragons, which are no less representations than is the golden dragon on Arthur's crest, though the dragons in the poem are fictionally meant to be real. For there are two representations here of dragons—the representation of the golden dragon on Arthur's crest, and Spenser's own representation of the dragon, which culminates in canto 11. If we are to ask how Arthur can appropriate the dragon without contaminating himself, we also need to ask whether and how Spenser can wield these images and whether they represent in his case, too, a potential threat to his poetic enterprise. The dragon crest can be seen, then, as simultaneously radiating a threatening mimetism and serving as an apotropaic talisman which reveals Arthur's capacity to deflect the power of the dragon even if he cannot defeat it outright.

"That Olde Dragon": Contaminating the Hierarchies of Typology

If Arthur's Dragon is to be related to "That Olde Dragon" fought by Redcrosse Knight, then it is presumably also connected to the great dragon of Revelations, and therefore to the "monstrous beast" (1.7.16) that Duessa rides on in canto 7—in fact, the canto organization here is helpful in highlighting the similarities. Duessa's beast is presumably the beast who rises out of the water in Revelations and becomes an assistant to the great dragon. Both have the same seven heads, so certainly this dragon would not physically provide a precise image to match Arthur's dragon crest. As it is compared to the Lernean hydra slain by Hercules, it would seem to be the opposite of anything that could be an emblem for Arthur, who is here made into a second Hercules, capable of conquering the dragon. We have seen, however, that the poet, in connecting the dragon crest through allusion to the great antagonists of the epic tradition, does insist on a connection of Arthur's crest to emblems of evil. Moreover, the poem makes the suggestion that all the many recurring dragons in Book I are versions of the great dragon, and this one is uncomfortably connected both to Arthur and to Redcrosse's dragon by its shining eyes (many other details also make it clear that this beast resembles very closely the dragon that Redcrosse Knight will kill). Spenser's description of Duessa's beast helps, then, to problematize stable notions of hierarchy in typology and to suggest why typological thinking tends to contaminate rather than purify the compared benevolent image that fulfills the type:

> His tayle was stretched out in wondrous length,
> That to the house of heauenly gods it raught,
> And with extorted powre, and borrow'd strength,
> The euer-burning lamps from thence it brought,
> And prowdly threw to ground, as things of nought;
> And vnderneath his filthy feet did tread
> The sacred things, and holy heasts foretaught.
> Vpon this dreadfull Beast with seuenfold head
> He set the false Duessa, for more aw and dread. (1.7.18)

The Dragon in Revelations is first described as "a great red dragon having seven heads, and ten hornes, and seven crownes upon his heads; And his taile drew the third part of the stars of heaven, and cast them to the earth" (Revelations 12.3-4). Revelations goes on to gloss the vision: "That great Dragon, that Old serpent, called the devil and Satan" (verse 9), and the Geneva gloss similarly identifies this dragon: "That is the devil, or Satan."[36] In the second appearance of the dragon, though, the dragon gives his power and throne and "great authoritie" to the beast who is worshipped. Of course, the

---

[36] *The Geneva Bible: The Annotated New Testament*, facsimile reproduction of the English Geneva Bible (1602), Gerald T. Sheppard, ed. (New York, 1988).

Geneva gloss identifies the beast as Rome, both the Rome of the Roman emperors and the Rome of the popes. The image of the "tayle" of Duessa's beast stretching all the way to the house of the heavenly gods owes something to the description of the dragon's tail in Revelations 12. Hamilton glosses the reference to the tail both by allusion to Daniel's vision of the goat with horns that reached up to heaven and to the description in Revelations of the dragon's tail. In trying to explain what might be meant by the tail drawing the third part of the stars of heaven and casting them to earth, the Geneva gloss reads:

> After the description of Satan follows this action, that is, his battle offered unto the church partly to that which is visible, wherein the wheat is mingled with the chaff, and the good fish with that which is evil: a good part hereof though in appearance it shineth as the stars shine in heaven, he is saide to thruste downe out of heaven, and so to pervert, for if it were possible, he would pervert even the elect.[37]

The Protestant interpreters had to struggle a little here, but the gloss does conclude that 1) the stars only appeared to be pure—they aren't the elect; 2) the church has within it those who appear to be elect, but are not and will be winnowed out by the action of the beast; 3) there is some threat implied here to everyone. This passage also works in a different way, though, to suggest that we might read the Spenserian dragon's "tayle" reaching to heaven as a kind of opposite image to that of the Goodly Golden Chain of Virtues that might reach from heaven to earth, or to Jacob's ladder, or to the stairs that angels go up and down on from earth to the heavenly city, or even to that darker version of the great chain of being, the great chain of ambition that Spenser tries to displace into Philotime's dark underworld garden. Typology, in other words, is both a temporal and a hierarchical system: if Arthur or Redcrosse is a type of Christ in his actions—Arthur as redeemer in canto 8 and Redcrosse in canto 11—then he is linking an earthly self with a heavenly action by a form of imitation, and therefore linking earth to heaven. The Dragon and the beast are the horrifying versions of that link, a kind of evil version of the Platonic ladder of hierarchies or of the chain of analogies that should lead from the earth (the letter) to the heavens (the proper spiritual reading)—a kind of contagious literalism where the dead letter reaches to the source of spiritual readings, suggesting the reach of the idol and the threat of imprisonment or petrification in the letter. This is the threat to our readings, our efforts to use the figure to make it all make sense.

This threat to the skies—Orgoglio "*seemd* to threat the skye" (1.7.8; my emphasis) but this beast of Revelations actually does so—is linked by the poem with filth and abominations: his filthy feet tread upon sacred things and the beast himself is bred in "a filthy fen" (1.7.16). The topic of filth and abomination is a familiar topos of Revelations, of course, especially as it is associated with the Cup of the Whore of Babylon ("a cup of gold in her hand

---

[37] Ibid., Gloss 7, Revelations 12.4.

full of abomination, and filthiness of her fornication" [Revelations 17.4]). The Geneva Bible reads these abominations as blasphemies and false doctrines (and the cup can be an allusion to the chalice used in the mass). But, in romance as well, dragons are associated with filth and pollution. Hamilton notes that the dragon slain by St. George in *The Golden Legend* lived in a "stagne" or pond like the sea, and we might note that in stories of foundation and origin both giants and dragons are usually associated with a kind of pollution that the founder must cleanse in order to define and begin the new society. (Orgoglio is a characteristic giant in this regard—his castle, we learn in canto 1.8.35, is richly furnished with arras and all, but the floor is defiled with the blood of guiltless babes.) Thus, in *The Golden Legend* St. George kills a "plague-bearing dragon" that lurks in a lake and devours human offerings in what becomes a kind of ritual of human sacrifice for the town of Silena. George wounds the dragon, temporarily saves the maiden about to be sacrificed, and says to her "Throw your girdle around the dragon's neck. Don't hesitate!" "When she had done this, the dragon rose and followed her like a little dog upon a leash." Her purity controls the dragon's threat temporarily— long enough for George to threaten the population. The multiple baptism that follows provides a description of this cleansing and purifying action on a different plane: "The Lord has sent me to deliver you from the trouble this dragon has caused you. Believe in Christ and be baptized, every one and I shall slay the dragon," says George, and "then the king and all the people were baptized, and George, drawing his sword, put an end to the beast and ordered him to be moved out of the city" (they need four yoke of oxen to drag him out of town).

When Spenser comes to retell the story of George and the dragon, he deletes some of the comic details, and focuses on Redcrosse's need to purify himself rather than on a forced mass-conversion scene as the cost of saving the population.[38] Is the threat represented by Spenser's dragon one of defilement, pollution, and the abominations of idolatry—the evil of Catholicism, perhaps, as a central threat to any sense of the purity of the nation? Or does the dragon represent the body itself, the threat of earthliness, of the temptation to love this world and the things and images of this world too much? The identification of the dragon with the earth and the elements is made in the stanzas in which it is associated with water, earth, air, and fire (1.11.20-23), but the dragon is also linked to the pollution of cannibalism—"yet trickling bloud and gobbets raw / Of late deuoured bodies" still appear in his iron teeth (1.11.13). This dragon's tail does not reach to heaven but "sweepeth all the land behind him far"—it

---

[38] See Susannah Brietz Monta's "The Conversion of the Saints: Testifying to Sanctity in Early Modern England" (Ph.D. dissertation, University of Wisconsin, 1998), for an argument about the ways in which Spenser's rewriting of the St. George story may represent an effort to rewrite and render Protestant the Catholic legends of the saints. Spenser's use of typology too can be seen to be an effort to create a Protestant revision of a Catholic figurative strategy. I have learned a great deal about Spenser's rewriting of the St. George of *The Golden Legend* from the very fine chapter on this topic by Monta in her dissertation.

lacks only a bit of 3 furlongs (11). Spenser seems to combine here a dragon associated with earthliness and the things of this earth, including tangled and enfolding tails/tales, with a more apocalyptic horror, which becomes a figure for the kind of abominations associated with Duessa and her beast.

The actual dragon that Redcrosse finally fights has a number of connections to Arthur, but perhaps most striking is a similarity in the poet's description of the armor of the two: Redcrosse Knight's sword bounces off the dragon's armored hide, which is completely impenetrable by such weapons, and is described "as if in Adamant rocke it had been pight" (1.11.25). Arthur's shield, as we have seen, has been "hewen out of Adamant rocke":

> But all of Diamond perfect pure and cleene
> It framed was, one massie entire mould,
> Hewen out of Adamant rocke with engines keene,
> That point of speare it neuer percen could,
> Ne dint of direfull sword diuide the substance would.
> (1.7.33)

If Arthur's shield indicates the invulnerability of his faith—its "entire" shape or wholeness—the dragon's diamond-seeming armor suggests that such evil appears invulnerable. The description of the powers of Arthur's shield creates a tension between its destructive and its creative powers. Like the Medusa's head it can petrify; like the dragon it can turn men to dust. As has proven true even of the explicit biblical typologies, then, the similarity between the dragon itself and Arthur's shield and helmet uneasily and uncannily warns that his power has much in common with the power of "That Olde Dragon," and that he is both the typological opposite and yet also the fulfillment of this kind of invulnerable force—that he is, in fact, the dragon of his nation.

The Tudor Dragon

For Arthur's dragon crest can also be interpreted through the contemporary political and social context of the Tudor monarchs. Indeed, this is no doubt the most obvious and immediate interpretation of it. To read the dragon in this way we turn not to the Bible, not to classical epic, not to myth nor to saints' lives, but to the Welsh sources of Arthurian legend, and to the Tudor appropriation of Arthur as a mythic predecessor. To explain the presence of the crest in this way is seemingly simpler, since the Arthurian sources tell us that Arthur had a helmet with a dragon crest. Henry VII made much of his descent from the Welsh Owen Tudor, and at his coronation in 1485 had displayed a banner with the red dragon of Cadwallader on it. Giving the son born in 1486 the name of Arthur only seemed to extend the myth of the once and future king. There is not space here to catalogue the importance of the resurgence of interest in

Arthur in the course of the sixteenth century, or the debates that followed Polydore Vergil's attack on the matter of Britain.

Not only do the sources tell us of Henry VII's efforts to link himself in general with Arthur. They also show that actual dragon crests on decorative helmets became popular in the late medieval period (see figures 8.1-3), while Henry VII himself used a badge that displayed the red dragon of Wales (see figure 8.4). Read in connection with the Elizabethan revival of chivalry and the art of heraldry, Arthur's dragon crest echoes the late medieval custom of using decorative crests in tilting and ceremonial armor, and alludes to the descent of the Tudors from Arthur. The Tudors were not unique in using the sign of the dragon: Harold Godwinson used a dragon ensign at the Battle of Hastings, Richard I carried one in 1190 as he besieged Messina on his way to Jerusalem and in the third crusade, his brother John used a dragon ensign. But the Tudors were unusual in the extent to which they strengthened their claims to legitimacy by allusion to the prophecies of the Arthurian legends and the matter of Britain. In the manuscript of Prince Arthur's book, particularly rich in examples of heraldic art from the Tudor period (perhaps, as Arthur Foxe-Davies speculates, originally written for Henry VIII and Katharine of Aragon)[39] we see examples of ceremonial crests, as well as pictures of "the supporters"—animals holding banners. The red dragon was one of the supporters of the Tudor Kings, and Elizabeth I continued to use the dragon as a supporter, though she changed its color to gold.[40]

The use of crests represents an extension of the art of heraldry from the needs of identification in battle to the claims of social position, right, rank, and obligation which were expressed when late medieval and Tudor nobles used arms and heraldic symbols ceremonially and in tournaments and in other moments of display.[41] Foxe-Davies argues that crests were never worn in battle,[42] and almost certainly served to denote aspects of rank or position:

---

[39] Arthur Charles Fox-Davies, *The Art of Heraldry: An Encyclopedia of Armory* (London, 1904), pp. 427-8.

[40] Indispensable in the study of English heraldry are the two volumes by Fox-Davies, *The Art of Heraldry* (op. cit.) and *A Complete Guide to Heraldry*, rev. and annotated by J.P. Brooke-Little (London, 1969; 1st pub. 1909). See p. 169 of *A Complete Guide* for a brief account of the Tudor use of dragons as supporters and for the history of the use and augmentation of the Royal Badge for Wales (the "red dragon passant"). See the entry under "dragon" in Bradford B. Broughton, *Dictionary of Medieval Knighthood and Chivalry* (Westport, Ct., 1986) and J.P. Brooke-Little, *Boutell's Heraldry*, rev. ed. (London and New York, 1950; rev. ed. 1954, 1973), pp. 211-13. Brooke-Little lists as Royal Supporters, "Henry VII—a dragon gules and a greyhound argent; two greyhounds argent; a lion or and a dragon gules." For Henry VIII, "a lion or and a dragon gules; a dragon gules and a bull sable, a greyhound argent or a cock argent." Edward kept the "lion or" and the "dragon gules," and so did Mary, though she also used the supporters of Phillip of Spain, an eagle and a lion. Elizabeth I used "a lion or and a dragon or" and "a lion or and a greyhound argent" (p. 212).

[41] See Foxe-Davies, *A Complete Guide*, ch. 20, "The Heraldic Helmet" (pp. 228-44) and ch. 21, "The Crest," pp. 245-53. These chapters provide a detailed history of the rise of the crest and the use of the helmet and crest as markers of rank.

[42] Foxe-Davies, *Art of Heraldry*, p. 257.

> Then comes the question: what did the crest signify? Many have
> asserted that no one below the rank of knight had the right to use a
> crest; in fact, some writers have asserted and doubtless correctly as
> regards a certain period, that only those who were of tournament
> rank might assume the distinction, and herein lies other confirmation
> of the supposition that crests have a closer relation to the tournament
> than to the battle ... There is no doubt, however, that whatever the
> regulation may have been—and there seems little chance of our ever
> obtaining any real knowledge upon the point—the right to display a
> crest was an additional privilege and honour, something extra and
> beyond the right to a shield of arms ... whilst we find that in the
> latter part of the fourteenth century that all the great nobles had
> assumed and were using crests, we also find that the great bulk of the
> lesser landed gentry bore arms but made no pretension to a crest.[43]

He speculates that the bearing of a crest was perhaps valued beyond the shield
of arms, for those who aspired to a crest were of such rank that a shield of arms
was a matter of course. In Elizabethan and Stuart times, the granting of a crest
to ancient arms became a widespread practice. Figures 8.1-3 display several
examples of actual dragon crests from the medieval period, including the
impressive dragon (or wyvern) crest of Thomas, Earl of Lancaster, taken from
his seal of 1301. (A wyvern is a dragon with only two legs.) The lion crest of
Thomas of Mowbray from 1389 similarly shows how the crest functioned to
distinguish, identify, and honor the bearer. Arthur's crest is described as a great
deal larger and more all-encompassing than these crests, but these examples do
show how his can be identified with the use of symbolic crests in ceremonial
armor and with the Elizabethan ceremonial revival of late medieval chivalric
custom.

By placing Arthur in the context not of an allegory of grace but of
allusion to the Elizabethan vogue for chivalry and tournament, and by
identifying him with the symbols of a Welsh past—to be treated in the next
section—and a Tudor present, a monarch who claimed to be his descendant,
Spenser underlines the political prophecy implicit in the figure of Arthur, and
he also provides a new twist on Arthur's own inability to read his arms or crest.
Fictionally at this point in the poem, Arthur still does not know who he is, and
therefore cannot have any reason to attach any special lineal or familial
meaning to the dragon; politically, we can see that he cannot understand the
full meaning of his crest because he cannot see prospectively—by definition he
cannot know the full Tudor meanings of his own prophetic role. The Tudor
prophetic claims associated with Arthur again raise questions about how we
should connect the religious and the political meanings in the poem: does the
political allegory re-enforce the Protestant reading of the poem, as if to insist
that only a Protestant royal family can guarantee an uncorrupted nation? Or
does the political suggest an alternative way in which redemption may
sometimes have to occur? The sense that redemption may need to come from

---

[43] Fox-Davies, *Art of Heraldry*, p. 258.

Figure 8.1
Crest of Roger de Quincy, Earl of
Winchester (d. 1264), from his seal

Figure 8.2
Crest of Thomas, Earl of Lancaster,
from his seal (1301)

Figure 8.3
Crest of Thomas de Mowbray, Earl of
Nottingham and Earl Marshal (1389),
from his seal

Figure 8.4
The cross of St. George, the crowned rose of
York and Lancaster, the red dragon of
Wales, the greyhound, the sunburst, and the
crowned portcullis, all badges used by
Henry VII. The dragon is in its oldest and
best form, according to Fox-Davies.

Figures 8.1-4
Illustrations reproduced from Arthur Charles Fox-Davies, *The Art of Heraldry: An
Encyclopedia of Armory* (London, 1904), figures 695, 696, 699 and 1040

political conquest perhaps explains some of the darker aspects of both Arthur's representation—the iron pen writing in his heart (1.8.44) seems inappropriate for the redemptive agent of grace—and the representation of his shield, a shield of faith in the Pauline sense perhaps, but one which Spenser endows with remarkably destructive capacities.

The Welsh Dragon

Perhaps the best way to consider the power of political prophecy and agency in the case of Arthur is to look more closely at the Welsh myths of Arthur on which Spenser drew. This approach to reading the dragon on Arthur's crest requires that we start with the sources of the Arthurian stories in Geoffrey of Monmouth's *History of the Kings of Britain* and in Malory. These were not Spenser's only sources of Arthurian material, of course, but they do provide some critical linkages between the dragon helmet, stories of national origin and legitimacy, and the problem of prophecy. Arthur's helmet had to have a dragon crest, as we have seen, because that is what was described by Geoffrey of Monmouth as having been the decoration of Prince Arthur's actual helmet:

> On his head he placed a golden helmet, with a crest carved in the shape of a dragon; and across his shoulders a circular shield called Pridwen, on which there was painted a likeness of the Blessed Mary, Mother of God, which forced him to be thinking perpetually of her. He girded on his peerless sword, called Caliburn, which was forged in the isle of Avalon. A spear called Ron graced his right hand: long, broad in the blade and thirsty for slaughter.[44]

But perhaps even more important is the mythology and legend surrounding the actual stories of Arthur, especially since this lore is not only used by Spenser but is itself the source of Welsh claims to the dragon as symbol. Geoffrey of Monmouth, for instance, describes several crucial moments in which dragons come to define Arthur's identity. From the very beginning the dragon is associated with Merlin's prophecies, and serves as an emblem for both ruler and country:

> While Vortigern, King of the Britons, was still sitting on the bank of the pool which had been drained of its water, there emerged two Dragons, one white, one red. As soon as they were near enough to each other, they fought bitterly, breathing out fire as they panted. The White Dragon began to have the upper hand and to force the Red Dragon back to the edge of the pool. The Red Dragon bewailed the fact that it was being driven out and then turned upon the White One and forced it backwards in its turn. As they struggled on in this

---

[44] Geoffrey of Monmouth, *The History of the Kings of Britain*, trans. Lewis Thorpe (London and New York, 1976), p. 217.

way, the King ordered Ambrosius Merlin to explain just what this battle of the Dragons meant. Merlin immediately burst into tears. He went into a prophetic trance and spoke as follows: "Alas for the Red Dragon, for its end is near. Its cavernous dens shall be occupied by the White Dragon, which stands for the Saxons whom you have invited over. The Red Dragon represents the people of Britain, who will be overrun by the White One: for Britain's mountains and valleys shall be levelled, and the streams in its valleys shall run with blood ..."[45]

Here, the battle of the two dragons is read by Merlin immediately and as though it were a transparent figure for the battle between the Saxons and the Britons. Geoffrey's account of Uther seeing a meteor is well known, but we should notice how this account is similarly framed by Uther's nation-building battles, and by Merlin's prophecies:

While these things were happening at Winchester, there appeared a star of great magnitude and brilliance, with a single beam shining from it. At the end of this beam was a ball of fire, spread out in the shape of a dragon. From the dragon's mouth stretched forth two rays of light, one of which seemed to extend its length beyond the latitude of Gaul, while the second turned towards the Irish Sea and split up into seven smaller shafts of light.

This star appeared three times, and all who saw it were struck with fear and wonder. Uther, the king's brother, who was hunting for the enemy army, was just as terrified as the others. He summoned his wise men, so that they might tell him what the star portended. He ordered Merlin to be fetched with the others, for Merlin had come with the army so that the campaign could have the benefit of his advice. As he stood in the presence of his leader and was given the order to explain the significance of the star, he burst into tears, summoned up his familiar spirit, and prophesied aloud. 'Our loss is irreparable,' he said. 'The people of Britain is orphaned. Our most illustrious king has passed away. Aurelius Ambrosius, the famous king of the Britons has died. By his death we shall all die unless God brings us help. Haste forward, most noble leader! Haste forward, Uther, and do not put off for a moment making contact with the enemy. Victory shall be yours and you will be the King of all Britain. The star signifies you in person, and so does the fiery dragon beneath the star. The beam of light which stretches towards the shore of Gaul, signifies your son, who will be a most powerful man. His dominion shall extend over all the kingdoms which the beam covers. The second ray signifies your daughter, whose sons and grandsons shall hold one after the other the kingship of Britain.'

Although he remained in some doubt whether or not what Merlin had prophesied was true, Uther nevertheless continued to advance against the enemy as he had begun.[46]

---

[45] Ibid., p. 171.
[46] Ibid., pp. 200-201.

The ending of this passage somewhat comically casts doubt on how much to believe of these prophecies—the reading of the dragons is connected to a kind of political pragmatism in which Uther uses prophecy to support a plan he had already launched ("he continued to advance ... as he already had begun"). But when Uther finally comes to be king, he commemorates Merlin's prophecy by having the dragons crafted:

> With the agreement of everyone present he was appointed King. Mindful of the explanation given by Merlin of the star about which I have told you, he ordered two Dragons to be fashioned in gold, in the likeness of the one which he had seen in the ray which shone from the star. As soon as the Dragons had been completed—this with the most marvellous craftsmanship—he made a present of one of them to the congregation church of the see of Winchester. The second he kept for himself, so that he could carry it round to his wars. From that moment onwards, he was called Utherpendragon, which in the British language means 'a dragon's head.' He had been given this title because it was by means of a Dragon that Merlin had prophesied that he would become King.[47]

Merlin's prophecies in these instances seem more magical and much less certain than Spenser seems to allow in his descriptions of Merlin or Arthur. In Geoffrey's account Merlin reminds one more of the Spenserian sage wizard who interprets the appearance of a comet in Book III:

> But the sage wisard telles, as he has red,
> That it importunes death and dolefull drerihed. (3.1.16)

The poet satirizes his own prophetic powers here: readers should not, like the "sage wisard," interpret Florimell speeding by in this way—though perhaps we, too, must interpret her "as we have read." Since all mortals will die, and "dolefull drerihed" may be the way of the world, it could be said that Spenser's sage wizard, like other good oracles, has hit upon a formulation that is sufficiently universal while appearing unique that it stands as a good instance of prophecy. In the case of Geoffrey's Merlin, his many prophecies are so multiple and hallucinatory that many can be found to be true. The appearance of the comet quoted above seems to be a case in which Geoffrey's Merlin found two meanings for one astral event—the prophecy of "death and dolefull drerihed" ("by his death we shall all die") is quickly supplanted by a more politically efficacious one: although Geoffrey makes Uther's doubts about the prophecy clear, the second interpretation of the prophecy does tell him to do what he already intended to do.

A final example in Geoffrey of Monmouth of the dragon image as royal emblem occurs as Arthur sets sail to defend Britain from the Roman challenge:

---

[47] Ibid., p. 202.

Round about midnight, as he sailed briskly on through the deep sea, surrounded by ships too numerous to count, and following his course closely with joy in his heart, Arthur fell into a very deep slumber. As he lay lulled in sleep he saw a bear flying through the air. At the growling of the bear every shore quaked. Arthur also saw a terrifying dragon flying in from the west and lighting up the countryside with the glare of its eyes. When these two met, they began a remarkable fight. The dragon which I have described attacked the bear time and time again, burning it with its fiery breath and finally hurling its scorched body down to the ground. Arthur woke up at this point and described what he had dreamed to those who were standing round. They interpreted it for him, telling him that the dragon was himself and the bear some giant or other with which he was to fight. The battle between the two animals meant the struggle which was to take place between him and the giant, and the victory of the dragon was that which Arthur himself would win. Arthur, however, was sure that it meant something different, for he considered that this dream had come about because of himself and the Emperor.[48]

Here again the text is canny about the uncertainty of any particular strategy of reading the dream, but the prophecy fulfills itself anyway, not necessarily because it was true, but because it became a useful way after the fact of confirming the inevitability of the direction that things actually took. Like most such narratives, the story about the prophecy has a retrospective shape. In the case of Arthur's dream, a horrible giant appears almost immediately (and almost comically) in the narrative, and Arthur quickly defeats him, but the battle with the Romans occurs very soon too.

It is striking to see that, in Malory's accounts of the prophecies, Merlin is a disturbing and problematic figure. Merlin is responsible for the conception of Arthur, since he uses his magic to disguise Uther as the husband of Igraine—"ye shall be like the Duke, her husband" (the disguise is to appear in the likeness of the husband, suggesting again how a mirroring, the likeness of simile, can be a saving device)—and he thus displaces the threat of adultery and illegitimacy that hovers over the Arthur story in Malory's version, a hidden cause of the incest that marks Arthur's tragedy. For, like his father's, Arthur's sexual desire initiates and directs the narrative. His desire for King Lot's wife is apparently matched by hers for him: "For she was a passing fair lady, wherefore the king cast great love unto her, and desired to lie by her. So they were agreed and he begat upon her Mordred, and she was his sister, on the mother's side, Igraine." Immediately after this account, Arthur has a dream that land griffins and serpents had come to his land and burnt and slain the people, and he fought with them and finally killed them.[49]

---

[48] Ibid., p. 237.

[49] Sir Thomas Malory, *Le morte d'Arthur*, ed. Janet Cowen (London and New York, 1986), 1: 45.

Arthur's ignorance about his origins protects him from any guilt in this case of sleeping with the queen, and it is on the occasion that Merlin first tells him who he is and prophesies his end:

> 'But ye have done a thing late that God is displeased with you, for ye have lain by your sister, and on her ye have gotten a child that shall destroy you and all the knights of the realm ...'
> 'Ha,' said King Arthur, 'ye are a marvellous man, but I marvel much of thy words that I must die in battle.'
> 'Marvel not,' said Merlin, 'for it is God's will your body to be punished for your foul deeds ...'

Merlin concludes, "I shall die a shameful death to be put in the earth quick, and ye shall die a worshipfull death."[50] Here again we find an end and an origin confused, and a prophecy that describes the tragic end of the narrative only as it is validated retrospectively.

While the dragon crest on Arthur's helmet in *The Faerie Queene* seems to be present as a reminder to the reader that Arthur is the romance son of Uther Pendragon, it fails to function in this manner for Arthur as character, as he does not yet know his own origins. The announcement of his death in the moment that we meet him provides a clue not only for how to read Spenser's allegory—"But when he died, the Faery Queen it [his shield] brought/ To Faery lond, where yet it may be seene, if sought" (1.7.36)—but also a reminder of the odd convergence of destruction and celebration or glory in so many of Merlin's prophecies in Malory and in Geoffrey of Monmouth. Arthur's helmet is an incarncation, then, of Arthur's position in the midst of a prophetic narrative that will allow him to discover his identity but only at the cost of discovering his death.

These prophetic contexts shift our judgment of Spenser's Arthur, and help to intensify our critical debates about whether the poem works as a prophetic text in the sense of celebrating fulfilled prophecy, or whether it employs a prophetic structure to invoke for its darker powers of warning, criticizing, and reminding the nation, and the Queen, that prophecies will come true only if they are retrospectively made to do so.[51]

The interpretations of these dragons offered by Geoffrey's Merlin all reveal an essential ambiguity typical of oracular and prophetic utterances from the earliest days. The famous oracle described by Herodotus, but repeated frequently, exemplifies the doubleness of oracular utterance: "If he makes war

---

[50] Malory, 1: 48.

[51] See Richard McCabe's *The Pillars of Eternity* where he argues that each of the quests actually involves returning to the past—they actually go backwards towards origin: George goes back to Eden as if the past were a place to which one could return; Fradubio and Fraelissa, once redeemed, will be restored to former kind, and so on. Eventually, the whole poem will make it back to Gloriana's court. McCabe's analysis of the Arthurian moment brilliantly illustrates the temporal complexity by which Spenser writes a prophetic narrative aware of its own retrospective fulfilling of the prophecy. See also Dobin's *Merlin's Disciples*, *passim* and throughout, on the political valences of prophecy.

on the Persians, he will destroy a great empire." Such an utterance will remain true regardless of who wins the battle. Like this oracular statement, the prophecies of Geoffrey's Merlin seem always capable of validation by events no matter what their outcome. Similarly, in Malory's accounts, Merlin's visionary powers create both greatness and loss, provoking Arthur to heroic deeds, but also to an act of incest that will destroy his accomplishments. In a study of oracles, Michael Wood has written that "the promise and the ruin of the promise speak the same language. When you consult an oracle, you are promised what you want and get what you have feared. Only in the form of riddling words can necessity and chance, fear and desire, be made to coincide."[52] This complex interpenetration of the words one wants to hear with the horror that one fears perhaps best captures the double way in which Spenser's poem makes use of prophecy, both within the chivalric story and for its contemporary English readers. Arthur's dragon, then, is both the prophesied dragon of the nation and a representation of the greatest evil. Temporarily in his control and yet also itself constituting part of his identity and armor, it marks what will make him both succeed and fail in his future beyond the poem.

Tentative Conclusions

These differing ways of reading the dragon crest or the poem cannot easily be made to be congruent. The religious allegory in Book I, cantos 7-8, ties the dragon on the crest to the Great Dragon of the Apocalypse, and raises questions about how to understand, from a theological perspective, the poem's apparent desire to harness and use at least the illusion of evil if not aspects of its power. The political allegory, on the other hand, presents a different and perhaps more complex picture of Arthur as the ancestor of Elizabeth I and originator of her line. In that the dragon crest seems to import into the poem a certain scepticism about the temporal relation between royal emblems, royal authority, and prophecy, it also invokes a way of reading that would foreground the poem's darker forebodings about the uncertainty of its own prophetic fulfillment.

Typology in this analysis is less a clarifying and authorizing interpretive schema than a means of generating deeply ambivalent and ambiguous images, which, like the word "shamefastness," seem to include their own opposites. The use to which Spenser puts these images suggests, also, that the only way to avoid dualism is to produce multiplicity and ambivalence. If an image can be used apotropaically, to deflect or defuse a threat that is to be imagined as controlled or harnessed, it can also serve to

---

[52] Michael Wood, public lecture, Bread Loaf School of English, Middlebury, Vermont, July, 1996.

infect or disrupt the coherent structuring of meaning which it may have been invoked originally to sustain.

Prophecy, too, has an ambiguous effect in the case of Arthur, both in the earlier Arthurian texts and in Spenser. To suggest that prophecy is retrospective, depending on a retrospective authorizing and selection of meanings, is both to remind readers of the need to take action to make the prophecies come true, and to expose the fictional nature of the project of making a national identity (or legitimizing political authority). Like typology, then, prophecy is metaleptic; that is, both systems of generating meaning depend on a retrospective re-examining of complex utterances that cannot be made to express a given meaning until a later event clarifies the earlier statement. Placing both Arthurian and typological prophecy alongside a national myth helps to show that to invoke either kind of prophecy is a risk, rather as Stephen Mullaney (following Puttenham) and Howard Dobin have suggested in a different context.[53] The riddling traditions of prophetic language come to Spenser both through the Bible and through the epic tradition.[54] By devoting a sparkling stanza to the dragon crest, Spenser invokes both these traditions, insisting that Arthur be understood as participating in this doubled prophetic tradition even as he presents Arthur as the hero of a new national epic. How much do the doubts about prophetic authority and the echoes of the Apocalypse qualify or limit the political myth incarnate in Arthur? We see here a locus of disjunction and moral tension that points to a deeper, unbridgeable break in the Protestant and national ideology which the poem invokes and to some extent helped to articulate.

The description of Arthur as he enters the poem urges the readers to read in this multiple sense, and not to collapse the differing kinds of symbolic and mythical allusion into a single, simplifying meaning. The dragon crest, in particular, shows that the political and the religious are as often opposed as they are congruent in this great allegorical epic. The rereading of prophecy provided in this episode qualifies and challenges the apparent union fashioned in the poem between Arthur as a political and national symbol and Arthur as a representative of the work of redeeming Grace. Arthur's own ignorance of his identity may figure the narrator's methods of eliding this difference for us and for his readers at court, just as Arthur's happy ignorance of his own role in an allegorical scheme allows the chivalric plot to displace tensions between the epic and allegorical roots of the poem.

To insist that the political and the religious do coincide, then, seems to me itself to be an ideological move, whether by poem or by reader, and, in so far as the poem does elide the differences between the political and the religious, it provides another instance of the epic's avoidance of and erasure of

---

[53] On ambiguity or "amphibology" as the trope of the traitor, see Stephen Mullaney, *The Place of the Stage: Licence, Play and Power in Renaissance England* (Chicago, 1988), p. 120.

[54] The oracle about Lavinia in *The Aeneid* has a similar doubled meaning.

origins.[55] The reader, on the other hand, needs to be alert to that process of elision, because the poem also calls attention to its own method of constructing meaning, and thereby allows us to see both the wish—that the Prince Arthur of the poem that was never completed could actually fulfill the chivalric and national prophecies about him while also serving as a figure for the efficacy of God's grace—and the fear, that there can be no way to wed the religious allegory and the national prophetic and authorizing narrative.

---

[55] See my "Epics and the Politics of the Origin Tale" in *Epic Traditions in the Contemporary World: The Poetics of Community*, Margaret Beissinger, Jane Tylus and Susanne Wofford, eds. (Berkeley, 1999), pp. 239-69.

9

The Postures of Allegory

Kenneth Gross

Borne along around allegories, or dragged behind them like a shadow, is a structure of attitudes, a trailing history of demands which follow them, like a company of faithful retainers, even into the wilderness. A cosmic, yet portable theater crystallizes around even small traces of allegorical expression, forcing the world into new forms around them, hollowing out or animating spaces once solid. Allegory in the end comes to compete with its own creations; it does battle with its own residues. The demon of allegory must sometimes "course his own shadow for a traitor"—to quote the fiend-haunted Edgar in *King Lear*, who, despite his desolation, his manic and mantic gestures, offers fragments of personification and Aesopian emblem such as let us take him for an allegorist: "Who gives anything to Poor Tom? Whom the foul fiend hath led through fire and through flame, through ford and whirlpool, o'er bog and quagmire ... false of heart, light of ear, bloody of hand; hog in sloth, fox in stealth, wolf in greediness, dog in madness, lion in prey."[1] Here, allegory seems to belong, if only for an interval, to the domain of derangement, the fiction of demonic possession. Allegory is a mask of madness.

I want by my title to constellate together several senses of "posture," at once touching and cutting across our familiar pictures of allegory. First, the dramatic or sculptural connotation, in the sense that allegorical figures strike a pose, carry meaning through signifying gesture and emblematic form, through the way that they comport themselves in imaginary space or lay claim to an imaginary body. The postures of allegory aspire to be what Wittgenstein calls "forms of life," embodied ideas and intentions, pictures of a soul, masks of will, spiritual dispositions, however ambiguous they may appear: St. George riding his horse, Isis footing her crocodile, Melancholy holding his head in his hands, Rage tearing her hair. Exposed to our gaze, such postures fix themselves against time; they are things to be catalogued, also assembled and disassembled. "Posture," however, slides into something more suspect: the universe of allegorical imposture, the domain of meanings imposed on a text or a mind. The word in this sense points toward the subterfuges of which allegory is capable, the masking of the body's more disorderly impulses, the mind's mask of its own confusion. Here, it is the posture of the allegorist that counts as well,

---

[1] *King Lear*, ed. R.A. Foakes (New York, 1997), 3.4.50-52, 90-92.

the complex stance that the allegorist takes up towards the materials of allegory.

Finally, the idea of posture should invoke the idea of "positing," in the sense of a speculative, sometimes metaphysical placing or naming of objects; it touches the ability of language to give us a world we can know, or a world behind the world we know. The world-making tropes of Renaissance poetics are relevant here (for example, Philip Sidney's image of poetry delivering a golden world in place of a brazen one), but for the moment I'm thinking rather of the philosopher W. V. O. Quine's sparer sense of "the posit," by which he means a name or word whose referent "can be admitted to be forever unobservable without yet being repudiated, like blue apples, as non-existent."[2] A "posit" in this sense is not just something given. It is, like allegory, a made thing, a way in which we create and organize a world, structure our beliefs (whether the posit is "mama," "water," or "mankind"). To call a posit a posit is not to patronize it, Quine insists. We take pains over our posits. We build them into networks of connected meaning. Posits can also be tested, repudiated as partial or inadequate; a fresh posit is something we may have to break through to, often by finding new names for objects in the world, or by dividing old names from the imaginary objects into which they tend to collapse. The posit is thus a thing subject to revision, whether by experience or hypothetical reason. It is also capable of catastrophe. For one thing, Quine writes, "we have had the wit to posit an ontology massive enough to crumble of its own weight."[3]

I

Sitting at my desk, leaning over a copy of *The Faerie Queene*, my shoulders and head frame a roof over the book. The pencil I take notes with writes much less than it gets fiddled with, poking the air, or skittering blindly over an invisible, embroidered surface. My hand itself seems half a prop, a prosthesis or a phantom limb, even an arcane writing instrument. I find myself straining to inscribe a posture on the air with my shoulder or chin. At moments, my limbs assume unnatural curves, as if they could magically conjure around them a world to fit the shape they have thrown themselves into—the image of some external order, but also like an impulse of the body to adjust itself to an interior pain. It feels as if I were trying to stand at once inside and outside a mirror; as if I wanted to make myself transparent to an opaque world.

Allegorical texts like Spenser's are designed to draw one into a world of parts; the mind shrinks toward small bits of meaning, gets scattered among fragments of gesture, story, and emblem. But allegorical writing also invites one to assume a part in an order or a consciousness large enough to contain those parts; and it generates a theory or a story that lets one connect the parts to

---

[2] W.V.O. Quine, *Ontological Relativity and Other Essays* (New York, 1969), p. 13.
[3] Quine, *Ontological Relativity*, p. 17.

a larger whole, even if that whole remains something of a riddle. This double gift helps bind you to an allegorical world, lets it claim you. Allegory demands scrupulous, "stupendous" researches, but it should also bolster your confidence that you belong to that world, and can move fluidly within it—as if, at a chessboard, you were at once the player and the pieces, at different moments a pawn, a queen, a knight, at once enabled and endangered by the movements of other pieces. (Allegorical parts, however, tend to project a deranged or incomplete whole, a ruined order, one reason for the ambivalence that allegory attracts, and a reason for the sense of something killing within its animations. The allegorical cosmos can seem as much a Gnostic prison as a harmonious, Neoplatonic palace.)[4]

Looking even at something so conventional as the personifications of the seven deadly sins in the House of Pride, one is drawn into a complex game of moral thinking, at once rigid and chaotic. Here are some lines about a particularly crucial Spenserian enemy:

> And next to him malicious *Envie* rode
> Upon a ravenous wolfe, and still did chaw
> Betweene his cankred teeth a venemous tode,
> That all the poison ran about his chaw;
> But inwardly he chawed his own maw...
>
> All in a kirtle of discoloured say
> He clothed was, ypaynted full of eies;
> And in his bosome secretly there lay
> An hateful Snake, the which his taile uptyes
> In many folds, and mortal sting implyes. (1.4.30-31)[5]

How, in all the series of these "sins," does one fix the relation of the emblematic face, the physical gesture, the symbolic props, the costume, the beast, the particular disease? The text asks the reader to leap between emblems of quite different range and genealogy; it is the force of their accumulation and even redundancy that counts.[6] One can list the "facts" about envy gathered

---

[4] In these reflections, as throughout this essay, I am indebted to Angus Fletcher's *Allegory: The Theory of a Symbolic Mode* (Ithaca, 1965).

[5] All quotations of Spenser's poem are from *The Faerie Queene*, ed. J.C. Smith, 2 vols. (Oxford, 1909).

[6] On the workings of such personifications, which he refers to as "grotesques," John Ruskin comments: "A fine grotesque is the expression, in a moment, by a series of symbols thrown together in bold and fearless connection, of truths which would a have taken a long time to express in any verbal way, and of which the connection is left for the beholder to work out for himself; the gaps, left or overlooked by the haste of the imagination, forming the grotesque character." This works "with a delightfulness—in the higher instances with an awfulness—which no mere utterance of the symbolized truth would have possessed, but which belongs to the effort of the mind to unweave the riddle, or to the sense it has of their being an infinite power and meaning in the thing seen, beyond all that is apparent therein." From *Modern Painters*, vol. 3, ch. 8, par. 5, quoted in *The Literary Criticism of John Ruskin*, ed. Harold Bloom (Gloucester, Mass., 1969), p. 60. One of Ruskin's chief examples for analysis is the description of Envie quoted above.

here: its viciousness, its paranoia, its secrecy, self-damage, its endless twists of fantasy. But one also wants to know how the different parts of this corpse-like assemblage entail each other, work as cause or effect; who eats whom, who poisons whom? Who or what is inside whom, for that matter? Where is the "inward," so folded and implied, hiding a mortal sting? As reader, I may see fragmentary anticipations of other quests, other agents, as if this Envie were a grotesque knot or seed of larger narratives. I also recognize in Envie a mode of allegorical perception, allegorical desire, that at once gives birth to and defiles a signifying posture, transforms its object and gets transformed by it. The knot of emblems aims at convincing me that my own body, my tongue and my eyes, my diseases, my interiority, not to mention my own clothes and possessions— that all these are likely to be allegorical props and prostheses, anything but natural. Allegorical envy both has a disease and is a disease; the lines even suggest a diseased passion lurking at the origins of allegory itself. I say this because of the eerily personal note that breaks through at the end of the second stanza, where one hears echoes of an angered, spiteful soul that hurls this vicious emblem against the world in a gesture of both recognition and revenge: "So every good to bad he doth abuse; / And eke the verse of famous Poets witt / He does backbite, and spightful poison spues / From leprous mouth on all, that ever writt" (1.4.32). The emblem thus contains a seed of the Blatant Beast, with whose iconoclastic rage the poet comes to identify.[7]

II

The paradoxical embodiments of allegory exert a rigid, often strangely inhuman pull on our impulses and gestures, our bodily and emotional accidents, also our inherited stories. Hence the images of reduction, abstraction, entrapment, and violation that are often used to characterize the work of allegory.[8] But such embodiments also work to lend a human

---

[7] I have discussed the vexed relations between Spenser's poetic project and the work of the Blatant Beast more at length in my *Spenserian Poetics: Idolatry, Iconoclasm, and Magic* (Ithaca, 1985), pp. 224-34, and "Reflections on the Blatant Beast," *Spenser Studies* 13 (forthcoming).

[8] Gordon Teskey powerfully explores the darker framings and appetites of allegorical figuration in *Allegory and Violence* (Ithaca, 1997). What he calls the "allelophagic" aspect of allegorical figuration, its tendency to devour other bodies, forms, and allegories, is particularly suggestive in this context.

The image of allegory as itself a dead or tyrannical mode of reading and writing has its own complex history, of course. Protestant reformers, for example, saw in Catholic allegoresis a species of idolatry, a device that pretended to open up hidden, even iconoclastic senses within the literal text of scripture, but in fact subdued that text's truths to imposed doctrinal errors and fictions. The hidden senses supposedly discovered in the sacred text thus offered only an imaginary salvation, like the "whorish" representations of the mass. Romantic critics, in a related way, often characterized allegory as a kind of rationalistic machine, a way of imposing dead meaning on a living image or of keeping meaning and substance abstractly aligned, something which was opposed to the mutual, vivifying interaction of meaning and

substance, a human face or gesture, to ideas, energies, structures, and influences, which otherwise seem to live a different life, a less or more than human life (for instance, an idea of perfect justice, a principle of superhuman vengeance, a suspicion of occult sympathies in matter). These embodiments give form to things otherwise inarticulate, and invisible—things that might, if revealed in a less mediated way, endanger a human life, or be themselves in danger of violation, such as divine presence or ancient wisdom.[9] Emerging at the vexed crossing point of such intentions, allegory seems paradoxically a mode of both purification and contamination, caught between idealism and illusion, given to posing as both a veiling and an unveiling, both humanizing and dehumanizing.

The stakes are high, because of allegory's capacity not just to incarnate moral ideas but to shape more archaic demands. Allegories give form to our wish to know where the mystery sits, where the veil or mirror stands, what a hidden intention amounts to, what others cannot see. They seek to bridge gaps in our experience—between the known and the unknown, the visible and invisible, the human and the divine (often at the cost of deforming or rationalizing such gaps).[10] Systematic allegories like Spenser's offer to tell us

---

substance made possible by the "symbol." On allegory as idolatrous in Christian tradition, see my *Spenserian Poetics*, pp. 53-77. For an important analysis of Romantic debates about the contrast between allegory and symbol, see Paul de Man, "The Rhetoric of Temporality" in *Blindness and Insight: Essays in the Rhetoric of Contemporary Criticism* 2nd rev. ed. (Minneapolis, 1983), pp. 187-208.

[9] The idea of allegory as a figured veil or shell that protects sacred truths from vulgar readers, even as it tests the wisdom of an interpretive elite, is an ancient one; versions of this story show up, for example, in Augustine's *De doctrina christiana*, and in the mythographic encyclopedias of Fulgentius, Boccaccio, and Natales Conti, to name just a few sources. Francis Bacon probes the myth in his preface to *De sapientia veterum* (1609), clearly wanting to believe that there is a "hidden and involved meaning" in ancient myths, which are "as sacred relics and light airs breathing out of better times," even though he also sees that the allegorical interpretation of such myths allows later writers to "gain the sanction and reverence of antiquity for doctrines and inventions of their own." In the end, what interests Bacon is the formal ambivalence or contrariness of allegorical fables—their ability at once to veil and illuminate the truth. As for real antiquity of the wisdom which ancient writers put into such myths, it is "either great or lucky: great, if they knew what they were doing and invented the figure to shadow the meaning; lucky, if without meaning or intending it they fell upon matter which gives occasion to such worthy contemplation." See *Francis Bacon: A Selection of His Works*, ed. Sidney Warhaft (New York, 1965), pp. 274-8. As Angus Fletcher comments (*Allegory*, p. 236), the mixed pleasure and pain of exegetical labor, the sheer cognitive difficulty of allegory, will almost inevitably give us the sense that we are encountering in allegorical texts something taboo or sacred.

[10] Allegorical images can also to give sharper, daemonic form to such gaps. In *The Gazer's Spirit: Poems Speaking to Silent Works of Art* (Chicago, 1995), John Hollander cites a passage from Ralph Waldo Emerson's "Experience," describing an engraving by Henry Flaxman of a scene from *The Eumenides* of Aeschylus: "Orestes supplicates Apollo, whilst the Furies sleep on the threshold. The face of the god expresses a shade of regret and compassion, but is calm with the conviction of the irreconcilableness of the two spheres. He is born into other politics, into the eternal and the beautiful. The man at his feet asks for his interest in the turmoils of the earth, into which his nature cannot enter. And the Eumenides there lying express pictorially this disparity" (p. 23). One wants to ask: Does this wounded need to give form to the disparity between human and divine experience help to explain why the mythic

where to stand, where threshold of the temple lies, but also where the battlefield is, what weapons to employ, who our enemies are, what wounds they can inflict, where our secret sources of strength are. (With a consistency that would require a longer essay to make clear, these sources of strength are often depicted as lying within the work of allegory itself, that is, within the work of composing or unfolding its enigmatic images—one reason why the theory of allegory tends to take a resolutely allegorical form.) Allegory also offers to wrench readers free of any more conventional or naturalistic diagram of history. If they cannot quite reinvent the world, allegories often seek to re-diagram a history, a soul, a sacred text, reinventing its meaning according to the lineaments of a prophetic or divine intentionality.[11] Indeed, the self-referentiality or other-referentiality of allegory is in part a way for later allegorical texts to defend themselves against the opacity or authority, or the simple priority, of their sources.

To illustrate, consider a text crucial to Spenser, the description of spiritual battle from St. Paul's epistle to the Ephesians. Addressing a persecuted religious community, the text strategically re-maps an earthly, factional conflict as a battle in the sky, an engagement with daemonic hierarchies: "For we wrestle not against flesh and blood, but against principalities, against powers, against the rulers of the darkness of this world, against spiritual wickedness in high places" (Ephesians 6.12, King James). The early church's historical conflict with Rome and the Synagogue, read first as a wrestling match, veils another war that is hidden behind it, at once more drastic and more ambiguous. The description, indeed, echoes the language of Gnosticism, with its hierarchies of cosmic demons entrapping and tormenting the pieces of a fallen light.[12] The cosmological drive upward, however, is matched by a corresponding drive inward. Having redrawn the conceptual battle lines, the author urges his listeners to reconceive their interior, spiritual gifts as furnishings of warfare: the whole armor of God—the shield of faith, the breastplate of righteousness, the helmet of salvation, the sword of the Word. The concreteness, the abstract but still material cast of the allegorical weaponry shapes a powerful, but equally ambiguous stance of spiritual readiness, one that is underlain by a kind of historical and ideological paranoia, mere flesh and blood disappearing below the spiritual armor.

---

emblems of that disparity, the Furies, take the form of creatures who are themselves vengeful, personified curses that pursue and harass the living? And further, could the conversion of the *Erinyes* into the *Eumenides* be seen as an emblem of a traditional tendency to rationalize or purify the more violent capacities of allegorical expression?

[11] Erich Auerbach, "Figura," in *Scenes from the Drama of European Literature* (New York, 1959), notes that especially in typological allegory the events of sacred history "are considered not in their unbroken relation to one another, but torn apart, individually, each in relation to something other that is promised and not yet present" (p. 59).

[12] Hans Jonas, *The Gnostic Religion: The Message of the Alien God and the Beginnings of Christianity*, rev. ed. (Boston, 1963), pp. 268-9, comments on the Gnostic tonalities in Paul, especially in a shared contempt for the created cosmos, something which includes a contempt for the demonically manipulated structures of the fallen psyche.

III

It is useful to remember that, for all of its power to moralize, allegory does violence to certain kinds of moral reasoning. Allegory's rationality is often fantastic, formally barbaric, rationalizing. As an illustration: I remember vividly the note of frustrated protest, even the tone of disgust, that I elicited in a friend of mine, a philosopher, when I tried once to connect Aristotle's analysis of what in Greek is called *akrasia* to Spenser's Circe-like witch Acrasia, who turns humans to beasts. Aristotle describes *akrasia* in Book VII of the *Nichomachean Ethics* as a troubling blank space or weakness within human will, something that lets us act against what we know are the true goals of virtue.[13] This *akrasia* is not a blind passion, however, but a species of "involuntary ignorance"; it is a tendency given especially to making mistakes about the place of pleasure in relation to human ends. Aristotle does not assume that he knows the final cause of this weakness in the will; his intricate analysis of *akrasia*, indeed, suspends absolute answers. At the same time, however, Aristotle does keep faith with the possibility of a rational account of virtue and its failures. Hence, to my friend, I suppose, who had struggled with this complicated notion in Aristotle, Spenser's allegory must have felt as if it had got everything wrong, not inadvertently, but by some perverse and self-indulgent "design." For one thing, to make a relational paradox called *akrasia* into a personal agent named Acrasia posits an illusory ground for an effect that should remain, philosophically, in question—as if the allegory itself were shamefully yielding to easier conceptual pleasures. Spenser's Acrasia is not entirely dependent on a philosophical abstraction, of course (whether found in Aristotle or his commentators, such as Aquinas). As an allegorical character, she also echoes a more Pauline or Augustinian idea of "Sin," something that can itself emerge quite explicitly as a personification, and is not so susceptible to strictly rational analysis. And in any case, this transference of name and agency is a common enough allegorical trope. But I am not sure I want to take embarassment of reason by allegory entirely for granted. In some contexts, the work of allegory upon reason can seem both perverse and opportunistic. The business of giving a label to a void or blank space within experience can be a way to keep that void alive, rather than making sense of it; allegory empties things out, rather than filling them up with meaning, veiling that emptiness at the same time.

Vital sections of Spenser's poem do, of course, work to teach us about ethical, political, and religious ideas. It anatomizes moral acts and attitudes; it can illuminate the figurative shape of our moral language; it gives freshly fictive shape to old diagrams of value and puts inherited ideas on new stages. This is part of the analytic or critical cast of allegory, even if it co-operates with allegory's authoritarian coloring. In Isis Church, for example, the heroine

---

[13] See *The Basic Works of Aristotle*, ed. Richard McKeon (New York, 1941), pp. 1036-58.

Britomart dreams that she is turned into the statue of a goddess symbolizing Equity. The crocodile at her feet devours a storm of fire that bursts from below her altar, and turns his rage on Britomart herself. Beaten back, the monster turns amorous and begets a lion upon her. The allegorical aim of the text is to take an elusive, often technical principle of jurisprudence—that is, equity, the accommodation of fixed legal rules to particular circumstances—and lend it a more dynamic, mythic, and sexual cast, making equity an agent within a prophetic, nationalist history. But as Spenser designs it, the episode also helps us to think about equity's powerfully ambiguous status as cause and effect of justice, as principle of both order and disorder within the work of law.[14]

At certain moments, however, the energy of Spenser's personifications, especially the making up of agents out of abstract nouns and qualities, makes their meaning feel oddly opaque; it unsettles one's sense of "how" the words mean. Our words for certain states, feelings, or virtues lose their transparency when they become names for creatures who both suffer from and provoke those states and feelings.[15] Nouns can become curiously faceless, mute, hard to use in moral sentences, when they are made into things with faces. Their given meanings turn into something epiphenomenal, at once compensatory and infectious. This is perhaps why slowing down over a procession of personifications like that in Busyrane's house can make one feel slightly mad:

> With him went *Daunger*, cloth'd in ragged weed,
> Made of Beares skin, that him more dreadfull made,
> Yet his owne face was dreadfull, ne did need
> Straunge horrour, to deforme his griesly shade;
> A net in th'one hand, and a rustie blade
> In th'other was: this Mischiefe, that Mishap ... (3.12.11)

The dangerous posture of Daunger is clear enough, as is its place within this pageant of creatures derived from courtly love tradition—the procession of a love affair through stages of Ease, Fancy, Desire, Doubt, Daunger, Fear, Hope, Dissemblance, Grief, Fury, and so on. Still, with each frenetic embodiment, each arrival of figures masked in multiple, even competing figures of themselves, one feels not so much a greater richness of meaning as a sense of meaning turning against itself, as if the "meaningful" names had become merely masks—though masks of what is not at all clear. (What deforms the forms of danger?) Here, the pressure to make agents out of ideas threatens to

---

[14] On the analysis of equity in this episode, see Angus Fletcher, *Prophetic Moment: An Essay on Spenser* (Chicago, 1971), pp. 259-304.

[15] Samuel Taylor Coleridge thinks of such "confusion of agent and patient" in Spenser's allegory as a fault; he cites the description of Grief in Busyrane's pageant (3.12.16), which, he says, "represents two incompatibles, the grieved and the aggriever." Nevertheless, he acknowledges that such confusion "occurs so frequently in his allegorical personages that Spenser seems to have deemed it within the laws and among the legitimate principles of allegory." See *Coleridge's Miscellaneous Criticism*, ed. T.M. Raysor (Oxford, 1936), p. 39.

reduce both agents and ideas to a kind of nonsense.[16] Hence, perhaps, the pageant's ending with a crowd of "full many moe like maladies, / Whose names and natures I note readen well" (3.12.26), figures which themselves disappear quickly when Britomart breaks into the castle's center. Consider also the example of Malbecco, whose wounded desire and self-destructive envy help to transform him into a monstrous, stony figure named "Gealosie," confined to eating poisonous toads below a threatening cliff. This metamorphosis allows Malbecco to accomplish and yet put off his own death. Or rather, it realizes several deaths at once—physiological, psychological, moral—each further deforming him. But it seems a peculiarly allegorical oblivion when Malbecco, "transfixed" like Amoret, "forgot he was a man, and *Gealosie* is hight" (3.10.60). The name represents at once the exhaustion and the fulfillment of the allegorical activity. To whom does this creature's fixity belong, to Gealosie or to allegory? and what does it mean if we cannot distinguish between the two?

Perhaps, of course, my doubts depend on a false picture of how "ideas" work in allegory. Allegory is less about the meaning of ideas than about the fate of ideas. That is to say, allegories feed our fantasies that ideas have a fate distinct from their existence as verbal ciphers, that they can act, live a life of their own, that they can become warriors, lovers, swords, armor, chariots, traps; that they can become hells or heavens, blessings and curses, fountains pure or poisonous; that they can be possessed; that they can be built upon, produce offspring, or turn a person to stone. One additional desire fulfilled by allegory may be that ideas can work without our having to understand them. Allegories often seem to be too soaked in meaning, bristling with significations like an over-armed soldier or robot; yet the appetite for allegory also grows out of a loathing of meaning, a defense against its burdens.

This helps to account for the sense of something dead or inert in allegorical writing. Its rigidly diagrammed actions seem a mode of exhausting imaginative energy; what animation it has can feel inhuman, mournful, as if the life of allegory were always an afterlife. (This deadness is thus somehow built into allegory. It is not simply the result of an exhaustion of mythological meaning by history, as Walter Benjamin argues in *The Origins of German Tragic Drama*.[17] It also entails more than the merely strategic emptying-out of prior texts that occurs in much typological allegory.) All allegorical agents, in this view, can start to look like Spenser's monster Maleger—that uncanny,

---

[16] I am reminded here of Henry James's complaint about allegorical writing, that it is "apt to spoil two good things—a story and a moral, a meaning and a form," *Hawthorne* (New York, 1961), p. 58. This is admittedly said about allegorical narrative in general, rather than personification, but it helps illustrate my point nonetheless.

[17] Walter Benjamin, *The Origins of German Tragic Drama*, trans. John Osborne (London, 1977), p. 226.

unkillable composite of cadavar, skeleton, ghost, and shroud.[18] But even granting this, we still have to make sense of the real fascination of Maleger, or of Malbecco turned Gealosie. For the scandalous fact is that the fixities of allegory are, however deathly, something to be desired. They are not just imposed on the mind. Instead, the mind happily yields itself to them—as in Ovidian metamorphosis, where victims slide into the shroud of a mythic form that can be at once a substitute for death, a punishment, a release from pain, a fulfillment of desire, and a triumphant reinvention of form (and self).[19] Spenser's fiction overtakes and analyzes our attachment to allegorical death. But it continually indulges that attachment, in all its potential shame. To yield to the logic of a personification in Spenser also entails a release into new, more complex systems of fate, or helps us momentarily join conflicting desires. Our attachment to Spenser's eerie, often static postures—which so multiply themselves in the poem—may itself entail a distinctly erotic attachment, however fetishistic or perverse it may appear. Yielding ourselves to the postures of allegory may be a way of putting off alternative demands, a way of taking up for a moment an answering, resistant fixity—as in the mode of the sublime, where the mind's experience of being overwhelmed by prior, external forms entails a compensatory discovery of imaginative and conceptual power.[20]

IV

I want to turn, a little abruptly, to some passages from William Blake. Blake's prophetic poetry is unimaginable without Spenser's, and it shares his preoccupation with the life and death of allegory. But it follows these through in extreme ways, and casts light backwards on Spenser's ambitions.

At the opening of Blake's *Book of Urizen*, a "shadow of horror" arises in Eternity. "Some said, / 'It is Urizen'. But unknown, abstracted, / Brooding secret, the dark power hid" (plate 3, ll. 5-8). Urizen is described as an opaque, soul-shuddering vacuum, a shadow "dark revolving in silent activity, / Unseen in tormenting passions, / An activity unknown and horrible / A self-contemplating shadow, / In enormous labours occupied" (ll. 18-22).[21] He is an

---

[18] James Nohrnberg, *The Analogy of* The Faerie Queene (Princeton, 1976), speaks suggestively of Maleger as an entity "created out of the almost pure ectoplasm of allegorical 'otherness'" (p. 321).

[19] This helps explain why the fictions of metamorphosis serve as a model for what Dante calls the "counterpass" or *contrapasso*, that process by which damned souls are punished after death by being transformed into animate allegories of their own sinful desires and erring beliefs. For more on this connection, see my "Infernal Metamorphoses: An Interpretation of Dante's 'Counterpass,'" *Modern Language Notes* 100 (1985), 42-69.

[20] I am thinking of Kant's formulation of the structure of the Sublime in *The Critique of Judgement*, especially as this is analyzed by Thomas Weiskel, *The Romantic Sublime: Studies in the Structure and Psychology of Transcendence* (Baltimore, 1976), pp. 37-50.

[21] All quotations are from *The Complete Poetry and Prose of William Blake*, ed. David V. Erdman, rev. ed. (Berkeley, 1982).

opacity that contains a void, a will that seeks a solid without fluctuation yet is itself in continual motion. Urizen is manifestly a part torn in violence from a cosmic whole—"leaving ruinous fragments of life" (plate 5, 9). Yet he is also a part setting itself up as a singular measure of "all" creation, passionately at war with his own children. Urizen's world "teemd vast enormities / Frightning; / faithless; fawning / Portions of life; similitudes / Of a foot, or a hand, or a head / Or a heart, or an eye." Urizen is a creator god, but he also manifests himself as a rebellious, Satanic son who, falling into a "stony sleep," suffers a horrific, painful series of re-creations. His body is reshaped by the hammer of the smith-God named Los, who howls during his work in jealousy and fear. It gets distorted into what is, for Blake, our own false picture of fallen, limited, natural senses. This is how the sense of hearing "develops": "The pangs of hope began. / In heavy pain striving, struggling. / Two Ears in close volutions. / From beneath his orbs of vision / Shot spiring out and petrified / As they grew" (plate 12, ll. 19-24).

Urizen is both Satan and Jehovah, and also a satire on Enlightenment deification of natural reason, as many critics have noted. He also offers a bitter self-parody of Blake's activity as solitary, brooding poet–prophet. Yet reading these riddling stanzas, I feel something odder. It is not simply that Urizen is an allegorical picture of allegory, or a vision of the entrapping allegory our bodies can become. Rather, it is an account of what it would feel like to be an allegorical personification, what it would feel like, from the inside, to "live" the life of an allegorical schema, its ambitions, its sins. Urizen's history suggests how a wounded part of existence transforms itself into a whole, a creative energy forming itself within a rift of creation, a void "margined by ruinous fragments."

In *The Marriage of Heaven and Hell,* Blake mocks our habit of taking fictional deities as gods, "choosing forms of worship from poetic tales" (plate 11), but forgetting their origin in human fantasy. Urizen, in a sense, shows us the will to allegory imposing its abstractions, its forgetting of origins, on itself as well as on others. Urizen, abstracting himself into a mental deity, is a picture of allegory's way of existing in the world, intending towards the world. But again, Blake's dramatic sense means that he wants us to feel this from the inside. For all the rage of his satire, Blake tries to invest Urizen with a certain pathos: this stony world, fallen petrific womb, appears also "like a human heart struggling & beating" (plate 5, 36).

The eerie pathos of Urizen points to a major difficulty in reading Blake's allegory. For elsewhere, not vague pathos, but the most raucous and moving dramatic voices—rivalling those of Job or Lear—break forth from figures who are clearly ciphers, obscurely-named fractions divided away from some larger symbolic whole. These voices show Blake's allegorical figures strikingly present to their history; they can speak with ecstatic ferocity about the errors of mind and heart that "created" them, limited or bound them—in part aspects of a world produced by the posits of allegory itself, "where the horrible darkness is impressed with the reflections of desire" (*Visions of the Daughters of Albion*, pp. 7, 11). Indeed, the energy and knowledge of these speeches are a function of how fully these allegorical characters have begun to "live" what is inescapably an allegorical existence. At the same time, Blake also tests our very trust of dramatic "hearing" by so ambiguating those voices. He shows us speakers whose extreme cries remain unheard, or are violently misheard by those sharing their world; he suggests even that the speaker may not be present to his or her own truth. Take, for example, the grand and vituperative speeches of the female character Oothoon in *The Visions of the Daughters of Albion*. Oothoon has been "rent" by the thunders of a storm-demon called Bromion, cast out by her envious lover Theotormon, and somehow bound by both. She is able, nevertheless, intricately to survey the different worlds that human imagination produces, and the fear of this difference that produces human law; she darkly mocks the elements of hypocrisy, jealousy, and secrecy in human desire that entrap her, and even reserves enough joy to project a vision of human love freed of jealousy. We as readers hear her speak of such things. But within the fiction, her jealous lover only hears her words as a love song to his rival, while the chorus of the Daughters of Albion only hear a pathetic, passive "lament," sighs that they echo back each morning. Oothoon is understood, if at all, only by her rapist Bromion, who under her influence reveals himself as Urizen. The effect is to make one question what it is, after all, that anyone in this fiction hears, what we are hearing, even how Oothoon might hear her own voice.

To call such a voice "subjective" would be grotesque. Its dramatic and conceptual form is too precise; it demands too much of us, and wounds us too much. Part of what it demands is that we trust this voice, even as we understand that it is no more than a vision of what is possible; that it is a possible posture of voice. Oothoon's voice reminds us that our listening is, in a sense, a transitive or allegorical listening—as when in another poem, the fearful virgin Thel is found "listening / Dolours and lamentations" in the fallen world outside her garden, lamentations that are distorted versions of her own voice echoing back to her from her tomb ("The Book of Thel," plate 6, ll. 6-7). Unlike Spenser, Blake lacks even a residual trust in forms of order prior to what the imagination makes for itself; he asks us to see all forms of "oppression" as forms of weakness, things we have made and imposed on ourselves. He makes it so that one is aware of having invented one's own demons and angels. The added difficulty is that, for Blake, the appeal to interiority is never enough; one can only engage with such creatures as entities that speak from the outside, as Job confronts the voice of Yahweh (though without the imagination's abasing itself before them).

Blake, in ways that often resemble Spenser, wants to examine the "obscure contiguities of schematization and consciousness"; he investigates those places where an allegorical schema might itself begin to be "lived," and conversely those places where lived experience schematizes itself, "merges into the design it unconsciously plays out."[22] But Spenserian allegory cannot, or does not try to, find a voice for Amoret, bound bleeding to a column in Busyrane's house. Nor does it allow Malbecco/Gealosie to offer an apologia (however deluded) for his fixed existence under a rock. Nor does the text tell us what Busyrane's voice sounds like when he "reads backward" the spell written in Amoret's blood—the only moment when Britomart, who has spent the whole day examining the chamber of horrors, manifests any real terror at what she encounters. Blake, by contrast, does invent voices for characters in such situations, though those voices scarcely free them from their allegorical bondage; in fact, ordinarily, we are meant to overhear in their words some trace of the errors which create and perpetuate their often ecstatic entrapment.

In the end, I am not certain what to make of the contrast, or of my own impulse to weigh such different modes of writing one against the other. Blake suggests that it is only by living the forms of allegorical death that his characters can break through to something more radical or liberating. Spenser lacks these terrible, extravagant voices. The scope of his allegory may thus appear less extreme. But I wonder, after all, whether Spenser is not in some ways more ruthless and honest. There is often a suspicious circularity in Blake's voicings. The cries he evokes from his allegorical creatures can seem willful and arbitrary, not to mention melodramatic. In *The Faerie Queene*, by contrast, the terrible face of allegory remains mute.

---

[22] Weiskel, *The Romantic Sublime*, p. 66.

Afterword

10

A View of the Present State of Spenser Studies: Dialogue-Wise

Andrew Hadfield and Willy Maley

WILLY: But if that field of Spenser Studies of which you speak be of so goodly and commodious a soil as you report, I wonder that no course is taken for the turning thereof to good uses, and reducing that corpus to better government and civility. What evils prevent its reform?

ANDREW: I will declare the evils which seem to me most hurtful to the corpus of that man, and first those that are most ancient and long grown. And they are of three sorts: The first in colonialism, the second in gender, and the last in religion.

WILLY: I remember at Kalamazoo I saw an old professor take up *The Faerie Queene* and tear his hair, crying that the new historicists were not fit to have it.

ANDREW: "The past quarter of a century has witnessed a striking growth in the study of Edmund Spenser, where the centre of interest has perhaps been shifting from England to America."[1]

WILLY: That strikes me as a fairly uncontroversial opening gambit, Andrew.

ANDREW: But Willy, those words were written by Frederic Ives Carpenter in 1923!

WILLY: That puts paid to any notion of Spenser as a narrowly English author. In fact, his work appears to appeal most emphatically to Irish, American, and Irish-American critics.

ANDREW: The essay by an American that casts a shadow over virtually all subsequent work on Spenser has been Stephen Greenblatt's "To Fashion a Gentleman: Spenser and the Destruction of the Bower of Bliss" (1980) in his

---

[1] Frederic Ives Carpenter, "Desiderata in the Study of Edmund Spenser," *Studies in Philology* 19 (1922), 238.

Renaissance Self-Fashioning, which opened out the poem to three interrelated contexts—"New World" travel literature; Reformation iconoclasm; and English colonial activity in Ireland.

WILLY: Perhaps we should start with Ireland, and with Greenblatt's conclusion: "Ireland is not only in Book V of *The Faerie Queene*; it pervades the poem."[2] The appeal of Ireland worries me and I would like to sound a note of caution here. Ten years ago a publisher told me that a book on Spenser and Ireland would be "sexy," and not because the goatee was making a comeback, but because there was something naughty about Ireland—the frisson of the Troubles, the threat of political violence that would lend an aura of worldliness to an academic text. There is a very real sense in which *The Faerie Queene* is a work that, in recent criticism, cannot fail to be marked by contemporary events. Itself produced in a period of intense conflict, it has arguably become caught up, four centuries on, in the present state of Ireland. Ireland sells well, and while it might have been one way for critics and readers interested in things other than poetry—politics, history, colonialism and so on—to get a handle on Spenser, it arguably leads to a bias toward contextual criticism that talks readers around *The Faerie Queene*, rather than taking them into the text.[3]

I think both Greenblatt's article and Nicholas Canny's influential essay, "Edmund Spenser and the Development of an Anglo-Irish Identity," serve to suggest that a reading of Spenser that does not foreground Ireland is somehow deficient or dishonest.[4] Whether seen as a representative of the New English, or more generally as the architect of a colonial politics, Spenser is being made to bear the burden of a history that is presented as self-evident, or at least accessible to scholarship in a way that I find questionable.

The Faerie Queene is, on one level, a poem about reading, and while reading "Ireland," in all its complexity, in Spenser's life and texts may be a fruitful exercise, it can never exhaust the range of meanings in the poem. *The Faerie Queene* is not "all about Ireland." Even Book V addresses a range of other issues. Michael O'Connell and Julia Lupton have argued for the integrity of the poem in terms of Book VI building on and counterpointing Book V.[5]

---

[2] Stephen Greenblatt, *Renaissance Self-Fashioning: From More to Shakespeare* (Chicago, 1980), p. 186.

[3] Recent books on Spenser and Ireland include, Patricia Coughlan, ed., *Spenser and Ireland: An Interdisciplinary Perspective* (Cork, 1989); Claire McEachern, *The Poetics of English Nationhood, 1590-1612* (New York and London, 1996); Andrew Hadfield, *Spenser's Irish Experience: Wilde Fruyt and Salvage Soyl* (Oxford, 1997); Willy Maley, *Salvaging Spenser: Colonialism, Culture, and Identity* (Basingstoke, 1997); Christopher Highley, *Shakespeare, Spenser and the Crisis in Ireland* (Cambridge, 1997); David Baker, *Between Nations: Shakespeare, Spenser, Marvell and the Question of Britain* (Stanford, 1997); Andrew Murphy, *But the Irish Sea Betwixt Us: Ireland, Colonialism, and Renaissance Literature* (Lexington, Ky., 1999).

[4] Nicholas Canny, "Edmund Spenser and the Development of an Anglo-Irish Identity," *The Yearbook of English Studies* 13 (1983), 1-13.

[5] Michael O'Connell, "*The Faerie Queene*, Book V" in *The Spenser Encyclopedia*, ed. A.C. Hamilton (London and Toronto, 1990), pp. 280-83; Julia Reinhard Lupton, "Home-

This is an advance on the view that The Legend of Justice is an anomaly infected by its Irish elements, but it leaves intact the idea that Book V is fundamentally different in tone and tenor. My own feeling is that Ireland is beginning to colonize Spenser in a way that I find rather alarming. This may be poetic justice, but it also carries with it the risk of reduction and oversimplification. For too long Spenser has been the writer most likely to be singled out and scapegoated when critics of English colonial rule in early modern Ireland were looking for a whipping boy. Recently, two changes have occurred to complicate the picture. If one move in recent years is towards a less pejorative criticism with regard to Spenser and Ireland, then a concomitant shift has occurred in the direction of a more inclusive and comparative literary context, as other key canonical figures are read in relation to Spenser, writers such as Donne, Jonson, Milton, Marvell, and Shakespeare. Both these shifts in perspective, the move towards a more sympathetic portrait of Spenser's experiences as a planter in Cork, and the drawing in of key contemporaries in the realm of English Renaissance literature, are encapsulated in the work of David Baker, Christopher Highley, Claire McEachern and Andrew Murphy.[6] Their contributions have ensured that Spenser is no longer singled out for attention. Rather, his work now clearly has to be set in the context of wider Renaissance attitudes to Ireland. The easy language of condemnation yields to a growing appreciation of the ways in which Spenser's work was traversed by Ireland and the extent to which he was not anti-Irish in any simplistic sense. (Indeed, this new criticism would suggest that his chief targets in relation to Ireland were an earlier wave of English settlers, the metropolitan government, and the Scots.) Criticism of Spenser's Irish experiences, if it is to bear fruit, has to be rooted in cultural complexity rather than seen in simplistic terms as character defect or individual opportunism.

ANDREW: I think you have vastly overstated your case, old chap. *The Faerie Queene* is not just "made in Ireland"—in the sense that its composition was rendered possible by Spenser's presence there and his acquisition of an Irish estate. Spenser himself was "made in Ireland." Everyone knows that Ireland literally afforded Spenser the means to pursue a literary vocation, and that in a very material sense his epic poem, and all that he wrote subsequent to settling there, is undoubtedly the "fruit of savage soil." Moreover, your charge that Ireland is now the main preoccupation of Spenser studies overlooks the fact that much recent criticism displays a blithe disregard for any Irish dimension. While it might be all right to discuss a large number of relevant Spenser concepts—numerology, Neoplatonism, patristic writings, pictoralism, for example—without having to drag Ireland in willy-nilly, it is wrong-headed to ignore the central presence of Ireland and the Irish in the poet's imaginative

---

making in Ireland: Virgil's Eclogue I and Book VI of *The Faerie Queene*," *Spenser Studies* 8 (1990), 119.
   [6] See above, n. 3.

geography. What about the Blatant Beast? The Mutability Cantos? The large number of savages throughout the pastoral book who threaten settlers? *Colin Clouts Come Home Againe*? Or, to carry on with Professor Greenblatt, the witch Acrasia?

Spenser's marginal position as a writer on the fringes of court society, his involvement with the Protestant factions and, yes, his role in Ireland, establish a hermeneutics of suspicion in his works—for both writer and readers—partly owing to fear of censorship, which forces us to read his work obliquely as literary forms (from my perspective this usually means that Spenser is invariably writing with one eye on Ireland even when the immediate context would suggest otherwise). We all know how difficult it was to write about Ireland in the 1590s. This is a problem, even now, for many critics, some of whom tend to take the narrator's statements as the expressions of Spenser himself.

Spenser's tangential situation has been elaborated upon in a series of important articles by Louis Montrose, and is a staple of New Historicist concerns with the question of power and literature.[7] A further relevant point that needs to be made about *The Faerie Queene* is that it appears to have aroused most disapproval in Scotland via the threats of James VI who was outraged at the representation of the trial of his mother at the court of Mercilla in Book V.[8] Again, this points to the need for more readings of the poem in a British context.[9] In fact, Willy, one way of countering the Hibernocentrism you detect is to open out the Irish context to a British one. Spenser is developing a complex British mythology, drawing on Brutus, as well as Arthurian and Tudor material.[10]

WILLY: You say Spenser is writing about Ireland even when he is not. My argument would be that he is writing about England even when he is not. But this approach—the text says what it does not say—is another contextual impasse, another way of not reading, which is why I feel that the revenge of the textual scholar has proven timely. Jean Brink's argument concerning the problematic nature of the Spenser canon is of importance here.[11] How can we decide how texts need to be read if we do not even know the circumstances of

---

[7] Louis A. Montrose, "'The perfecte paterne of a Poet': The Poetics of Courtship in *The Shepheardes Calender*," *Texas Studies in Language and Literature* 21 (1979), 34-67; "The Elizabethan Subject and the Spenserian Text" in Patricia Parker and David Quint, eds., *Literary Theory / Renaissance Texts* (Baltimore and London, 1986), pp. 303-40; "Spenser's Domestic Domain: Poetry, Property, and the Early Modern Subject" in Margreta de Grazia, Maureen Quilligan and Peter Stallybrass, eds., *Subject and Object in Renaissance Culture* (Cambridge, 1996), pp. 83-130.

[8] Richard McCabe, "The Masks of Duessa: Spenser, Mary Queen of Scots and James VI," *English Literary Renaissance* 17 (1987), 224-42.

[9] For recent readings, see Baker, *Between Nations*, ch. 2.

[10] See Hadfield, *Spenser's Irish Experience*, ch. 3.

[11] Jean R. Brink, "Constructing the *View of the Present State of Ireland*," *Spenser Studies* 11 (1990), 203-28 and (1994), 216-23.

their production? Brink notes with distaste that "it has become increasingly fashionable to use the *View* to interpret Spenser's biography and to explicate *The Faerie Queene*" (p. 203). She reminds us that the *View* is a text "first attributed to Spenser thirty-five years after his death and one for which there is no holograph manuscript" (p. 204). She might have added that we have none of Spenser's poetry in his own hand, and that *The Shepheardes Calender* was published anonymously, as were the translations of epigrams and sonnets in *A Theatre for Worldlings* (1569), and that a fragment of Book VII of *The Faerie Queene*—"Two Cantos of Mutabilitie"—was appended to the poem posthumously. How certain can we be that Spenser was sole author of the letters signed by him in the published correspondence between himself and Harvey? These were, after all, as Harvey says, "Patcheries, and fragments." In short, Spenser's corpus is and always has been in a state of flux.

ANDREW: As has Spenser criticism. Yet there are problematic areas of consensus. Many critics who have written on the *View* have assumed it was censored because it is such a nasty piece of work. I would agree that the *View* is a nasty piece of work, but there is not any direct evidence that it was suppressed. All we know is that after being registered by the Stationers' Company it did not appear as a printed work. This happened to other works for various reasons. It may be significant that the *View* was entered by Matthew Lownes, who had gotten himself into trouble for pirating editions staked out by the more powerful William Ponsonby. Whatever the chain of events I would hazard a guess that trying to publish a work on Ireland in 1598 was no mean feat, particularly if its author had just been rebuked by the King of Scotland. The title of the *View* may have been enough to get it banned. If the word "present" was the problem for Ware—it does not appear in his edition, remember—then the word "Ireland" alone could have confined a text to manuscript in the 1590s.[12]

However, Professor Brink is undoubtedly right to conclude that more careful textual scholarship needs to be undertaken in sorting out the manuscripts of *A View* and relating them to Spenser's poetry. Brink's claim that Spenser may not have written *A View* cannot be ignored, since it constitutes the most direct challenge by a textual scholar to the largely contextual work on Spenser and Ireland, but I am not convinced by her arguments—emphatically unconvinced in fact. It is almost as if she does not want the *View* to have been written by Spenser, a claim that suits those who wish to minimize the impact of Ireland on Spenser. I have not consulted the holograph of Brink's essay, so I cannot be completely sure of its authorship. We will have to wait until all the manuscripts for *Spenser Studies* have been

---

[12] See Brink, "Constructing the *View*," pp. 204-9; Andrew Hadfield, "Was Spenser's *A View of the Present State of Ireland* Censored? A Review of the Evidence," *Notes and Queries* 239 (December 1994), 459-63.

collated before it can confidently take its place as part of the canon of Spenser criticism.

There remains the question of how we read a prose dialogue by a poet fond of ironic juxtapositions. The problem of Spenser's irony is both peripheral and central. Peripheral, as it is difficult to see how the question can ever be resolved; central, in that it is impossible to write on Spenser without making an assumption one way or the other, a problem highlighted by the arguments of the deconstructionist critics, an aporia which is perhaps inevitably inscribed in the process of reading.[13]

WILLY: Another problem in Spenser studies—and one that may be resolved soon—is the lack of a proper, factually-based, integrated biography. The exciting work of Richard Rambuss is a useful corrective to the line taken by critics such as Richard Helgerson, David Lee Miller, Michael O'Connell, and Patrick Cheney, that Spenser wanted to be a poet first and foremost, but his assumptions that Spenser valued his career as a secretary as much as that of a writer have been too much for some tender-hearted reviewers to stomach.[14] The problem is that we do not know accurately enough yet how people perceived themselves or their work in the early modern period, or even which genres carried most weight (hardly surprising given the intellectual flux of the early modern period and the uncertainty of the value of literature). In some ways we have not advanced beyond what C.S. Lewis and Yeats said of the poet versus the colonial official.[15] The impending biography by Jean Brink and the collection of essays published by Massachusetts will go some way towards breaking down this binary division.[16]

Spenser the poet and Spenser the planter coincide in the figure of Spenser the Puritan. Religion remains a key problem. It has received sporadic attention since first being examined by Grace Landrum and Virgil Whitaker.[17]

---

[13] See, for a recent example, Elizabeth J. Bellamy, "The Vocative and the Vocational: The Unreadability of Elizabeth in *The Faerie Queene*," *English Literary History* 54 (1987), 1-30; Elizabeth J. Bellamy, *The Limits of Eroticism in Post-Petrarchan Narrative: Conditional Pleasure from Spenser to Marvell* (Cambridge, 1998). The classic study is Jonathan Goldberg, *Endlesse Worke: Spenser and the Structures of Discourse* (Chicago, 1981).

[14] Richard Helgerson, *Self-Crowned Laureates: Spenser, Jonson, Milton and the Literary System* (Berkeley, 1983); David Lee Miller, "Spenser's Vocation, Spenser's Career," *English Literary History* 50 (1983), 197-231; Michael O'Connell, *Mirror and Veil: The Historical Dimension of Spenser's* Faerie Queene (Chapel Hill, 1977); Patrick Cheney, *Spenser's Famous Flight: A Renaissance Idea of a Literary Career* (Toronto, Buffalo and London, 1993); Richard Rambuss, *Spenser's Secret Career* (Cambridge, 1993).

[15] W.B. Yeats, "Edmund Spenser" in *Essays and Introductions* (London, 1969), pp. 356-83; C.S. Lewis, *The Allegory of Love: A Study in Medieval Tradition* (Oxford, 1959; rpt. of 1936), p. 349; "Edmund Spenser, 1552-99" in *Studies in Medieval and Renaissance Literature*, ed. Walter Hooper (Cambridge, 1966), pp. 121-45.

[16] Judith H. Anderson, Donald Cheney, and David A. Richardson, eds., *Spenser's Life and the Subject of Biography* (Amherst, Mass., 1996).

[17] Virgil K. Whitaker, *The Religious Basis of Spenser's Thought* (Stanford, 1950); "The Theological Structure of *The Faerie Queene*, Book I," *English Literary History* 19

Anthea Hume's book attempted to show that Spenser's poetry was inherently and polemically Puritan in orientation, a position challenged by John King who has suggested that Spenser is a much more mainstream Protestant.[18] Such views have been recently countered in different ways which seek to open out the question of Spenser's religious beliefs. Harold Weatherby has argued that much of Spenser's poetry owes as much to patristic theology as to Protestant writings, which, he claims, were widely known at Spenser's Cambridge.[19] Weatherby's book is refreshingly new, often fascinating and clearly deserves to be known, but suffers from his deliberate decision not to interpret the theology but simply note its presence in Spenser's writings.

In marked contrast is Darryl Gless's *Interpretation and Theology in Spenser* which wants to place the act of interpretation at the center of the problem, arguing that theological texts should not be relegated to the background as static works against which the changing literary text should be read, but read as part of the same hermeneutic order.[20] For Gless, there was no stable Elizabethan orthodoxy. For some, double predestination was all the rage; elsewhere, a stress on Erasmian free will can be found. Gless tries to extract himself from the moral maze of interpreting which line Spenser took by creating an ideal reader—or set of readers—who read the text "correctly." But, as ever, one is brought back to the question of the narrator's control over the narrative. Does Spenser fashion his readers by leading them to the truth, or do they fashion his texts? Equally important is Richard Mallette's *Spenser and the Discourses of Reformation England*, a work which, like Gless's, suggests that reading an orthodoxy against Spenser's works is doomed to failure. Mallette shows how *The Faerie Queene* not only represents the discourses of the Reformation, but also in the process of using them, transforms, distorts, and applies them to new situations and problems. There are some astute observations on marriage as a desirable state of companionship for the godly Protestant couple, a pointed contrast to the cruel Petrarchan conception of love.[21]

ANDREW: Staying with religion, I am going to bring the question round to Ireland once again. Brendan Bradshaw has argued that Spenser belongs to that radical Protestant grouping who favored the use of force rather than the Erasmian humanist faction who preferred persuasion to convert the Irish and

---

(1952), 151-64; Grace Warren Landrum, "Spenser's Use of the Bible and his Alleged Puritanism," *Publications of the Modern Language Association of America* 51 (1926), 517-44.

[18] Anthea Hume, *Edmund Spenser: Protestant Poet* (Cambridge, 1984); John N. King, *Spenser's Poetry and the Reformation Tradition* (Princeton, 1990).

[19] Harold L. Weatherby, *Mirrors of Celestial Grace: Patristic Theology in Spenser's Allegory* (Toronto, Buffalo and London, 1994).

[20] Darryl J. Gless, *Interpretation and Theology in Spenser* (Cambridge, 1994).

[21] Richard Mallette, *Spenser and the Discourses of Reformation England* (Lincoln, 1997).

establish English rule.[22] Bradshaw argues that such opinions are found
throughout both *The Faerie Queene*—notably Book V—and *A View*. But are
all these attempts to sort out Spenser's religion putting the cart before the
horse? In *A View*, Irenius argues that religion cannot be established in Ireland
before the groundwork has been done, that is, the land reduced to civil order,
so that religion cannot be separated as a category on its own in that text.
Moreover, Spenser is critical of Protestant preachers in the dialogue. Similarly,
The Faerie Queene moves from an explicitly religious allegory in Book I to a
second edition which appears less concerned with problems of religion, in fact,
explicitly qualifying incidents in that book in terms of later episodes; Una's
sojourn with the satyrs, for example, appears to demand a consideration in the
light of the religious allegory of Book I, but it also needs to be read in terms of
the appearances of satyrs later on—the end of Book III, when Hellenore leaves
Malbecco to live amongst them—and the savages who are scattered throughout
the pastoral world of Book VI, most importantly the experience of Serena with
the cannibals. Once again, neglect of the Irish context leads to a distortion of
the interpretative matrix of the poem.

The question of genre and the problem of identity cannot be separated.
This point has been made by many recent studies. The interpretation of
Spenser's use of genres is, of course, intrinsic to an evaluation of the trajectory
not just of his career, but also in the establishment of his sense of identity, a
point I would like to highlight. Probably the most significant thinker along
these lines has been Richard Helgerson, whose analysis of Spenser's poetic
forms and their political significance, first in *Self-Crowned Laureates* and,
more recently, *Forms of Nationhood*, has radically altered the ways in which
Spenser's career and identity have to be analyzed.[23] In *Forms of Nationhood*,
Helgerson has argued that *The Faerie Queene* is a reaction to Tasso's
Gerusalemme Liberata, a gesture of independence from "the epic and its statist
ideology" (p. 54).

Helgerson's argument that *The Faerie Queene* represents a "nation of
indistinct boundaries" is one that appeals to me. After all, what was Spenser's
nation? In *Colin Clouts Come Home Againe* it seems to me that Spenser
fashions himself either as Anglo-Irish (using this definition of identity in its
simplest and least specific form) or an exiled colonial subject of the Queen
(probably both). What is the nature of fairyland in the poem? It might be best
to suggest that it represents a series of alternative Englands and Britains, past,
present, future (as has long been recognized), plus a series of displaced and
possible nations which overlap, conflict and intermingle. In this scheme of
things Ireland and England face each other as opposite poles: Ireland is the

---

[22] Brendan Bradshaw, "Sword, Word and Strategy in the Reformation in Ireland,"
Historical Journal 21 (1978), 475-502; "Edmund Spenser on Justice and Mercy," *The Writer
as Witness: Literature as Historical Evidence: Historical Studies XVI*, ed. Tom Dunne (Cork,
1987), pp. 76-89.
    [23] Richard Helgerson, *Forms of Nationhood: The Elizabethan Writing of England*
(Chicago, 1991), pp. 1-62.

land of savagery to England's civilization. Conversely, English Ireland stands as a corrective to England's decay. Spenser would undoubtedly have known the story told in Holinshed's Irish Chronicle of the foolish English lord who travelled to Ireland and found that he could understand the natives of Wexford quite well. Whilst he imagined that he had somehow acquired Irish, in fact he failed to recognize an English which was more pure and authentic than his own.[24] For Spenser, perhaps, the English colonial community were the true English, hence the shocking, strange, and aggressive form of *The Faerie Queene*, a poem of exile and eccentricity.

Much excellent work has been done on the strange status of *The Faerie Queene* and its experimental nature, notably by Colin Burrow. His magisterial survey, *Epic Romance: Homer to Milton*, shows how the pathos and sympathy of the romance hero actually emerged out of complex rereadings of a classical epic tradition. Burrow argues that the pattern of Spenser's politics developed as a mixture of military rigor and clemency. Once violent English conquest has been effected then the victors can "offer mercy and clement conditions of peace."[25] Burrow's insights might be read alongside David Quint's argument that the history of epic is a battle between the Virgilian, imperial epic of the winners and the Lucianic, republican epic of the defeated.[26] Quint only makes passing mention of *The Faerie Queene*, but his analysis of a vast literary tradition might help to explain further the odd nature of Spenser's *magnum opus*. It was certainly not obvious to Spenser that the English were going to triumph over the Irish in the late 1590s. Furthermore, even if they did, it was not clear whether the main benefit would have been to New English planters in Ireland like Spenser or the forces of the crown (whom Spenser blames for the precarious situation in which he found himself).

Helgerson has suggested that Spenser was keen to represent the power of great men, a sort of residual feudalism against the centralizing modern state, but can we be so sure? What about Spenser the republican, exploding the myth of the monarchy from within? Deborah Shuger has pointed to Spenser's use of classical republican sources in the *View*, which emerges in her reading as primarily an anti-aristocratic tract, while I have traced the impact of anti-monarchical ideas in the poetry, arriving from a different perspective at a similar conclusion about Spenser's indebtedness to, and embeddedness within, a complex republican cultural matrix.[27] Shuger sees the central contrast in a *View* as that drawn between a warrior aristocracy and a rural gentry, with Spenser on the side of the latter. Her key point is that the "georgic vision" of

---

[24] For analysis, see Willy Maley, "Spenser's Irish English: Language and Identity in Early Modern Ireland," *Studies in Philology* 91 (1994), 417-31.

[25] Colin Burrow, *Epic Romance: Homer to Milton* (Oxford, 1993), p. 131.

[26] David Quint, *Epic and Empire: Politics and Generic Form from Virgil to Milton* (Princeton, 1993).

[27] Deborah Shuger, "White Barbarians: Irishmen, Indians and Others in Spenser's *View*," *Renaissance Quarterly* 50 (1997), 494-525; Andrew Hadfield, "Was Spenser a Republican?" *English: The Journal of the English Association* 47: 189 (1998), 169-82.

peace and civility through cultivation—in all its senses—"ranges itself against a still-powerful attraction, even among scholarly humanists, to heroic barbarism."[28] In this version of the seduction narrative that C.S. Lewis and Stephen Greenblatt advanced, the one that had Spenser the Englishman succumbing to Irish wildness, Spenser the aspiring English gentleman is turned on by the power of the very over-mighty subjects who impede his progress in Ireland. This opposition creates productive tensions, in prose and poetry alike. In mapping out his distance from the court, and in representing in esthetic terms a feudal culture to which he was politically opposed, Spenser found reserves of social energy that play and pulsate in his work. The old royalist and imperialist tags simply do not square with this highly localized ideological ambivalence and hybridity, composed of an anti-metropolitan attitude which might be termed "colonial republicanism." Barnaby Rich wrote that what passed for treason in England was merely table-talk in Ireland[29]; Felix Raab in *The English Face of Machiavelli* has pointed to the paucity of references to Machiavelli in English political writing of the late sixteenth century, despite the fact that, as Gabriel Harvey testified, people obviously read his works.[30] In Ireland this was clearly not the case as numerous treatises, most in manuscript, refer to Machiavelli, one being Spenser's *View*. Spenser was related by marriage to Geoffrey Fenton, who translated Guicciardini, and Spenser's fellow undertakers on the Munster plantation—William Herbert, Lodowick Bryskett, Richard Beacon—were clearly conversant with Italian political thinking and keen to explore the question of the forms which political opposition could take. Such connections need investigation, as does Spenser's connection with Robert Devereux, Second Earl of Essex, whom he appears to recommend for the office of viceroy at the end of *A View*.[31]

WILLY: You bring yourself well into the way, Andrew, not that you were ever out of it. Not really. Your idea of Spenser as ironic and subversive recalls another one of Greenblatt's claims—that Spenser was turning into an Irishman. It is, of course, one of the tenets of deconstruction that you become like the thing you ostensibly oppose. Speaking of which, another objection to Greenblatt's essay is that it enacts a displacement of gender that was part of the

---

[28] Shuger, "White Barbarians," p. 519.

[29] Cited in Andrew Hadfield and Willy Maley, "Introduction: Irish Representations and English Alternatives" in Brendan Bradshaw, Andrew Hadfield and Willy Maley, eds., *Representing Ireland: Literature and the Origins of Conflict, 1534-1660* (Cambridge, 1993), p. 10.

[30] Felix Raab, *The English Face of Machiavelli: A Changing Interpretation, 1500-1700* (London, 1965), p. 86. Harvey noted the popularity of Machiavelli and other European political theorists; see *The Letter-Book of Gabriel Harvey, A.D. 1573-1580*, ed. Edward John Long Scott (London, 1884), pp. 79-80.

[31] For details of Spenser's Irish circle, see Willy Maley, *A Spenser Chronology* (London, 1994), pp. 85-108. See also Hadfield, *Spenser's Irish Experience*, ch. 1. Paul Hammer discusses Spenser's relationship to Essex in *The Polarization of Elizabethan Politics: The Political Career of Robert Devereux, 2nd Earl of Essex, 1585-1597* (Cambridge, 1999).

original incorporation of sexual difference into a discourse of colonialism. I am thinking here of responses by Margaret Waller, Patricia Parker, and Clare Carroll.[32] I am also thinking of Jonathan Goldberg's work on Colin and Hobbinol.[33] Both feminism and queer theory suggest that sexual politics ought not to be read solely as an allegory of colonial politics.

Sheila Cavanagh's recent book, *Wanton Eyes and Chaste Desires*—a long overdue attack on Spenser's misogyny—makes the assumption that Spenser is not in control of the representations he fashions in his narrative and analyzes these as a series of separate and separable groups.[34] In other words, the narrative is read straight and the narrator perceived as a mouthpiece for Spenser. On the other hand, Lauren Silberman's *Transforming Desire* regards Spenser as a subtle ironist whose works have to be very carefully decoded before his critique of gender stereotypes and stress on the importance of the hermaphrodite can be understood.[35] For Silberman, the narrator's comments are almost always in need of careful scrutiny and the onus is on the reader to read and see all the false examples of human behavior exposed and pick out the good ones.

In volume 2 of his *History of Sexuality*, Foucault points out that [for the Greeks] "... immoderation derives from a passivity that relates it to femininity. To be immoderate was to be in a state of non-resistance with regard to the force of pleasures, and in a position of weakness and submission; it meant being incapable of that virile stance with respect to oneself that enabled one to be stronger than oneself. In this sense, the man of pleasures and desires, the man of nonmastery (*akrasia*) or self-indulgence (*akolasia*) was a man who could be called feminine, but more essentially with respect to himself than with respect to others."[36] Now if this recalls the destruction of the Bower of Bliss, Acrasia's Bower, where we see just such an exercise of self-mastery by Guyon, the Knight of Temperance, it also reminds us that the whole of Spenser's epic revolves around control of sexual desire in the interests of imperialism and political action. We are being immoderate, however, when we see the poem as "all about Ireland," rather than seeing Ireland as an example of

---

[32] Marguerite Waller, "Academic Tootsie: the Denial of Difference and the Difference it Makes," *Diacritics* 17 (1987); Patricia Parker, "Suspended Instruments: Lyric and Power in the Bower of Bliss" in *Literary Fat Ladies: Rhetoric, Gender, Property* (London, 1987), pp. 54-66; Clare Carroll, "The Construction of Gender and the Cultural and Political Other in *The Faerie Queene* V and *A View of the Present State of Ireland*: The Critics, the Context, and the Case of Radigund," *Criticism* 32 (1990), 163-91.

[33] Jonathan Goldberg, "Spenser's Familiar Letters" in *Sodometries: Renaissance Texts, Modern Sexualities* (Stanford, 1992), pp. 63-101.

[34] Sheila T. Cavanagh, *Wanton Eyes and Chaste Desires: Female Sexuality in* The Faerie Queene (Bloomington and Indianapolis, 1994).

[35] Lauren Silberman, *Transforming Desire: Erotic Knowledge in Books III and IV of* The Faerie Queene (Berkeley, 1995). See also John Watkins, *The Spectre of Dido: Spenser and the Virgilian Epic* (New Haven, 1995).

[36] Michel Foucault, *The Use of Pleasure: The History of Sexuality*, trans. Robert Hurley (Harmondsworth, 1985), 2: 84-5.

the "New World" and the perils of promiscuity. *The Faerie Queene* is all about sexuality.

ANDREW: Thank you, Camille Paglia. Your presence has been sorely missed. It is a question, surely, not of choosing between discourses, but of resisting representations, and negotiating between desires—colonial and sexual. The pitfalls of privileging one over the other, or of misreading their complex interaction, is all too evident in Robert Welch's novella, *The Kilcolman Notebook,* an imaginative reconstruction of Spenser and Ralegh's voyage to London in 1589 when Spenser brought the first copy of *The Faerie Queene* to the Elizabethan court.[37] The novel concludes with Spenser having a bizarre dream in which he kills a hermaphrodite and argues with a naked young woman who turns into a tumescent Walter Ralegh. Pretty run-of-the-mill Spenserian fantasy really.

WILLY: I have obviously led a sheltered life. The focus on colonial history—in fiction or in criticism—is a good thing, provided that the reader is made aware of the fact that this history, no less than Spenser's allegory, is anything but "thinly veiled," and is as open to dispute now as it was in Spenser's day. Clare Carroll makes the forceful claim that "The resistance to topical readings of Spenser's allegory is a symptom of a larger denial" of "the historical and political function of criticism" (p. 169). *The Faerie Queene* is all about history and politics. I am also in agreement with the suggestion that on one level the focus on colonial matters can be a way of presenting, without fear of punishment, a critique of the court. As Brendan Bradshaw says, "the intellectual history of the colony cannot be understood in isolation from the intellectual history of the metropolis."[38] Discussing Ireland is thus a way of speaking about England, but what originated as the ploy of dissidents—using Ireland as a cover, a front, a beard—has become critical orthodoxy. Readers continue to focus on Ireland and let England off the hook. This calls to mind Linda Gregerson's compelling work on idolatry.[39] Gregerson argues that Spenser tried to train his readers out of their idolatrous assumptions that the truth was in the text rather than, as both he and Milton as radical Protestants insisted, out in the field. Critics who obsess about Ireland to the exclusion of other issues are making an idol of what ought to be an angle. One might detect in the critical commodification and fetishizing of Ireland in recent Spenser studies an idolatrous approach, in which Ireland, rather than being seen as one national paradigm, is regarded as the key to all the mythologies of *The Faerie Queene.*

---

[37] Robert Welch, *The Kilcolman Notebook* (Dingle, Co. Kerry, 1994).

[38] Brendan Bradshaw, "Robe and Sword in the Conquest of Ireland," in Claire Cross, David Loades and J.J. Scarisbrick, eds., *Law and Government under the Tudors: Essays Presented to Sir Geoffrey Elton on his Retirement* (Cambridge, 1988), p. 162.

[39] Linda Gregerson, *The Reformation of the Subject: Spenser, Milton and the English Protestant Epic* (Cambridge, 1995).

ANDREW: In other words, *The Faerie Queene* is all about England. Or rather, *The Faerie Queene*, including Book V, is all about Scotland, Wales, England, Europe, the New World, and, of course, Ireland. The risk is that "Ireland" becomes a con-text or pre-text that is also a "passe-partout," a frame in the pictorial and criminal sense, and a skeleton-key that opens all of the doors to the poem. So you are saying that having spent so much time talking about Ireland, we have to get back to the world?

WILLY: I am saying that the best way to approach "Spenser" and "Ireland" is to assume, first of all, the complexity of both. James I, inspecting the documents stored in Whitehall on his accession to the British throne declared: "We had more ado with Ireland than all the world besides."[40] This could be the cry of a future Spenser bibliographer or editor. We have to put *The Faerie Queene* back into the world, and back among the disciplines, which means not just history, but anthropology, geography, ethnology, and so on. But again we are back with Greenblatt, because his essay was interdisciplinary in a way that some of the work that it inspired has not been, and he did treat the Irish dimension as an example of "New World" colonialism. Again, I do not think it is a matter of looking for alternatives to Ireland in terms of critical focus. I think it is a question of bringing together two apparently opposing sides. Annabel Patterson has well shown that Irish historians have relied on conventional Spenser criticism, while it could be argued that New Historicists have chosen a rather simplistic version of Irish history. Contextual critics have gone overboard about Ireland, while textual scholars may take their revenge by robbing them of their mainstay, the *View*. Perhaps it is time for a dialogue.

ANDREW: I am not entirely convinced, but I thank you, Willy, for your gentle pains. Not forgetting withall that we shall have to hammer all this out again on like good occasions, as you have promised.

---

[40] Cited in J.H. Andrews, "Appendix: The Beginnings of the Surveying Profession in Ireland—Abstract," in Sarah Tyacke, ed., *English Map-Making, 1500-1650* (London, 1983), p. 20.

Index